Michael Irving Jensen holds a Ph.D. in Middle Eastern Studies from the University of Copenhagen and a Masters in Developing Studies from SOAS, University of London. He is currently a lecturer in Middle Eastern History and Politics at the University of Copenhagen and runs the private consultancy Middle East Awareness.

LIBRARY OF MODERN MIDDLE EAST STUDIES

See www.ibtauris.com/LMMES for a full list of titles

THE POLITICAL IDEOLOGY OF HAMAS

A GRASSROOTS PERSPECTIVE

MICHAEL IRVING JENSEN

TRANSLATED FROM DANISH BY SALLY LAIRD

I.B. TAURIS
LONDON · NEW YORK

Reprinted in 2010 by I.B.Tauris & Co. Ltd.
6 Salem Road, London W2 4BU
175 Fifth Avenue, New York NY 10010
www.ibtauris.com

Distributed in the United States and Canada Exclusively by Palgrave Macmillan
175 Fifth Avenue, New York NY 10010

First published in 2009 by I.B.Tauris & Co. Ltd.

Library of Modern Middle East Studies: 64

ISBN: 978 1 84511 059 8

A full CIP record for this book is available from the British Library
A full CIP record is available from the Library of Congress

Library of Congress Catalog Card Number: available

Printed and bound in India by Replika Press Pvt. Ltd.
from camera-ready copy edited and supplied by the author with the assistance of Kalligraf DK-7800 Skive

CONTENTS

PREFACE AND
ACKNOWLEDGEMENTS

This book has, as so much other research, been born out of wonder and curiosity. The initial curiosity was raised during a stay on the occupied Palestinian West Bank back in 1991. We were a small group of foreign students who had ignored the first Intifada, which at this point was at its peak, and had chosen to study during the summer at the Bir Zeit University north of Jerusalem. One night, during a seminar on the countless Israeli offences against Palestinian human rights, a small group of masked Islamists entered the room, equipped with large machetes, and broke off the seminar and read out a handbill. The message was clear and simple: "AIDS infected decadent westerners – you have 24 hours to pack your clothes and leave this area, otherwise Hamas will take its precautions." Only a few students followed the request, while the main group stayed put to witness the political aftermath unfold over the next couple of days. Apparently, the incident was broadcast on Israeli TV. It also reached the highest level of the National Palestinian Leadership in the occupied territories. Two days after the incident, the late Faisal Husseini came to visit and put forward an unreserved apology on behalf of the Palestinian people. This was followed by discussions and showdowns in the Palestinian camp. Hamas came forward with an apology and assured us that the incident was not backed by their leaders, but was an independent act of young kids belonging to the movement. At first the incident sharpened my interest in the Islamic Resistance Movement in Palestine and in particular in the movement's political and social functions. This interest later resulted in several stays and studies on the West Bank and in the Gaza Strip, both during the first Intifada and after the Oslo Agreement in 1993 and the Aqsa Intifada. My interest in political development in the Palestinian occupied and autonomous areas and particularly the development within the Islamic movement Hamas has only increased since then. The Hamas electoral victory in 2006 made my desire to publish my work on Hamas in

English even stronger. This book is a revised and updated edition of my book originally published in Danish, *Hamas i Gazastriben* (2002), based on the fieldwork I conducted in relation to my Ph.D.

During the years I spent on the project I have received inspiration and support from a number of colleagues both in Denmark and abroad. First and foremost I wish to thank my mentor throughout the years, the former Director of the Danish Institute in Damascus and current Professor at Carsten Niebuhr Institute, University of Copenhagen, Jørgen Bæk Simonsen for moral and professional support. I would also like to extend my acknowledgements to my colleagues at the Carsten Niebuhr Institute, University of Copenhagen: Anette Haaber Ihle, Lene Kofoed Rasmussen and Daniella Kuzmanovic for prolific discussions during the process. I am also grateful to journalist and scholar Birgitte Rahbek for repeatedly having found time to read through parts of my publications.

I wish to acknowledge a number of other colleagues at the Carsten Niebuhr Institute, the Danish Institute for International Studies as well as at the Danish Center for Culture and Development (in alphabetical order), i.e. Hanne Adriansen, Christel Braae, June Dahy, Jakob Feldt, Maria Fodeh, Thomas Illum, Mahmoud Issa, Abdul Rahman Jabari, Nathalie Khankan, Mogens Trolle Larsen, Gry Krogager Lund, Helle Gudio Nielsen, Ivan Smilianov, Anne Stadil, Svend Maan Søndergaard and others.

Among my foreign colleagues I would like to extend my sincere appreciation to Professor Michael Hudson of Georgetown University, who on several occasions encouraged me to publish my study of Hamas in English. I also wish to thank Professor Ahmad Moussalli from the American University in Beirut, who like Michael Hudson was visiting Professor at Copenhagen University. Furthermore I would like to extend my acknowledgement to Professor Francois Burgat (Aix en-Provence) and Professor Augustus Richard Norton (Boston University) for supporting the project through seminars and conferences.

I wish to thank the many young Islamists and their leaders in the Gaza Strip, who, despite the pressing and tense political situation in the area, received me with open arms and participated in a series of interviews constituting the backbone of this study. A great thanks also to the Board of the Islamic University in Gaza, the Head of *al-Jam'iyya al-Islâmiyya* Sheikh Ahmad Bahr, and especially to the late Hamas leader Ismael Abu Shanab, who through a long series of interviews openly sought to extend his views on the political reality in Palestine. This project would not have been possible without their kindness. Furthermore I wish to thank everybody who either supported, listened or discussed with me during my stay in the Gaza Strip (in alphabetical order): Dr Ziad Abu Amr (Bir Zeit University, PLC member and former Minister of Foreign Affairs), Dr Iyad Barghouti (Najah University, Nablus), Ashraf Joudah, Muhammad Joudah, Ali Khilleh, Director Dr Iyad Sarraj (Gaza Community Mental Health Clinic), Director Raji Sorani (Palestinian Center for Human Rights), Middle East Correspondent and analyst Graham Usher and others. Finally I wish to extend my gratitude to my interpreter Hassan, who was an important asset in building trust in the Islamic environment.

I also wish to thank Sally Laird, who translated the book from Danish with great thoroughness and precision into comprehensive English. Parts of the book, however, have been revised and updated since Sally Laird handed in her final translation.

I owe the greatest acknowledgement to Mette Søltoft and my two children Johan and Frida, who on several occasions have travelled with me to Palestine. Mette has followed the project closely, and has contributed with analytical comments and constructive input and ideas. I would not have been able to accomplish this project without her professional and moral support.

Finally, I would like to thank the Danish Arts Council, the Danish Institute for International Studies and the Plum Foundation for the financial support of the publication of this book.

ABBREVIATIONS

CIA	Central Intelligence Agency
DFLP	Democratic Front for the Liberation of Palestine
DGI	Danish Gymnastics and Sports Association
EU	European Union
FBI	Federal Bureau of Investigations
ICG	International Crises Group
IDF	Israel Defence Forces
IIRO	International Islamic Relief Organisation
IUG	Islamic University of Gaza
JSI	Jamîyyat al-Salâh al-Islamiyya
NGO	Non-Governmental Organisation
PA	Palestinian Authority
PBH	Peace be Upon Him
PFLP	Popular Front for the Liberation of Palestine
PLC	Palestinian Legislative Council
PLO	Palestine Liberation Organisation
PNC	Palestine National Council
PNGO	Palestinian Non-Governmental Organisations Networks
UN	United Nations
UNLU	United National Leadership of the Uprising
UNRWA	The United Nations Relief and Works Agency for Palestinian Refugees

1

ISLAMISM IN PALESTINE AND THE QUEST FOR THE SOUND MUSLIM

"Hamas is one of the deadliest terror organisations in the world today"[1]
George W. Bush, President of the United States of America

In late January 2006 Hamas once again made the headlines in the news all over the world. The Palestinian Islamist movement won a landslide victory in the second Palestinian Legislative Council elections, sweeping away Fatah's monopoly of power. Hamas won no fewer than 74 out of 132 seats. This stunning victory indicates a new phase in the history of Palestinian Islamism and constitutes a major challenge to the Palestinian Islamists, as they now have to take important responsibility for developments within Palestinian society in an international environment which is very hostile to Islamism in general and to Hamas in particular. The United States, Israel and the EU all consider Hamas a terrorist organisation and as a consequence of this they are not willing to engage officially with the movement. The elections also marked the end of almost half a century in which the Palestinian national movement was dominated by secular nationalism and the beginning of a new phase in Palestinian politics dominated by Islamist political culture. However, as the change was not easily accepted by the Palestinian nationalists and the international community the situation developed into Palestinian civil strife between Fatah and Hamas in the Gaza Strip during June 2007. The strife resulted in a divison of the Palestinian occupied territories leading to an isolated Hamas-controlled Gaza Strip and a West Bank controlled by Mahmoud Abbas and Salam Fayyad fully supported by the international community.

As a result of these significant changes in the Palestinian political landscape it is now more important than ever to understand the politics of Hamas and understand how deeply the movement is rooted in Palestinian society. What is Hamas about? Will Islamism in Palestinian society be imposed from above? Where will its war with Israel most likely travel?

In order to gain an in-depth understanding of Hamas and its impact in Palestinian society, it is necessary to analyse how Islamist leaders have been working during the past decades to implement the Islamist utopia. We also need to look at the motivation of sympathisers of the movement. This book concerns Hamas and how the movement has organised itself in Palestinian civil society during the "old order" where the secular dominated Fatah movement was in control of the Palestinian National Movement and the Palestinian Authority.

Hamas in the limelight

Around 9.15 p.m. on 19 August 2003 a huge bang resounds through Jerusalem. It can be heard both in the eastern Palestinian parts and the western Jewish parts of the city. For the first few moments after the bang you clutch at the hope that perhaps this was a fighter plane passing through the sound barrier. Seconds later an uneasy feeling starts to spread. An *infijar*. The Arabic word for a suicide action, or rather an explosion. On the terrace of the exclusive Arab Ambassador Hotel most people hold their breath a moment longer – and then the sirens start. Now everyone knows. Yet another young Palestinian man or women has blown himself – or herself – to smithereens. What no one knows at this point is that around 20 Orthodox Jews – on their way home from praying at the Wailing Wall – have gone with the bomber to their deaths. More than 100 have been wounded.

There was no trace of triumph or jubilation among the many Palestinian guests at the hotel. A state of shock and frustration prevailed. At the same time virtually every mobile phone was in use. What's happened? Where exactly? How many killed? How many wounded? And the counting went on in both Hebrew and Arabic. An acquaintance who had just returned from a stressful tour of the northern part of the West Bank, where he had been gathering information and talking with Palestinian farmers who in recent weeks and months had lost virtually everything they owned as a result of the Israeli government's erection of a so-called "security fence" – what the Palestinians call a "wall of apartheid", arrived at the hotel less than ten minutes before the explosion. When the truth dawned on him he put his head in his hands, rubbed his tired eyes and said, "This life is soon going to be bloody well unbearable. Our life is hell, and this won't make things any easier." Not only was he, like everyone else, certain that an as yet unknown number of Israelis had lost their lives, but he also knew that the so-called *hudna* (cease-fire) that had come into force at the end of June 2003 was over.

Twenty minutes after the explosion the first helicopters could be heard over the city. Were they on their way to Gaza, Ramallah or Hebron? In the first instance they simply circled over the city, but it was thought to be only a matter of time before Ariel Sharon's government would launch a fresh attack on the occupied Palestinian territories. The Palestinians feared what tomorrow would bring. To start with, the control of the more than 100 Israeli checkpoints on the West Bank would be tightened, even though everyone knew it was possible to sneak round them.

Just two hours before the explosion a Palestinian acquaintance had been explaining how he had managed without problem to get to Jerusalem from Ramallah, avoiding several Israeli checkpoints. He said with a smile that it was quite easy, since the occupying forces could not begin to match his knowledge of the terrain. And the soldiers knew this. Indeed, in the last few days Israeli soldiers at the biggest checkpoint – Qalandia between Jerusalem and Ramallah – had quite openly been encouraging Palestinians with no permission to visit Jerusalem to bypass the checkpoint. This could mean one of two things: either going over the fields or taking a two-hour detour. The soldiers recognised, in other words, that the many checkpoints were first and foremost a demonstration of power and a symbolic attempt to convince large sections of the Israeli population that the country was now more secure.

Outside the Ambassador Hotel a young boy comes to meet us. He imitates machine gun fire and advises us not to go any further. Just 30 minutes after the explosion most of the Palestinian part of the city has been cordoned off. There are police everywhere. All cars are stopped. Everything is checked.

Back at the hotel, where we are staying, the mood is subdued. Outside around 40 young Palestinian men are arrested. The usual suspects. They are certainly not the only ones to be arrested that evening. After a couple of hours, as information about the explosion and the steadily growing number of dead and injured whirrs around, discussions begin among some of the hotel's Palestinian guests. Not all the attitudes that emerge are easy to accept.

Ayman is the harsh type: "We have to continue until the message goes in. Fuck them. We can't carry on living with things as they are now!" But he is more or less alone in this uncompromising attitude. Hussam interrupts: "No. What we're doing is wrong. If the Israelis are so dumb that they're incapable of stopping this vicious circle, we'll have to do it. It boomerangs back on us. It's not taking us anywhere. They have families like us as well." Hassan is more reflective: "Israel is building a wall, confiscating our land, carrying on with their liquidations, and the Palestinians have basically seen no improvement over the last couple of months of the cease-fire. This is the result."

Ziad butts in and tries to explain: "We Palestinians also have a life here." This life will not be any easier after the explosion. Yassir's last words that evening were: "I know that he [the suicide bomber] is going to end up in hell. He's committed a crime. I know it."[2]

I wrote this brief essay just hours after an explosion in late August 2003. Usually Hamas has made the headlines across the world in relation to its attacks on Israeli civilians and it is often portrayed in the West as a terrorist organisation. It is true that the movement's armed wing, *Kata'ib Izz ad-din al-Qassam*, has been involved in numerous actions easily defined as terrorism. Despite this militant record, the roots of Hamas, which originated from the Muslim Brotherhood, have not been abandoned. Thus Hamas is at the same time involved in facilitating a number of important social services for the Palestinian population. The so-called social infrastructure of Hamas and other Islamist movements has been discussed intensively ever since the terror attacks in Washington and New York in 2001.

Even before 11 September 2001, however, many regarded Hamas as a terrorist organization that needed to be fought. Witness, for example, former US Secretary of State Madeleine Albright's speech in 1998 to the Israel Academy of Arts and Sciences in Jerusalem. Albright said among other things:

> ... fighting terror is not a part-time job. Fighting terror is not something you do only when it is convenient. Fighting terror is a twenty-four-hour-a-day, 365-day-a-year responsibility, and for any partner in peace, fighting terror is a sacred obligation. Fulfilling that obligation means identifying and seizing terrorist weapons and supplies. It means arresting and prosecuting those involved in planning, financing, supplying or abetting terrorism. It means sharing information and co-ordinating law enforcement actions. And it means getting out the message over and over again that those who commit terrorism in the name of the Palestinian cause are committing terrorism against the Palestinian cause.[3]

Politicians in Israel, the United States and elsewhere appear to have been inspired by media coverage[4] of Islamism and/or the kinds of research generated by security policy, which looks at Islamism primarily in terms of the threat it poses, to US interests in the Middle East on the one hand, and to the state of Israel on the other. Basing his judgement on accounts in the media and elsewhere, Glenn Robinson has described Hamas as one of the least understood social movements today.[5]

Against the background of these political developments, and the massive international attention Hamas has generated both in politics and the media, it is not surprising that over the last decade a great many scholars have published monographs and articles on the Islamist movement in Palestine. It is this movement and its engagement within the framework of Palestinian civil society that is the subject of the present book.

The diversity of Islamism

Islamism has multiple meanings, and political strategies among Islamists vary considerably. In this book an Islamist is defined as a Muslim "who regards Islam as a body of ideas, values, beliefs and practices, encompassing all spheres of life including personal and social relations, economy and politics".[6]

Islamist movements throughout the Middle East share the common goal of establishing an Islamic state (such a state being defined, however, only in terms of its adherence to *sharî'a*, or Islamic law). Where the various Islamist groups and movements part ways is on the means to be used in achieving this goal.[7]

Moderate Islamists strive for the creation of an Islamic state by means of a political strategy based on a process of islamisation at the grassroots level. Thus moderate Islamists seek to (re-)islamise society from below through preaching, but also by putting pressure on the ruling elite to promote Islamism from above. In this sense the moderate Islamists differ from the more radical adherents of Islamism, who share the same goal, but seek to bring about an Islamic state through revolution from above, which would subsequently lead to the islamisation of society. Through a political strategy that seeks to persuade individual men and women to adopt "true Islam" (*al-Islâm al-hanîf*), moderate Islamists hope to lay the foundation for the future Islamic state. The creation of *sound Muslims* at the individual level is a precondition for the success of this moderate strategy and for the realisation of a moral society based on *sharî'a*. *Sharî'a* as an Islamic normative system is addressed first of all to the individual, secondly to society and last of all to the state. The *sound Muslim* in this context should be treated as synonymous with an Islamist. The task for leading Islamists is thus to create *sound Muslims*. The concept should be understood at two levels: partly in terms of a system of thought, or more precisely an ideal; partly in terms of lived social practice. The *sound Muslim* should thus be created in a dialogue between leading Islamists and followers of Islamism.

Research on Islamism has occupied a central place in Middle East studies ever since the revolution in Iran in 1978–79. During this period scholars have produced a number of articles and monographs that throw light on the genesis, development and ideology of Islamism. They have also contributed a great deal to our understanding of the way Islamist groups function as political opposition movements. Research has been done on Islamism and democracy/pluralism, on Islamic economy, the islamisation of science and education, and lately on the trans-national Islamism inspired by the thought and acts of Usama Bin Laden.[8] Despite this wide-ranging literature, however, relatively few studies have been devoted to the Islamist movements' engagement in society and their efforts to create *sound Muslims*. Fewer still look at what motivates the movements' followers and "consumers" to become involved in Islamist contexts, and what use they make of the various Islamist institutions.

A common feature of most studies in the field hitherto is that they are based on elite sources, that is to say, on interviews with the movement's leaders and on texts written by them. Islamist studies relating to Palestine are no exception in this regard. The popular level is ignored. Thus we still lack analyses of the way that rank and file followers perceive Islamist movements. How do they assess these movements' strengths and weaknesses, and what enables such movements to attract ordinary people at all?

Grassroots work in the local community constitutes a significant ingredient in the political strategy of the moderate Islamist movement in the Palestinian context, namely Hamas as well as for other moderate Islamists.[9] Thus in large parts of the Middle East Islamist groups – including the Hamas movement – have set up medical clinics, kindergartens, schools, sports clubs, computer centres, choirs, old people's homes and hospitals. In addition they provide social support for some of the weakest groups in the community. In this sense Islamist institutions play a significant role in civil society in the Middle East, which I define here as a place "where a mélange of groups, clubs, guilds, syndicates, federations, unions, parties come together to provide a buffer between the state and the citizen".[10]

Scholars of Islamism often describe Islamist social institutions as being crucial to the effectiveness of the Islamist movement. Emile Sahliyeh, for example, writes of the Palestinian Islamists:

> Many of the activities of Hamas and the Muslim Brotherhood on the West Bank and in Gaza centred on the mosques. A vast network of daycare agencies, religious schools, youth and sports clubs, clinics, nursing homes, and financial programmes were established. The creation of the

Islamic Centre [*al-Mujamma' al-Islâmî*], the Islamic University in Gaza and several Islamic colleges, in the West Bank provided the Muslim Brotherhood with an additional means to advance their political agenda. These institutions served as mechanisms for the recruitment of new members and their *indoctrination* along Islamic lines.[11] (My italics).

The conclusion is clear: these institutions are crucial to the popularity of the movement, this is where they recruit new members, and where indoctrination takes place. The only thing missing is empirical evidence for these claims. Some researchers like Matthew Lewitt (2004) even argue that:

The charity committees, mosque classes, student unions, sports clubs and other organizations run by Hamas all serve as places where Hamas activists recruit Palestinian youth for positions in Hamas *da'wa*, for terrorist training courses in Syria or Iran, or for suicide or other terror attacks.[12]

Researchers on Islamism thus recognise and stress the importance of these social institutions, as a form of self-legitimisation, in the Islamists' political strategy, while failing for the most part properly to investigate and analyse the Islamists' social work within a given socio-economic and historical context.[13] Expanding on this, Richard Augustus Norton writes:

Scholarship on the Islamists has, however, been overtly textual, too inclined to report the words of the ideologues and the spokesmen, and insufficiently sociological, in terms of failing to look at the motives of those who lend their support to the Islamist movements.[14]

Over and above the need concretely to analyse how these movements work towards the realisation of their Islamic utopia, it is important to our proper understanding of Islamism and its power and influence within the community to focus on what motivates the movements' followers.

Instead of constructing stereotypes about Islamism we need to analyse it, and this need has not been diminished by 11 September 2001. The aim of the present book is thus to analyse the reasons behind the Islamic leaders' engagement in Palestinian civil society. In the course of my analysis, I will look at the ideologically conditioned initiatives Islamists have taken to make themselves visible in the socio-political space surrounding the Palestinian population.

There is a consensus in the literature that the Islamists' engagement in

Palestinian civil society has enabled them to spread the Islamist message. This occurs, it is claimed, through Islamist indoctrination[15] in various institutions.[16] A further aim of this book is therefore to look at what motivates followers to participate in a number of Islamic initiatives, in order to understand how they respond to and absorb the leadership's efforts to carry out islamisation. In addition, I will examine how Islamist sympathisers define themselves in relation to their political opponents, i.e. the secular forces mainly represented by Fatah.

The purpose of the project is therefore not to describe "reality", but to show how the actors involved, in this case the Islamists in the Gaza Strip, describe, define, understand and manoeuvre in relation to various events and other actors. In order to gain greater understanding of Islamism and its impact, we need concretely to analyse how Islamist leaders work to implement the Islamist dream and to look at the motivation of sympathisers. In the chapters that follow I will discuss in particular the underlying motives of young Islamist sympathisers who become involved in the movement, setting their motives and patterns of behaviour in the specific historical, social and cultural context in which they operate. This is important in order to achieve a more profound understanding of Islamism and its penetration of society. Basically, it will give us an idea of what Hamas is all about. The material presented in the book in based on extensive fieldwork within two major institutions within Palestinian civil society ruled by the Islamists, namely the sports club of *al-Jam'iyya al-Islâmiyya* and the Islamic University of Gaza.[17]

Hence, the book thus deals exclusively with the social aspects of Hamas as opposed to its military (or, in the prevailing hegemonic parlance, terrorist) side. Manifestly it is difficult, at least on the surface, to distinguish between the two. My reasons for doing so have first and foremost to do with security. It would quite simply have been dangerous to research the military side. Moreover I take the view that the primary focus of the Muslim Brotherhood, from which Hamas springs, has been on social work. It was not until 1987 that the Brotherhood took the decision to participate in the resistance struggle against the Israeli occupation. This struggle is provisional in character and came about as a result of an "abnormal" situation – namely the Israeli occupation. So long as the occupation continues, military action will continue as well. And as I discuss in the chapter on context (Chapter 2), Hamas will be disposed to halt its struggle the day Israel withdraws from the West Bank, Gaza and East Jerusalem. Its social and educational activities, however, will continue to play a central role.

Structure of the book

Chapter 2 provides a historical background on the development of Islamism in Palestine during the twentieth century. The main focus is on the development post-1987, i.e. after the establishment of Hamas. This chapter is based both on the existing literature as well as on interviews with high-ranking Hamas leaders such as the late Ahmad Yasin and Ismael Abu Shanab. The aim is to place the empirical data to be presented in a historical-political context.

In Chapter 3, which is based primarily on interviews with Hamas leaders (e.g. Abdel Aziz Rantisi, Ismael Haniyya, Ismael Abu Shanab and Mahmoud Zahhar) and the writings of Hamas leaders (e.g. Abdel Fattah Dukkhan), I seek to address the Islamists' conception of both Islam and history. This understanding is a precondition for understanding their involvement in civil society. The aim of this involvement is to create the *"sound Muslim"* who, it is argued has for hundreds of years been detached from Islam due to what the Islamists perceive as an "ideological invasion" led by the West. This western "invasion" has resulted in a gap between Islam and Muslims, and civil society is seen as a tool by which to rescue the latter.

Chapter 4 is based solely on participant observation and qualitative interviews with leaders and players in a Hamas affiliated football club. I focus here on a number of questions: does indoctrination take place in the club? Why had the young men who played in the club ended up in an Islamist soccer club? I also seek to arrive at a deeper understanding of the relationship between the standard Islamist narrative of Islam and the social praxis of the players, as well as to examine in what ways – if any – the young men adopt the discourse of the leaders of the club. Finally, since the Islamist discourse, like all other such discourses, is based on exclusion, this chapter also deals with how the players perceive the secular Palestinian Authority and other central actors.

The material presented in Chapter 5 is based solely on fieldwork conducted at the Islamic University during the spring term of 1998. In this chapter I present three spheres in which Islamist schooling takes place at the Islamic University of Gaza (IUG). Thus I focus on: (1) the activities of the student council, which is controlled by *Kutla Islamiyya*, which is the student organisation of the Muslim Brotherhood (Hamas); (2) the obligatory courses in Islamic studies (*islamicum*), which are a kind of pendant to courses on Western Civilisation and (3) the courses offered in the English Department where I did my fieldwork. The chapter not only focuses on the way in which Islamist schooling is conducted, but also on how the students respond to and adopt the administration's aim of creating *sound Muslims.* Finally the chapter discusses the students' perception of other central actors such as the Palestinian Authority (at that time controlled by Fatah) and the West.

Chapter 6 is a brief conclusion that also focuses on what the future holds for Hamas in the wake of their landslide victory during the election in January 2006, as well as the Palestinian civil strife during June 2007. Hence, it takes a closer look at what we can expect a Hamas-run Palestinian Authority to look like. Finally, it assesses the direction in which its war with Israel is travelling.

In the Appendix I present a brief background of why the selected institutions were chosen. Furthermore I present how I was admitted into the selected institutions. Finally, I discuss the fieldwork in practice in the football club as well as at the IUG.

2

THE CONTEXT

The Development of Palestinian Islamism and the
Relationship with the Palestinian Authority during
the 'Old Order'

The aim of this chapter is first and foremost to place the empirical data gathered in the course of my research in a historical-political context. I will therefore begin by summarising the history of Islamism in Palestine since 1945, when the first branch of the Muslim Brotherhood was established, until the landslide victory of Hamas in early 2006.[18] The chapter also includes a section describing the measures taken in the late 1990s to block the funding of Palestinian Islamism and the social institutions associated with it. While the first part of the chapter draws on secondary sources, sections of the second part are principally based on information gathered through qualitative interviews conducted during my fieldwork in the Gaza Strip.

The Brotherhood's First Decades in Palestine

The Muslim Brotherhood from which the Hamas movement sprang was established in Ismailiyya in Egypt by Hassan al-Banna in 1928.[19] Its first official contact with Palestinian society was made in August 1935, when the Egyptian branch sent two of its leaders on a mission to Palestine. They were warmly received by the then *mufti* hajj Amin al-Husseini.

The first Palestinian branch of the Brotherhood was set up in 1945.[20] Like the Egyptian organisation, the Palestinian Brotherhood grew rapidly, and by 1947 over 25 local branches had sprung up all over Palestine. Between them they had some 12,000–20,000 active members.[21] However, it was not until during and immediately after the first Arab-Israeli war in 1948–49 that the Brotherhood really made its mark on the political scene in Palestine. Its attitude towards the Palestinian question undoubtedly strengthened the movement's popularity among Palestinians. In 1947, after the UN passed Resolution 181, under which the British mandate in Palestine was divided into two states, one Jewish, one Arabic, the Brotherhood embarked on a campaign to launch a *Jihâd* against the new Jewish state of Israel. Among other things it created brigades of volunteers to wage war against Zionism. At this point Hassan al-Banna proposed to the League of Arab States that the Muslim Brothers send 10,000 men to join in the struggle.[22] The atmosphere that the Brotherhood created in Egypt undoubtedly stimulated public interest in the Palestinian question, which in turn put pressure on the Egyptian government to participate actively in the war against Israel.[23]

Following the Arabs' defeat in the first Arab–Israeli war of 1948–49 – a war which came to be known as *al-nakba* (the catastrophe) – the former British Palestinian mandate was divided into three parts: the state of Israel, the West Bank and the Gaza Strip. In the immediate aftermath of the war the West Bank, which is a geographic area of 5,800 square kilometres on the West Bank of the Jordan, was administered by Transjordan. In 1950 Transjordan annexed the area, changing its name to the Hashimite Kingdom of Jordan. In the period from 1948 to 1967 the Gaza Strip, a 360-square-kilometre strip of land that runs along the Mediterranean coast and borders on Egypt, was administered by the Egyptians. The division of Palestine had far-reaching consequences for the political development of Palestinian society. For the Muslim Brotherhood – as for many other political movements – it brought marked changes in the conditions under which the organisation operated, since it was subject to the policies of the respective regimes in question. The third geographical area established after 1948, Israel, will not be discussed here.

The Brotherhood on the West Bank (1948–67)

Since Jordan annexed the West Bank in 1950, it is not surprising that the story of the Palestinian Brotherhood in this area is closely bound up with that of the Jordanian branches of the organisation. The Brotherhood enjoyed relatively good relations with the Hashimite royal family for most of the period 1948–67. Unlike many other political movements, it operated legally throughout this period, a distinction due mainly to the nature of its activities, which were confined to publishing and distributing Islamic literature and carrying out various social initiatives.[24]

However, its relations with the royal family were not always straightforward. Despite the fact that the Brotherhood has been described as a "loyal opposition", there were disagreements between the two parties. Like the Arab Nationalists, the Brotherhood was opposed to the King's close alliances with the West, particularly Great Britain. In 1954 members of the Brotherhood demonstrated against the presence of British officers in the Jordanian army; as a result, they were put under surveillance and some of their leaders were arrested. But when the Brotherhood supported the King in a showdown with the Arab nationalists, relations between the two parties improved. Thereafter the Brotherhood was the only legal opposition movement in the country. One of the leaders of the Brotherhood in Jordan explains its non-confrontational policies as follows:

> The Muslim Brotherhood did not provoke the King. We had a truce with him, because we were unable to open fronts with all sides at one time ... We stood with the King in order to protect ourselves, because if Nasir's followers had risen to power, or a pro-Nasir government had been established in Jordan, the Muslim Brotherhood would have been liquidated, as they were in Egypt.[25]

In the period 1948–67 the membership of the Brotherhood declined, falling to only around 1.000 members in 1967.[26] One reason for this lay in the Brotherhood's traditionally strong ties to King Hussein, who unlike the Arab nationalists enjoyed little support from the Palestinian population in the 1950s and 1960s.

The Brotherhood's activities in the Gaza Strip (1948–67)

The development of the Brotherhood in the Gaza Strip differed from that on the West Bank. In Gaza it was generally subject to the same conditions as its parent organisation, which had its headquarters in Cairo.

In the late 1940s the Brotherhood was suppressed by the Egyptian regime, led by King Farouk. Following the coup that brought Nasser and the Free Officers to power in 1952, the situation changed.[27] Several of the officers had close ties with the Brotherhood, and in the first years after the coup the two parties co-operated; indeed, the Brotherhood was seen by many as being part of the government.[28] The organisation expanded its activities and its membership significantly increased. Thus in the immediate aftermath of the 1952 coup the Brotherhood was one of the most influential movements in the region, including the Gaza Strip. But it did not remain so. After Gamal Abd al-Nasser had got rid of most of the opposition and banned all political parties, the Brotherhood too was suppressed. In 1954 Nasser accused the

Muslim Brotherhood of backing an attempted coup against the regime. He banned the movement, which thereafter went underground. Nasser proceeded to crack down on the Brotherhood's members; thousands were arrested, and several of the movement's leaders were executed. It is therefore paradoxical that the Brotherhood's most conspicuous political activities were initiated in the Gaza Strip after 1954. In 1955, along with other political groups, the organisation took part in mass demonstrations against a plan aimed at relocating Palestinian refugees from Gaza to the Sinai Peninsular – a plan that was eventually withdrawn under pressure from public opinion. The following year members of the Brotherhood were active in the resistance against the short-lived Israeli occupation that resulted from the Tripartite Invasion of Egypt in 1956.[29] In the late 1950s the Brotherhood had largely played out its role as a factor in the power politics of Egypt and the Gaza Strip. Apart from the massive repression of its members, there was another important reason behind the Brotherhood's loss of influence: namely, that Nasser's pan-Arabic ideology had gradually taken hold not only among intellectuals but also among ordinary people throughout the Middle East. From the late 1950s and throughout the 1960s themes such as Arab nationalism, Arab unity, socialism and the liberation of Palestine were high on the political agenda of the Arab world – both in government circles and among general Arab population. The Brotherhood, by contrast, put less emphasis on these themes, focusing more on Islam as a frame of reference and as an aspect of identity.[30]

The Islamic movement's activities under the Israeli occupation (1967–87)

In the aftermath of the Arab defeat in 1967, Palestinian nationalism flourished,[31] and the PLO quite rapidly emerged the victor in the political power struggle waged against the royal family in the occupied Palestinian territories.

While this power struggle was still under way, the Islamic movements played only a minor role. It was not until the late 1970s that they once again came into the foreground in Palestinian society. Several external factors combined helped to give greater prominence to Islamism in the occupied territories:

1. The re-establishment of active Islamist movements in the surrounding Arab national states, such as Egypt and Syria.[32] These movements became particularly active immediately after the defeat of Pan-Arabism in 1967.
2. The economic support that the newly enriched Gulf oil states had provid-

ed since 1973 to the Islamist movements in the occupied Palestinian territories. As a result of the oil crisis in the West, the Arab Gulf states had experienced an economic boost on a scale unprecedented in their history. The Gulf states' support of the Islamist movements was motivated primarily by a desire to secure influence and legitimacy in the Arab-Islamic world for the countries of the Arabian peninsula.

3. The Islamist revolution of 1978–79 in Iran, which was presented as tangible proof of the potential of the Islamist project – a project aimed ultimately at securing power and establishing an Islamic state.

4. Hizballah's military activities, which were among the prime reasons for Israel's withdrawal in 1985 from large areas of Lebanon. In 2000 Hizballah's continued struggle against the Israeli occupation of Southern Lebanon led Israel to withdraw from Lebanon entirely. These activities convinced many Palestinians that Islam was a force capable of putting an end to Israel's occupation of Palestine.

5. Jordan's assistance to Islamist groups, aimed at maintaining Jordanian influence in Palestinian society. As the traditional, pro-Jordanian elite lost ground as a result of Israel's economic policy in the occupied territories, the Islamists became important players in the Jordanian royal family's game.

In the Brotherhood's view the defeat of 1967, and the resulting bankruptcy of Pan-Arabism, proved that all previous attempts to liberate Palestine had been mistaken. It was now high time to give Islam a chance. Although the Brotherhood found itself in the doldrums immediately after the war, by the following year it had already begun taking the initiative to establish philanthropic organisations, discussion clubs and so on in close association with the mosques. After 1973 these activities expanded as funds from the Gulf States began to pour in. In the mid-1970s the Brotherhood was reorganised, with the branches in the Gaza Strip and the West Bank joining forces to form a common organisation with the Brotherhood in Jordan.

The Brotherhood's strategy was to re-islamise Palestinian society through converting individuals. According to Sahliyeh, during this period the organisation worked on:

> regenerating Islamic society and creating an Islamic state. The Brotherhood was convinced that reform was a precondition for transforming society, and that individual liberation from corruption, fear, ignorance and materialism would lead to social reform. The Brotherhood believed that an Islamic reawakening could occur peacefully. They encouraged individuals to refrain from using violent or rev-

olutionary means. They believed moreover that the creation of an Islamic state would herald a wave of Islamic victories. [33]

The first social institution to be established on this basis in the wake of the Israeli occupation was *al-Mujamma'al-Islâmi* (the Islamic Centre). The initiative came from the leader of the Muslim Brotherhood in Gaza, Sheikh Ahmad Yasin, in the early 1970s. In the mid-1970s a number of similar Islamic institutions began to shoot up. Among the most important was *al-Jam'iyya al-Islâmiyya*, founded in 1976 by another influential Islamist, Khalil Quqa. Until his deportation by the Israeli occupying powers in the late 1980s, Khalil Quqa was employed as a schoolteacher in UNRWA (the United Nations Relief and Works Agency for Palestinian Refugees) and was likewise *khatîb* (prayerleader) in Masjid al-Shamali in the Shati refugee camp.[34] Since its foundation in 1976 *al-Jam'iyya al-Islâmiyya* has established a total of nine branches in the Gaza Strip. Another of the large and influential Islamic institutions in the Gaza Strip is *Jamiyyat al-Salâh al-Islâmiyya*, created in the Bureij camp in 1978. There is also an Islamic institution for women, *Jam'iyyat al-Shabât al-Muslimât*, which offers corresponding services for young Muslim women via a number of centres in various parts of the Gaza Strip.[35] In addition to these institutions there are several minor Islamist NGOs that – unlike those mentioned above – focus primarily on single tasks.

Thus in the course of the 1970s the Islamists succeeded in bringing themselves to the attention of the Palestinian population in the occupied territories. This happened not only within the sphere of social welfare, but also in the educational sector. In 1978 the Islamist movement co-operated with nationalist forces in establishing the first university in the Gaza Strip, the Islamic University of Gaza (IUG). In the early 1980s, after a long power struggle with the nationalists, the Islamists took control of the university.[36] According to Hamas spokesman Mahmoud Zahhar, the Islamist movements controlled 150 of the roughly 600 mosques in the Gaza Strip. The Waqf administered the remaining mosques.

The Islamists began making their mark on the social front in the mid-1970s, and in the educational sphere after 1978, but the time was not yet ripe for a political breakthrough. This was due primarily to the fact that, unlike the various fractions within the PLO, the Brotherhood was not involved in military activities against the Israeli occupation. At this stage its efforts were focused solely on the re-islamisation of society.[37] Not surprisingly, this gave rise to sharp criticism, particularly from left-wing members of the PLO. Thus in 1992 the PFLP's English-language publication, *Democratic Palestine*, wrote:

Aside from some exceptions meant for their own political purposes, 'the activities of this reactionary movement had, to a great extent, been in tune with the Zionist plans. From the very beginning, they directed their actions against the national institutions and figures to further deepen confessional feuds, to divert our people's struggle from its main course against occupation and to exhaust the national movement in minor disputes under the pretext of fighting atheism'. [38]

The PFLP's accusations against the Brotherhood are not without substance. In the course of the 1980s there were several respects in which – because of its struggle against "atheism" – its interests coincided with those of the Israeli state. Thus in 1980 Islamists were involved in an attack on the offices of the Red Crescent in Gaza, which they accused of being a communist concern. [39]

However, the Brotherhood was not alone in opposing the left-oriented forces within the PLO. The largest PLO fraction, Fatah, also periodically took issue with the left-wing part of the organisation. This coincidence of interests between Fatah and the Brotherhood led to a short-lived alliance between the two groups. In the late 1970s and early 1980s the two organisations entered into a coalition with several student councils at the Palestinian universities. [40] Fatah thus played an active role in strengthening the political credibility and legitimacy of the Islamist forces.

Islamic Jihad puts pressure on the Brotherhood

In 1980 a split occurred within the Muslim Brotherhood. [41] The breakaway group called itself Islamic Jihad (*Jihâd Islâmî*), and was strongly inspired by the Islamic revolution in Iran. Its two founders, Fathi al-Shaqaqi and Abd al-Aziz Auda, were also greatly influenced by the movement of the same name created in 1979 in Egypt, where both of them had studied in the late 1970s. [42]

Islamic Jihad takes a similar view of the Palestinian problem as the Brotherhood, likewise seeing it in religious terms. According to Islamic Jihad, the solution to the problem lies in an Islamic war of liberation aimed at establishing an Islamic Palestine. What is unique to this new movement is that it has succeeded in doing what neither the Brotherhood nor the nationalist PLO could do, namely in mixing Islamism with nationalism in the struggle against Zionism – and hence against the state of Israel.

Throughout the 1980s Islamic Jihad carried out a series of armed attacks on Israeli military targets, becoming especially active in 1986–87. Islamic Jihad thus played a central role in the period immediately before the first

Palestinian Intifada broke out in December 1987.[43] There is no doubt that the popularity and dynamism of this Islamist group played a crucial role in the Brotherhood's decision to participate actively in the resistance against the Israeli occupation. The numerous actions taken by Islamic Jihad were greeted with joy, deep respect and large-scale demonstrations of sympathy by the Palestinian population, which threatened the Brotherhood's position within the Islamist-oriented community in Palestinian society. Many forces within the Brotherhood, particularly among its younger members, began to press for a more active policy directed against the occupying power. The Intifada inevitably led to a change of strategy on the part of the Brotherhood, and from 1987 onwards it began to participate actively in the resistance against Israel.

The rise of Hamas as a movement

It is clear that people with links to the Brotherhood were active in the uprising that marked the beginning of the Intifada. As early as 8 December 1987 leading forces within *al-Mujamma' al-Islâmî* met in Sheikh Ahmad Yasin's home in Gaza.[44] A week later the first leaflet signed by *Harakât al-Muqâwama al-Islâmiyya* (the Islamic Resistance Movement) was on the streets. However, it was only the fourth such leaflet, dated 11 February 1988, that made clear the movement's association with the Muslim Brotherhood.[45] In this leaflet the initials HMS were used for the first time, and in the following leaflets the acronym Hamas[46] was adopted.

With this fourth leaflet a new phase in Hamas' story began. The movement started to call for strikes on fixed days and encouraged direct confrontation with the Israeli occupying forces. The younger and more activist-oriented forces within the Brotherhood had thus managed to force through their policy. If the Brotherhood had refrained from taking a more activist line, the movement would undoubtedly have lost influence. The "new" activist movement, Hamas, which from this point onwards totally eclipsed the Brotherhood, fought against the Israeli occupation on an equal footing with the nationalist forces within the PLO (and Islamic Jihad). Hamas was able so rapidly to take over the role of the Brotherhood precisely because it was not, in fact, a new movement at all. Right from the start, the organisation had made use of the Islamist network and the institutions established many years earlier by the Muslim Brotherhood.[47]

Despite ideological differences between the nationalist leadership and Hamas, a *modus vivendi* between the two groups and their respective supporters was established at the beginning of the Intifada. In the summer of

1988 a new phase of the Intifada began, marked by greater tension between Hamas and the United National Leadership of the Uprising (UNLU). Increasingly, Hamas began to present itself as an alternative to the PLO. In August 1988 the movement issued a 40-page charter setting out its aims and means.[48] The charter notably appeared just at the point where the PLO expressed a serious desire to participate in an international peace conference based on UN Resolution 242, i.e. on recognition of the state of Israel – an initiative that Hamas sharply repudiated. It is therefore plausible, as several researchers have emphasised, that the charter was timed to coincide with this shift in policy on the part of the PLO.[49]

Hamas and the peace negotiations

When the then PLO chairman, Yasir Arafat, decided to participate in the Madrid conference[50] in October 1991, despite internal opposition to the move, relations with Hamas were strained still further. Hamas was among the first to take a firm stand against the conference, both on the grounds that no one in their view had the right to relinquish Palestinian territory, due to the religious aspect by such an act,[51] and – equally important, if not more so – on the grounds that the conditions for Palestinian participation were too limiting. In Hamas' view, the premises of the Madrid formula made it impossible to achieve any positive result.[52]

In a leaflet issued in connection with the opening of the Madrid Conference, Hamas wrote that the purpose of the conference was primarily to give international legitimacy to the Zionist entity and to stop the Arabs' boycott.[53]

They went on to say that "the most that enemies of God and humanity" could propose was a sort of "self-government" (*hukm dhati*) for the Palestinians. Thus, "we are asked to sign our death sentence ourselves".[54] Three years earlier the leaders of the Hamas movement had already made clear what they thought of resolving the conflict through negotiation. The movement's charter stated that:

Those conferences are nothing but a form of enforcing the rule of the unbelievers in the land of Muslims. And when have the unbelievers justly treated the believers? [55]

As the peace negotiations in Madrid and, later, Washington failed to make any progress, and as Hamas' armed wing, *Kata'ib Izz al-Din al-Qassam*,[56] carried out several attacks on Israeli military targets, Hamas' position was strengthened among the Palestinian population. One result of Hamas' armed struggle was that its members were imprisoned in ever greater numbers by the Israeli occupying forces. This development enhanced the movement's prestige in Palestinian society. At the same time, Hamas became more aggressive in its criticisms of the PLO, which in the summer of 1992 led to regular conflicts with the PLO's Fatah wing.

Increasingly, Hamas was seen as an alternative to the PLO. But Hamas repudiated this position. The movement's former official spokesman in Jordan, Ibrahim Ghawsha, participated in negotiations with the PLO leadership in the early 1990s aimed at gaining acceptance of the Islamist movement within the PLO. Ghawsha says of these negotiations:

> We have had many meetings with Arafat. I have personally led several Hamas delegations and we have met with Arafat in Yemen, Sudan and elsewhere. He has done his best to have Hamas incorporated into the PLO. Of course he's done so out of his own self interest, so he can say to the Europeans and Americans: I've got all Palestinian society in my pocket. I control everyone.
>
> I remember how in April 1990 I got a message from Hamas to meet with the top man in the Palestinian National Council (PNC). He asked whether we wanted to be members of the National Council. We said OK, we would like to participate, but only on condition that members of the National Council would be elected through direct, free elections, involving all the Palestinian people – under these conditions we as Islamists would participate. But to say as they did, you can have 18 out of 480 seats on the National Council – naturally we rejected that. Subsequently one of the people close to Arafat contacted me and said: "OK, Ibrahim, we're ready to give you 25 seats." I replied: "Excuse me, but this institution is the Palestinian people's institution, we don't want any more seats that we have won and earned." He then responded that it was extremely difficult to carry out an election. Our position at that point was that if it was impossible to carry out a direct election, we would agree in the meantime to be members of the National Council, but we wanted 40 per cent of the seats on it. We put forward this demand on the basis that around 40 per cent of the Palestinian population at that point supported the Islamists. At present the support is around 50 per cent. Naturally Arafat refused, and we did too since we want our share of seats to correspond to the level of support in the population. Another key point is that we want to change Arafat's dictatorial style through the National Council. The other Palestinian groups

aren't in a position to do anything, but if we got 40 per cent of the seats, we could do something. This is the reason we refused to participate. We're not against the PLO.[57]

Despite failing to reach an agreement whereby Hamas would be included on the PNC, the two parties agreed after the unrest of summer 1992 that the power struggle between them had to take a peaceful form, unless they were bent on a self-destructive internal struggle that would only benefit the state of Israel, which after all was their common enemy. The basic disagreements remained the same. Hamas opposed the peace negotiations, whereas the PLO, and particularly Fatah, continued their efforts to achieve a break-through in the negotiations – a breakthrough that continued to elude them mainly because of opposition on the part of the Likud government in Israel.[58]

The Oslo Agreement

The situation became more tense when, in late August 1993, it emerged that the PLO and Israel had agreed to sign the Oslo I agreement at secret negoti-ations in Oslo.[59] Immediately before Oslo I was signed, Hamas issued leaflet No. 102, which declared among other things:[60]

The agreement is simply one more phase in the occupation, and you will see that the people who have surrendered through weakness will seek to present this agreement, which is miserable, as if it were an enor-mous gain. The reality is that the occupation continues. What is hap-pening is simply a reshuffle [of Israeli forces] and the establishment of limited autonomy, which in reality is controlled from outside. The Arafat leadership, which has surrendered, is seeking to destroy the PLO and to destroy the movement purely because of its economic crisis. We emphasise that the Arafat leadership and those who support it do not represent our people. They speak only for themselves because they have disregarded Palestinian society and its institutions ... they also declare that they wish to erase the Palestinian constitution simply to satisfy America and the Zionist entity.

The festivities and speeches offered by the Arafat leadership and those who support it in our holy land are intended only to present the agreement in a positive light to our people ... We ask why the occupy-ing powers allow this but don't allow the opposition, and particularly Hamas, to express their views. During the Madrid negotiations we expressed our attitude to this kind of solution, and said that we would not surrender an inch of Palestinian soil. We will therefore insist on ruining this agreement and continue our resistance struggle and our *jihâd* against the occupying powers. We reject any action leading to a Palestinian civil war, not least because the result would only be to the benefit of our Zionist enemy. The Arafat leadership bears responsibility for ruining Palestinian society and planting the seeds of disunity and a split among Palestinians.[61]Around the time that the agreement was signed on 13 September 1993, fears were expressed for the first time that civil war might break out in the occupied territories. In particular, the opposition groups were afraid that the strong police force that would have to be established in the autonomous areas would be used against them, since they intended to continue their armed struggle against the Israeli occupation. A statement from ten opposition movements, consisting of eight groups within the PLO – including the PFLP and DFLP, together with Hamas and Islamic Jihad – declared:

Arafat and his team of losers see themselves as being involved in creating a strong police force[62] to ensure the security of the Zionist entity, crush the Intifada and crack down on national and Islamic resistance … this will lead to civil war.[63]

During this period spokesmen from the Hamas movement repeatedly emphasised that Hamas "would employ all possible peaceful means in relation to the movements' disputes with all Palestinian groups".[64] Hamas' attitude towards the Palestinian Authority and Israel was based on the following logic: notwithstanding Oslo I and the subsequent agreements, Israel is still an occupying power which it is legitimate to combat, and the armed struggle therefore continues. If the Palestinian Authority opposes Hamas on these grounds, Hamas will remain passive in relation to the Authority, but will retaliate against the state of Israel, which was responsible in the first instance for forcing the Authority to crack down on the Islamist movement. By adopting this logic Hamas believed that they could safeguard themselves against the worst possible outcome from the Palestinian point of view, namely civil war. The late Hamas leader Abdel Aziz Rantisi expressed this rationale as follows:

Formerly it was Israel that cracked down on us, now it is the Palestinian Authority. Some believe this will lead to a Palestinian civil war. This will not happen. Despite the Authority's crackdown on Hamas, we will remain patient. We will continue our struggle against the enemy, the occupying power. We can put it like this – the Authority will continue to crack down on us, and we will continue the struggle against Israel. That is the principle.[65]

Hamas' strategic decision to avoid a civil war scenario at all costs has on the one hand proved a strength, in so far as any internal Palestinian conflict would only serve to promote Israeli interests, but on the other hand has weakened Hamas' hand in relation to the Authority. No matter what measures the Authority takes, it knows that Hamas is neither willing nor able to retaliate. The Hamas leadership itself is fully aware of this problem. Ghazi Hamad, the editor of the Islamist weekly *al-Risâla*, puts it as follows:

> The Authority is convinced that Hamas is sincere in saying that it doesn't want a civil war – we don't want to direct our weapons against the Authority. I believe that the Authority is exploiting the fact that Hamas doesn't want – will never want – to use force against the Authority, and is [therefore] exercising restraint. They exploit this form of weakness.[66]

The Authority's policy towards Hamas after 1994

Through its agreements with Israel the Palestinian Authority has committed itself to cracking down on "terrorism", which in practice means the Islamist opposition. This commitment was spelled out in the Hebron Protocol of January 1997. In the appendix to this agreement ("note for the record") the Palestinian Authority signed, among other things, the following pledge:

> The Palestinian side reaffirms its commitments to the following measures and principles in accordance with the Interim Agreement:
> [...]
> Fighting terror and preventing violence
> Strengthening security co-operation
> Preventing incitement and hostile propaganda, as specified in Article XXII of the Interim Agreement
> Combat systematically and effectively terrorist organisations and infrastructure
> Apprehension, prosecution and punishment of terrorists ...[67]

Roughly the same wording is used in the subsequent Wye River Memorandum, dated autumn 1998.[68] During the negotiation process

(1993–2000) the Palestinian Authority had committed itself to close co-operation with Israel on security matters. One of Israel's key demands in relation to the Palestinian Authority and the implementation of the signed agreement has been that the Palestinian authorities would seek to eliminate resistance against Israel and the agreements themselves; this applies particularly to the Islamist opposition.

After Hamas' armed wing *Izz ad-Din al-Qassam* carried out a new series of suicide attacks on Israel in 1996, this demand was stepped up. The suicide attacks represented a response to Mossad's liquidation of Yahya Ayash, alias *al-Muhandis* (the Engineer). The Engineer was at the top of Israel's list of wanted men and was said to have manufactured several bombs that exploded in various Israeli towns in 1994 and 1995. His death was bound to evoke a response from Hamas, as the Israelis knew very well.[69] Under an agreement previously contracted by Hamas and the Palestinian Authority, Hamas waited to deliver its response until after the Palestinian election, which was held in January 1996. But on 25 February 1996, the second anniversary of the Hebron massacre,[70] they launched a series of four suicide bombs over a period of less than two weeks. In the aftermath, disagreements within Hamas surfaced once again. While several of the movement's founders in the Gaza Strip appealed to the *Izz al-Din al-Qassam* brigades to stop reacting with bombs, the Hamas headquarters which was located in Amman at the time declared that no decision had been taken to stop or suspend actions directed against Israel.[71] These actions provoked a witch-hunt of Hamas members by both the Israelis and the Palestinians. More than 1,200 members were arrested, a number of Islamist social institutions were ransacked and subsequently closed down (the closures formally took place on 25 September 1997), and more important still, the private mosques that had hitherto been controlled by Hamas were put under the control of the Palestinian Minister of Religious Affairs (*Wazîrat al-Awqâf*). A further result of Hamas' military actions was that the leaders of 31 states – including a long list of then presidents and heads of states such as the American president Bill Clinton, the French Prime Minister Jacques Chirac, the British Prime Minister John Major, the German Chancellor Helmut Kohl, and most of the Arab leaders, together with Shimon Peres and the then-Secretary General of the UN, Boutros Boutros-Ghali – met in the Egyptian town of Sharm al-Sheikh on the Sinai peninsular for a one-day anti-terrorist summit dubbed "the Conference of the Peacemakers". The concluding statement from the summit, known as the Sharm al-Sheikh declaration, read as follows:

We decided: to support the Israel-Palestinian agreement, the continuation of the negotiating process ... and [to] prevent terrorist organisations from engaging in recruitment, supplying arms, or fund raising ... To exert maximum efforts to identify and determine the sources of financing for these groups and to co-operate in cutting them off, and by provide training, equipment and other forms of support to those taking steps against groups using violence and terror to undermine peace, security or stability.[72]

Concrete measures taken against the Islamists by the Palestinian Authority

The measures taken by the Palestinian Authority against the Islamists in the Palestinian areas stemmed first and foremost from the fact that neither Arafat, Israel nor the United States wished to acknowledge that, in the initial period after its establishment, the Authority did not enjoy a monopoly of power. Arafat on the contrary was concerned to stress that only one authority existed.

It was thus quite natural that the Authority should initially direct its attention against the armed wing of Hamas, *Izz ad-Din al-Qassam*. Each time *Izz ad-Din al-Qassam* carried out armed attacks or suicide bombings, Arafat launched a crackdown and arrested numerous members of Hamas' military wing. Arafat's strategy was thus to force the Islamists to give up the armed struggle. On principle, however, the Islamists have refused to renounce violence. Nevertheless, both Hamas and Islamic Jihad redefined their strategy around this time. As a direct result of pressure from the Authority, for example, the two movements decided in the late 1990s not to carry out attacks from areas under the Authority's control. Instead, these attacks were launched from areas B or C on the West Bank (cf. the Oslo II agreement signed 28 September 1995). This meant in effect that *Izz ad-Din al-Qassam* no longer played a significant role in the Gaza Strip.

As discussed in the previous section, the Authority during the late 1990s went further than simply suppressing and virtually eliminating Hamas' military infrastructure. In an attempt to force the Islamists to accept and adapt themselves to the new political "reality", they also cracked down on civil Islamist institutions. In September 1997, under pressure from Israel and the United States, the Authority closed down 16 key Islamic institutions in the Gaza Strip, including *al-Jam'iyya al-Islâmiyya*, *al-Mujamma' al-Islâmî* and *al-Jam'iyyat al-Salâh al-Islâmiyya*. The alleged justification for these measures was that, through the agreements it had concluded with Israel, the Authority had pledged to "break up" the so-called "Islamic infrastructure" or "the terrorists' infrastructure".[73]

In addition, the Authority sought to cut off the Islamists' funding, a move that will be discussed in more detail below. The result was an institutional weakening of the Islamic movement in relation to the Authority.[74] These measures also gave rise to a series of internal discussions and disagreements within Hamas. After 1996 Hamas split into two camps. One camp aims to exert its influence within the areas of civil society in which Hamas has always played an important role: education, social welfare and the family. This camp wishes to be involved in the political process and influence legislation, even though it remains on principle against the "peace process". The other camp is more uncompromising and seeks to continue armed military resistance against the continuing Israeli occupation of Palestinian territories. Geographically the first camp has its stronghold in the Gaza Strip, while the second is to be found among the exile leadership. In 1999 Hamas' leadership in exile was expelled from Jordan and now has its main base in Damascus. It should be added, however, that a number of hard-liners were to be found among the leaders in the Gaza Strip during the late 1990s, including for example the preacher Ahmad Nimr and Abdel Aziz Rantisi.

The Palestinian Authority and Palestinian civil society

Since my empirical data relate to Palestinian civil society, I will focus in what follows on the measures that the Authority has attempted to carry out in this area. Shortly after its establishment the Authority drafted legislation aimed at regulating Palestinian civil society. In contrast to many other parts of the Arab world Palestine had a well-developed network of NGOs, which had arisen as a direct consequence of the Israeli occupation. As an occupying power Israel maintained only the most basic public services for the Palestinian population. The various Palestinian NGOs – both secular and Islamic – were set up to fill the resulting vacuum. These organisations took on a number of functions within the fields of health, agriculture, education, leisure, social welfare and so on. According to Denis Sullivan (1996), when the Palestinian Authority was established in 1994 Palestinian NGOs were responsible for 60 per cent of healthcare, 50 per cent of hospital care, 100 per cent of care for the disabled, 100 per cent of agricultural development and 30 per cent of education (including virtually all kindergartens). It was quite natural that the Palestinian Authority should seek to regulate civil society; such regulation after all is a feature of states all over the world. The problem in the Palestinian context is that, through the various measures it has taken, the Authority has sought to exert full control over civil society and thereby undermined the possibility of democratic development.

In September 1995 the Palestinian Authority issued a draft law concerning charitable organisations, social agencies and private institutions, also known as the NGO law. The draft replaced an earlier version that had come under criticism from a number of Palestinian NGOs, but did not differ radically from it.[75] According to a Palestinian civil servant, these restrictive proposals were based on the following argument: "We do not wish Iran or other groups or countries to send money to Palestine with a view to undermining us, the government and society."[76] The whole spirit of the draft law was to prevent the NGOs from acting independently of the Authority. Under pressure from foreign donors, among others, both drafts were withdrawn, and it was decided that no NGO law should be passed until the election of the Palestinian Legislative Council (PLC), which took place on January 1996.[77]

By late 1993 a number of Palestinian NGOs had already formed an umbrella organisation, the Palestinian NGO Network (PNGO). Since then the PNGO has sought to co-operate with the Palestinian Authority on behalf of around 70 of the largest and most prominent secular Palestinian NGOs. One of the PNGO's main projects has been to build a good relationship with the Authority through meetings and discussions concerning the draft NGO law.[78] The PNGO aimed thereby to demonstrate that it was not a rival to the Authority, but rather complemented its work. However, the impression as of the late 1990s was that the Authority continued to nurture a profound mistrust of the NGOs. The Authority's policies, and its mistrustful attitude, were to be seen for example in its establishment of an alternative NGO forum in the Gaza Strip in 1996. This initiative was backed by no less a person than Tayyib Abdel Rahim, a prominent member of Fatah and secretary general of the President's office. All the members of the new forum were 100 per cent loyal to the late president Yassir Arafat and to Fatah. At the same time this new, loyal NGO forum treated the independent NGOs as competitors to the Palestinian Authority in the battle for funding, and as a hidden form of opposition. Finally, the loyal NGOs and the Palestinian Authority had great difficulty in accepting criticism, for example concerning violations of human rights. Certain representatives of the Authority evidently regarded such criticisms as an expression of fifth column activity.

Because of this ambiguous relationship with the Authority, the PNGO campaigned for a long time for an NGO law to be passed. The story surrounding this legislation gives a good picture both of the ambiguous division of competence between the legislative and executive branches of the Authority, and of the strength of the government's desire to control the

NGOs. Following a number of procedural mistakes and discussions in the Palestinian Legislative Council – and among the NGOs – a controversial NGO law was passed in 1999.[79] Many Palestinian critics, such as the former ombudsman Iyad Sarraj, believed that the campaign against the NGOs was an attempt to lay a smokescreen over the Authority's own scandalous behaviour.[80]

Developments within the Islamist sector of civil society

The Authority has thus sought to acquire control over civil society in general. However, during the period 1993–2000 their attention was directed particularly at the Islamist community. Among other things the Authority closed down 16 Islamic NGOs, including *al-Jam'iyya al-Islâmiyya, al-Mujamma' al-Islâmî* and *al-Jam'iyya al-Salâh al-Islâmiyya*. The leaders of the Islamic NGOs themselves found these closures incomprehensible. Sheikh Ahmad Bahr told me:

> It was a crisis for us when the Authority closed these institutions, because we are legal institutions in terms of the current, Ottoman law in the area. We provide a series of services for the families of martyrs, for orphans and poor families, and we also offer sports activities for young people. So these institutions perform humanitarian services for people. So we've been in a crisis since the closure … I believe the Authority carried out [the closure] under Israeli and American pressure. It's impossible to justify closing down these institutions.[81]

The same views could be heard from the leaders of the other Islamic NGOs and Hamas. However, the Hamas leaders also stressed that they had no institutional connection with the NGOs, and they rejected all implications that these institutions constituted Hamas' own infrastructure. Abu Shanab stated in this regard:

> This isn't the infrastructure of Hamas, but the infrastructure of the Palestinian people.

In an article from the end of 1997 entitled "For whose sake were the Islamic institutions closed?" the Islamic weekly *al-Risâla* raised a number of key questions concerning the closure:

Can the Palestinian Authority fill the vacuum that has arisen as a result of the closures? Who is going to suffer [as a result of the closures]? The people behind the bombings, or the orphans and poor people? Tell me, who?[82]

The newspaper went on to say that around 2,500 families in the Gaza Strip were financially dependent on the assistance provided by the Islamic institutions. Though the Authority formally closed the institutions, they still manage in practice to keep functioning, albeit at a lower level. The Authority of course knows very well that these institutions are still going. Through this ambiguous policy the Authority is able to claim to Israel and the United States that they are genuinely doing something to undermine the Islamists' infrastructure, while at the same time stopping short of cutting off all ties with the internal opposition. What has happened is that the institutions' offices have been sealed up, and their computers and cars confiscated, while at the same time efforts have been made to put people loyal to the Authority on the boards of the institutions – although this has not happened in the case of *al-Jam'iyya al-Islâmiyya*.

"Drying out" the Islamist NGOs

The blocking of financial support to the NGOs during the late 1990s played a crucial role in weakening the Islamist organisations. The funds have dried up not because Muslims the world over no longer wish to support the Palestinian people but because, on the contrary, various forces have sought to prevent them from providing that support.

The question of financial support to the Islamists is very sensitive, as can be seen in the answer I received on the issue in an interview with Sheikh Ahmad Bahr, leader of *al-Jam'iyya al-Islâmiyya*. Asked to what extent *al-Jam'iyya al-Islâmiyya* had been supported financially since its establishment in the 1970s, he replied:

We keep coming back to the same … interrogation. Are you conducting an academic study? This is unacademic. I'm an academic myself, so I know what I'm talking about. This is political.[83]

In Sheikh Ahmad Bahr's understanding, raising the question of the Gulf States' provision of financial support to the Palestinian Islamist NGOs is synonymous with the attempt to equate the Palestinian Islamic movement with the rest of the international Islamic community, which the West regards as a community of "terrorists". Earlier in the same interview Sheikh Bahr complained about my efforts to establish the connections between the various NGOs in the Gaza Strip. Apropos of this, he said:

> The questions you ask are the questions of an interrogator, and the final conclusion will be that we are terrorists ... maybe you are OK, but in the end it will turn out exactly as I've said ...[84]

And he continued:

> Everyone comes with the same questions, posed in various ways, and everyone says that they are journalists, researchers or professors at this or that university, and everyone arrives at the same conclusion ... that is my experience.

This interview demonstrates very clearly the lack of trust on the part of Islamists towards Western researchers and perhaps journalists in particular. Events in the Gaza Strip (and beyond) may mean that Islamists feel that it is essential to be on their guard.

In 1996 the Islamist NGO *al-Jamîyyat al-Salâh al-Islâmiyya* (JSI) issued a small pamphlet summing up the institution's activities. On the last page the JSI thanks the various agencies and institutions that have enabled them to offer diverse forms of assistance. It is noteworthy – or perhaps quite natural – that the JSI began first and foremost by thanking the late President Yasir Arafat, followed by a number of ministers of the Palestinian Authority. It then went on to thank the following institutions:

- *Lajnat al-Ightâha al-Islâmiyya* – Nazareth, Israel
- *Lajnat al-Ightâha al-Insâniyya* – Nazareth, Israel
- *Al-Jam'iyya al-Islâmiyya al-Ightâha al-Insâniyya* – Kfar Qasim, Israel
- *Jam'iyya Ri'ayat al-Sajîn wal-Aytîm* – Umm al-Fahm, Israel
- *Lajnat Zakat al-Naqab* – Negev, Israel
- *Al-Sandûq al-Filistîni lil-aghâtha wal-Tanmiyya* – London
- *Mu'assasat al-ard al-muqaddasa* – United States

After this pamphlet was published a number of the supporting organisations listed were closed down or investigated by various intelligence agencies. In 1996 Israel closed the following NGOs: *Lajnat al-Ightâtha al-Islâmiyya* – Nazareth, Israel; *Lajnat al-Ightâtha al-Insâniyya* – Nazareth, Israel; *Jam'iyya Ri'âyat al-Sajîn wal-Aytîm* – Umm al-Fahm, Israel.[85] Later, in spring 1997, the Israeli government prohibited a number of foreign Islamic NGOs from providing support to Palestinians in the occupied territories. This applied to, among others, *Al-Sandûq al-Filistîni lil-aghâtha wal-Tanmiyya* (London) and *Mu'assasat al-ard al-muqaddasa* (United States). On this occasion Israel made use of a law from the period of the British mandate, which enabled them to prohibit the activities of institutions deemed to constitute a threat to state security and public order.[86] Other Islamic NGOs – including the International Islamic Relief Organisation (IIRO) and The World Association of Muslim Youth – have likewise come under the searchlight of the Israeli and Western intelligence agencies. According to a Western intelligence source the IIRO is a clearinghouse for around 20 million American dollars a year in Saudi Arabian economic support to Islamists in Gaza and the West Bank.[87] The same Western intelligence source claims that a large proportion of this help is first transferred to bank accounts in London and Amman belonging to Islamic charitable organisations such as the Palestine and Lebanon Relief and Development Fund (Interpal).[88] These two organisations also figure on *al-Jamîyyat al-Salâh al-Islâmiyya*'s thank you list. The Israeli police accuse these organisations of being among the main contributors to Hamas; in particular, Israeli sources claim, they donate large sums to the families of martyrs. However, when the British Charity Commission carried out a three-month-long investigation of these organisations in 1996, it found no indications of donations to Hamas.[89] The leaders of the organisations in question also deny that there have been any such transfers of funds. Essam Mustafa, vice-chairman of Interpal, categorically denied that the latter was associated in any way with a political organisation. He argued in an interview that the funding gathered and distributed by Interpal was well documented, as were the sources and beneficiaries.[90]

However, it is not only the Palestinian NGOs in Israel and Western Europe that have come under scrutiny; NGOs in the United States have also been hit. The United States' then president, Bill Clinton, signed an "executive order" on 23 January 1995 freezing all assets belonging to a long list of organisations and individuals and prohibiting financial transactions with them.[91] The reason for introducing this executive order was allegedly that "grave acts of violence committed by foreign terrorists that disrupt the Middle East Peace process constitute an unusual and extraordinary threat to national security, foreign policy, and economy of the United States".[92] Among the organisations covered by the new law were Hamas, the DFLP, and the PFLP; while Ahmad Yasin was among the individuals targeted.

In January 1993 Israel accused the United States of being the fund-raising centre for Hamas. It is worth noting that Israel made these accusations less than a month after deporting around 400 Islamists to Marj az-Zuhour in Lebanon.[93] One of the NGOs that have been the focus of much attention in the American context is *Mu'assasat al-ard al-muqaddasa*, based in Ricardson, Texas. According to the *Washington Post*, this Islamic NGO is the biggest of its kind in the United States; the same source claims that it sends around two million dollars a year to the West Bank and the Gaza Strip.[94] In December 2001 US President George W. Bush decided to freeze all *Mu'assasat al-ard al-muqaddasa*'s assets because of the organisation's alleged links with Hamas.[95] Several Islamist NGOs and institutions in Chicago have also come under FBI investigation.[96]

One result of this campaign against Islamist NGOs in the West, and Israel's accusations against them, has been that legal Islamic NGOs in the West have also come under suspicion and been undermined. This has led to infringements of Muslims' freedom of action within Western civil society for the sake of Israel's "security". After 11 September the argument has naturally been that these rights have been curtailed for the safety of the nations in question. What is certain, in any case, is that such violations of freedom will lead in the long term to a sense of alienation among Muslims in the West, which may in turn give rise to new, hitherto unknown conflicts between the minority and the majority. The result of the campaign against the Islamist NGOs in the Palestinian context has been that the weakest groups in society have lost much-needed assistance from Islamist institutions.

Relations between Hamas and the Palestinian Authority during my fieldwork (1997–98)

During the period in which I was conducting my fieldwork, i.e. 1997–1998, the late Hamas leader Abu Shanab told me the following:

ABU SHANAB: I will be completely honest with you. We are a nation, and we are fighting for the same cause. We still have one enemy. The enemy is occupying our country; it is confiscating our land and judaising our country. It continues to kill our people. So in this context it is necessary to focus on the enemy, even if the Palestinian Authority is not acting properly. We don't want to go down that road. We will not let them make mistakes towards their own nation. And we will tell them that we are going to fight against our enemy. If we didn't have an external enemy, we would concentrate on our internal affairs.

MICHAEL: But that isn't the way the Authority looks at the situation. They no longer have an enemy. They seek peace with Israel, so they no longer have an enemy, which is tantamount to saying that you are the enemy ...

ABU SHANAB: You're right, but what we're doing is fair ... we don't want a confrontation. That's a one-way street. Although the Israelis are putting pressure on the Authority and the Authority is putting pressure on Hamas, Hamas won't put pressure on the Authority. It will put pressure on Israel. It's like a circle. We don't want to turn against the Authority, because that's precisely what Israel wants.

MICHAEL: But still you don't see this as a problem for Hamas. You draw a line in the sand first in one place and then in another. Where does it all end?

ABU SHANAB: Yes, we're losing, but we would lose still more if we confronted our brothers. So no matter what we do, we lose. In all aspects of every phase of life we're living in a crisis. That is the fate of Palestinians, so we are forced to choose between two bad choices, the bad and the worse.

MICHAEL: I've been talking with a number of young Hamas sympathisers. Several of them have stopped listening to the speeches of Hamas leaders. They have heard enough sensitive words without action. They say, politics, hmm, I can't be bothered with that any more, even though I support Hamas.

ABU SHANAB: We feel it's part of the price we have to pay; otherwise we'll have to pay an even heavier price. We make a choice. When these young people are a little older they'll understand that this is a wise choice, and we need to make wise choices.[97]

Another key figure in the Islamist movement, Ghazi Hamad, who since 1997 has been the editor of the Islamists' mouthpiece, *al-Risâla,* and latest spokesman of the Hamas-led government in the wake of the victory in the 2006 elections, says of the movement's relationship with the Authority during the late 1990s:

HAMAD: I think it's very cold. I believe that the Authority has chosen to follow the political game and ignore the opposition: ignore everything else. They want to achieve something through this political game. They take it for granted that the opposition or the Islamic movement don't offer any alternative. The Authority doesn't pay any attention to Palestinian society, and the rift between the Authority and the opposition, and particularly the Islamists, is therefore growing bigger. Nor do we hear anything about any kind of dialogue or at least meetings between the Authority and the Islamist movement. There's nothing.

MICHAEL: You mentioned that the Authority feels the opposition has no alternative. Do they have any alternative?

HAMAD: The opposition may have an alternative but the Authority doesn't believe in it. They quite simply don't want to believe in it. They take the view that the other side is of no account. This is particularly true now that they believe they have crushed Hamas' military wing and arrested the leaders. They believe [Hamas] will become more pragmatic and realistic and willing to co-operate with the Authority and turn its back on the military approach."[98]

There is no doubt that the Oslo agreements constituted a threat and great challenge to the Hamas movement. The PLO's peace initiatives and the obligations they have entered into to co-operate with the state of Israel have forced Hamas to think creatively and soften its uncompromising rhetoric. The movement has therefore worked out, if not a peace offer, then at least an offer that amounts to a long-lasting cease-fire with Israel.

Hudna: an Islamist solution to the conflict

In the early 1990s Sheikh Ahmad Yasin launched the idea of a *hudna* (cease-fire). Following his release from an Israeli prison in 1997, he made the following statement to that effect in a newspaper interview:

Islam permits a temporary truce for a limited period of time with the Jewish enemy if necessary ...We have said that Israel must carry out a complete withdrawal from the West Bank and Gaza, including holy East Jerusalem, dismantle all the settlements, release all the prisoners and detainees and open a safe passage for us between the West Bank and the Gaza Strip. It must not interfere in the affairs of the state we will establish, God willing. We must have total sovereignty over everything that is above and beneath the land, and we must have complete control of our borders and crossing points with the Arabic countries. If Israel did that then we would halt our military operations for a period of time, so that people can regain part of their normal life and stability and calm can prevail.[99]

Abu Shanab has stressed that for Hamas *hudna* is a strategic choice. Asked whether this represented an alternative to establishing peace with Israel, he replied:

ABU SHANAB: Yes. We wish to unite our nation because at the moment we are split, with some believing in negotiation and others not. The path of negotiation has failed. The national unity we seek has a strategy and a goal. We are compelled to change course and struggle to obtain our rights.

MICHAEL: Regardless of whether you support Hamas or the PLO, Israel exists. And the whole world supports Israel and the state's right to exist.

ABU SHANAB: But the world also recognises our rights, so we too have rights. We need to obtain these rights, and we will stick to this until Israel gives them to us.

MICHAEL: What I think I hear you saying are that you will accept a state on the West Bank and the Gaza Strip if Israel withdraws to the 1967 borders?

ABU SHANAB: Yes that is a compromise that won't apply forever. We call it *hudna* and we would accept such a compromise. What will happen from one generation to the next is anybody's guess.

MICHAEL: Thus we're talking of a *de facto* recognition?

ABU SHANAB: Yes, precisely because the state exists. *De facto* it is there, and we would not create problems for our neighbours and ourselves if we had a *hudna*. The concept of *hudna* is completely legitimate within the framework of Islam and would hold for at least this generation. Despite the fact that it does not give us all our rights, we hope for God's forgiveness. This takes us to the limits of what we can do. We have fought. We have fought up to this point. So we will keep to a *hudna* and live in peace and let others live in peace. Maybe we'll establish good connections, maybe not. I mean that this is something of a compromise.[100]

Thus there is no doubt that groups within Hamas have sought to adopt a pragmatic, *realpolitik* approach to recent developments. The movement has therefore shifted from a total rejection of the state of Israel's right to exist to *de facto* recognition. It is worth noting that Hamas' call to enter into a *hudna* is in full accordance with the UN Security Council resolutions on the Israeli–Palestinian conflict.[101] This is noteworthy precisely because, in its rhetoric, Hamas has been overly critical and sceptical towards the UN in general, particularly with regard to the UN's 1947 plan for dividing the territory. In the present situation, however, it makes good sense for Hamas to argue, as Yasin does, in favour of the UN's resolutions. This gives the movement a "double legitimacy", in the sense that the movement's proposal for a *hudna* is legitimate in terms of Islam, *and* has a basis in the UN's resolutions.

In principle, however, the strategy for achieving the creation of a Palestinian state on the West Bank and Gaza Strip is still to continue the armed struggle, since according to Hamas this is the only logic Israel understands. In this connection the movement sees Hizballah in Lebanon as a role model. Another spokesman for Hamas in the Gaza Strip, Mahmoud Zahhar, commented as follows on this aspect of the organisation's strategy:

They continue to extend their settlements. They kill us. They should be punished. They should learn their lesson. If you continue to kill, you must expect the same policy that we have seen in South Lebanon. Why is it only now, after 20 years of occupation, that they have started to consider UN Resolution 425? Why? Because of Hizballah! We are also Hizballah but we are not Shiites. We are Muslims. But we are following the same path as Hizballah: resistance until our country is liberated.[102]

Nevertheless, after the late 1990s Hamas toned down the military struggle. Several factors came into play here. Hamas was compelled to adapt to the new status quo that emerged as a result of the Oslo I agreement. The entire world was watching the Palestinian Authority, and this virtually forced Arafat to try to eliminate Hamas. Thus the security co-operation between the Authority, Israel and the CIA proved effective. But this was not the only reason for Hamas' greater moderation. The shift in policy was undoubtedly due to recognition, on the part of the Hamas leadership, that change was necessary if the movement was to survive at all. Abu Shanab acknowledged in an interview that in the short term Hamas had lost the fight, while in the same breath stressing that it was not going to lose in the long run.[103] Thus in recent years Hamas has moved towards a new role that can best be described as that of a "loyal opposition". High-ranking Hamas leaders do not however use the term loyal opposition themselves, describing the movement rather as a "positive opposition". Abu Shanab explained this term as follows in the above-cited interview, 5 July 1999:

> A positive opposition takes a different view of things. We don't just say "Yes, we're in opposition, so we are against [the Authority] on every level." On the contrary, we take a stance on [different] issues. Sometimes we oppose actions, sometimes we agree with them. This means that if, in our view, there is a good initiative, we will adopt the idea regardless of whether, for example, it is the Authority that has fostered it.

This development is undoubtedly based on a desire on the part of the Hamas leadership to maintain the organisation's influence in civil society. In other words, in the course of the late 1990s Hamas shifted back to the movement's original starting point – namely re-Islamisation from below, but things were soon to change.

The Aqsa Intifada and its consequences for the political development of Palestinian society

In the fall of 2000, the Oslo process failed and the second Palestinian Intifada – known as the Aqsa Intifada – broke out. As Graham Usher has noted, "what in the West had been seen as a 'peace process' was for Palestinians Israel's latest mode of colonial dispossession".[104] Initially the new Intifada was a popular revolt, but it soon grew into a significantly more militarised conflict, issuing in an almost unstoppable spiral of violence. Palestinian groupings – Islamist as well as secular – increasingly attacked Jewish settlements, especially in the West Bank. Hamas used suicide bombers against civilian targets in Israel, and the movement furthermore developed the so-called "Qassam" rockets, launched from the Gaza Strip at Israeli targets. These attacks in fact had a quite limited effect, but Israeli propaganda made the most of them.

There is no doubt that the outbreak and developments during the Aqsa

Intifada have in many ways suited Hamas. In a leaflet published at the beginning of the Aqsa Intifada, Hamas argued that it was essential for the Palestinian Authority to support the resistance, which in their words represented "the people's choice". The level of popular resistance in the Palestinian territories, and subsequent developments, suggest that Hamas was on to something important in delivering this message: namely, that the late Yasir Arafat and the Palestinian leadership were out of step with the demands and wishes of the people. In other words, it was not only Hamas and its supporters that were dissatisfied with the current state of affairs. Virtually all the Palestinian political parties and movements agreed with Hamas' criticisms. In connection with the Aqsa Intifada, parts of Fatah, for example, activated the armed militia, the Tanzim, who swore to carry on the Palestinian resistance. Another militant organisation rooted in Fatah has also since then come into existence – the al-Aqsa Martyrs' Brigade, which have been behind a great many of the armed attacks against Israeli targets in the West Bank as well as in Israel.[105] In late summer 2001, and for the first time since the signing of the Oslo Agreement in 1993, the polls showed, however, that more Palestinians in the Gaza Strip supported Hamas than Fatah.[106]

11 September – reactions and consequences for the Palestinians

Immediately after the attacks in Washington and New York on 11 September, it seemed fairly certain that Usama Bin Laden and his al-Qa'ida network had masterminded the attacks. This renewed and increased the focus on Islamism worldwide. In November 2001, the United States included Hamas and Islamic Jihad on their new extensive list of terrorist organisations and a few months later the US president spoke about a "terrorist underworld" consisting of among others Hamas and Islamic Jihad.[107] Thus, Hamas like most Islamist movements was lumped together with al-Qa'ida, reinforcing the need to dissolve and break up the Palestinian Islamist organisations despite the fact that they had nothing to do with the 11 September attacks and completely overlooking the fact that Hamas (just like Islamic Jihad) rejects the ideology of al-Qa'ida.[108] Since then the pressure on Hamas – as on other Islamist organisations around the world – has grown considerably. In December 2001, the EU also drew up its own "terror list". Only two of the organisations that figured on this list came from the Middle East, namely Islamic Jihad and *Izz-ad-Din al-Qassam*. It is worth noting that for a long time the EU had succeeded in maintaining a distinction between Hamas and *Izz ad-Din al-Qassam*. This can only be seen as evidence of the fact that strong forces within the EU are aware of the important social work that Hamas carries out. It also shows that the EU – as opposed to the United States – accepts the presence of the Islamists in Palestinian civil society, including their right to resist the Israeli occupation, though naturally within the framework of international law. In 2003, however, under pressure from Israel and the United States, the EU decided to add Hamas in its entirety to the list of terrorist organisations.[109] According to sources in the EU the pressure to add Hamas on the terror list also came from Fatah itself.[110]

As we have seen the central part of Hamas' activities consists of grass-root work in local communities. As in the late 1990s the Palestinian Authority has sealed the premises of various Islamic social welfare organisations on a number of occasions since September 2001. By January 2002 some 50 of these were closed and the assets of some 25 had been frozen.[111] Not only did the US and eventually the EU demand that the military branch of Hamas, *Izz ad-din al-Qassam*, should be eliminated; they also demanded that the civilian parts of Hamas should be dissolved. These steps caused widespread discontent among Palestinians in the occupied territories – especially since the Authority does not have the capacity to carry out the tasks that the Islamists undertake. According to a Senior EU official in Gaza:

> The organisations and the Palestinian Authority are constantly reshaping deals with each other since the Palestinian Authority cannot take responsibility for those left with nothing. It does not have the appropriate tools.[112]

During the Aqsa Intifada, the demands for food and "social benefits" increased markedly. In fact since 2000–3 the average income of Palestinians has declined by approximately 50 per cent and poverty levels have gone up from 21 per cent to roughly 60 per cent. Meanwhile, a quarter of the population is unemployed. As the demand for social services is enormous, the support of Hamas' institutions remains vital for hundreds of thousands of Palestinians.[113]

As Daniel Nepp (2004) has pointed out:

> It is unsurprising that many Palestinians have turned to Hamas ... the movement's network of schools and hospitals allows it to be seen almost as a structure parallel to the PA, one which has a reputation for probity and one which, unlike the PA, allows numerous opponents to the Oslo agreements to express their political opinion. The PA is now being torn apart by the old leaders who cling onto their positions of power

and the younger generations, who are more radical and whose political outlook is closer to that of Sheikh Yasin than to that of Arafat.

Bombs and *hudna* revisited

In spite of the change in Hamas' role and the re-emergence of more militant resistance against the Israeli occupation the movement is still prepared to accept a de facto recognition of Israel. The Hamas spokesman Mahmoud Zahhar has stated that the proposal for a *hudna* is still valid:

> Everyone in Hamas is ready for a *hudna*. But as long as the occupation and the expansion of the settlements continue, this will not happen. However, if Israel pulls back from the areas they occupied in 1967, including Jerusalem, we are ready to enter into a *hudna*.[114]

Even the hard-liner Abdel Aziz Rantisi stated in January 2004, just a couple of months before he was killed by the Israelis, that:

> We accept a state in the West Bank, including Jerusalem and the Gaza Strip. We propose a 10-year truce in return for [Israeli] withdrawal and the establishment of a [Palestinian] state.[115]

All Israeli Governments have so far been unwilling to accept the *hudna* proposal, arguing that this represents only a tactical move on the part of the Palestinians, and that the militants will eventually break the *hudna*. However, as Daniel Nepp (2004) has noted, this is the risk of any kind of truce anywhere in the world.

Despite these signals, the movement continued to use suicide actions as a means of resistance. The many suicide actions launched by Hamas during the height of the Aqsa Intifada have met with more Palestinian support than before. A total of 75 per cent of the population supported the actions in the first year of the Aqsa Intifada. For Hamas, the suicide attacks are not an end in themselves. From Hamas' point of view, the attacks are a means to establish a balance of terror or rather a balance of fear. Their purpose is to intimidate the Israeli population by making sure that the occupation will have consequences for each and every individual Israeli citizen. Hamas hopes thereby to ensure that the Israeli civilian population will put pressure on the government to pull back from the West Bank and the Gaza Strip. The Hamas leaders argue that only a strategy of this kind will terminate the occupation. By way of empirical example, they keep returning to the case of

Lebanon. According to Hamas, it was only as a result of Hizballah's resistance that Israel eventually withdrew in May 2000. Yet so far the strategy of suicide bombings by Palestinians has not had the desired effect on Israel.

The war on Iraq and the question of Palestine

In mid-January 2003 the then US Deputy Secretary of Defence, Paul Wolfowitz, stated that the United States would work intensively to create a Palestinian state as soon as the war in Iraq was over.[116] In Denmark and other European countries a number of politicians issued similar statements, and the prospect of peace between the Palestinians and the Israelis was used as an argument to justify the war against Iraq.[117] Despite the failure of the war in Iraq and the huge problems encountered by the United States and its allies in "post-war" Iraq, the question of Palestine is still very high on the agenda. Yet no progress has been made, notwithstanding the launch of a new plan – the so-called Road Map – for restarting the peace process.

As a continuation of the Oslo process the Road Map is another attempt to establish a hegemonic peace, and as such the whole process is best understood as an internal Israeli discussion of the following questions: "How much land shall we leave for the Palestinians? How many settlements are to be dismantled? And how many Palestinian refugees may return home – if any?" It is only through Israeli acquiescence that the Palestinians will be able to acquire anything. Meanwhile, as we all know, the Palestinians do not occupy Israel, nor do they have any illegal settlements in Israel, nor have they undertaken the ethnic cleansing of a large part of the Israeli population. The only negotiating leverage the Palestinians possesses lies in the small word "no".

Targeting Hamas

Although the IDF during the Aqsa Intifada initially focused on destroying the infrastructure of the Palestinian Authority, the spotlight eventually turned on Hamas, with a number of targeted killings of *Izz ad-Din al-Qassam* leaders. The IDF took their campaign further and in 2003 they began to target political leaders of Hamas. Ismael Abu Shanab fell victim to this campaign in August 2003, and shortly afterwards Israel threatened to kill the head of Hamas, Sheikh Ahmad Yasin. The latter was duly assassinated in March 2004. After Yasin was assassinated Hamas declared that Israel had "opened the gates of hell". During the weeks and months after the assassination most researchers and analysts agreed that it would inevitably give rise to acts of revenge. In this regard Nepp wrote:

It would be foolish not to expect a dramatic increase in the number, scale and severity in the coming days and weeks. A new cycle of violence has been initiated ...[118]

However, nothing happened and it seemed as if the movement was unable to react as they had threatened to do. This continued to be the case even after the killing of Yasin's successor Abdel Aziz Rantisi in April 2004. No doubt Hamas was in a state of shock. Despite this, and despite the fact that Hamas initially – out of fear – did not publicly appoint a successor,[119] the organisation still had a large and increasing constituency.

The legitimacy of Hamas increases

The reason why Israel's gross violations of the Geneva Convention and the resolutions of the UN Security Council have not had any consequences is that the various Israeli governments has been able to convince US President George W. Bush that his war against the Palestinians is identical to the war against terror led by the United States. Israel and the US are in the same boat. Thus to the Americans it is "understandable" that Israel takes action – and brutal action. There is no doubt that the United States' "either you're with us, or you're against us" policy has traumatised the Palestinians in the wake of the 11 September attacks. Sharon's and his successors' policies have likewise been a horrifying experience.

Since 11 September 2001 the Palestinians have found themselves in a no-win situation, and the war in Iraq has done little or nothing to change this. If the Palestinians continue their struggle for independence through armed resistance, they will be on the wrong side of Bush's "either-or" formula, and they will not receive support from either the United States or the EU, since terror cannot be rewarded. If the Palestinians choose to give up their fight against the occupation, they have no chance of reaching their national goals either. They will be at the mercy of the Israeli governments' whims.

One outcome of the Americans' and Israelis' simplified way of looking at the world is that Arab attitudes towards the West and Israel have worsened – not only among the Palestinians, but also in the Arab world as a whole. Another outcome is that support for Hamas has been strengthened. The Aqsa Intifada has injected Hamas with new life and new hopes, and on the domestic front the state of crisis that the movement found itself during the late 1990s has been transformed into success. However, this victory was blurred by the increasing international focus on Islamism in general and Hamas in particular, which again was closely connected to the events that followed 11 September, the suicide attacks in Israel, and developments in Iraq. Because of the Aqsa Intifada, the changes that Hamas, as I have argued earlier, was on the brink of making at the end of the 1990s – i.e. the shift in focus away from militant resistance against the Israeli occupation towards the preservation of their institutions within the framework of the civil society – have been brought to a standstill. Hamas was now fighting and working within civil society simultaneously, with an emphasis on armed struggle.

However, the death of Yasir Arafat in November 2004 opened up a new political space, which brought Hamas back to its old more traditional Brotherhood discourse and even in to the game of political participation. During the early months of 2005 the movement's new leaders repeatedly stated that Hamas was ready for a cease-fire (*hudna*) with Israel and they henceforth kept a new unilateral Palestinian cease-fire for more than a year. The local council elections held in late 2004 and early 2005 indicated that Hamas was now willing to join the political game. During these Hamas, to the surprise of many, fared surprisingly well. Local elections were held in December 2004 in 26 municipalities on the West Bank: the first such elections to be held in the occupied territories since 1976. With an overall turnout of over 80 per cent Hamas' candidates defeated Fatah in nine out of the 26 local constituencies.[120] It was widely believed that Fatah chose to focus on the cities in the West Bank where they were confident of winning. Thus it came as a surprise to most observers that Hamas was capable of winning such a high proportion of the votes in these areas. And there were even greater surprises in store for Fatah. On 27 January 2005 Palestinian voters in 10 local communities in the Gaza Strip went to vote in the first local elections to be held there. The various political parties competed for 118 seats in these constituencies. Hamas won 77 out of the contested 118 seats in the Gaza Strip municipal elections, while Fatah won only 26 seats.

However, the biggest victory for Hamas came on 25 January 2006 when, Hamas candidates won 74 seats in the 132-member Palestinian parliament. It was a victory that exceeded their wildest dreams. Ghazi Hamad, a Hamas leader stressed the new agenda for Hamas in the wake of victory:

We said negotiations alone are not enough to achieve our rights. What is needed is a new Palestinian strategy, with a genuine national consensus over aims and a proper balance between political and military struggle.[121]

Summary

Islamism has a long history in the Palestinian context. By the 1930s there were already examples of Islamic resistance to Zionism and the British occupation of Palestine. The first branch of the Muslim Brotherhood was established in the mid-1940s. Islamism is thus an integral part of the social and political life of Palestinian society. The Hamas movement, which sprang out of the Muslim Brotherhood, is in many ways unique as a movement, in so far as it has sought since its establishment in 1987 to combine a strategy based on the islamisation of society from below, through work in social, religious, educational and cultural institutions, with an armed struggle against the continuing Israeli occupation. Until Hamas' foundation in 1987 the nationalists had had a monopoly on active resistance against the Israeli occupation.

After signing the Oslo I agreement in 1993, and the agreements that followed, the various camps in Palestinian society switched roles. Throughout the 1970s and 1980s the Brotherhood's non-activist policies had led the nationalists, as represented by the PLO, to accuse the Islamists of being agents of Israel. With the signing of Oslo I, the PLO suddenly found themselves in the position of co-operating with Israel, while Hamas pursued the struggle against the occupation. In this connection it became clearer that Hamas' policies were largely identical to those of the PLO in the early 1970s, albeit spiced with a good dose of Islamist rhetoric. Hamas thus opposed the peace conference; they oppose any division of Palestine; they seek to continue the armed struggle, and finally they act as the mouthpiece for over four million Palestinian refugees, articulating their right to return to Palestine.[122]

Particularly since the establishment of the Palestinian Authority in 1994, the relationship between the PLO and Hamas has been strained. This is due to the fact that, despite the PLO's commitment to combat "the opponents of peace", Hamas continued the armed struggle even after the agreements were signed. The PLO's agreements with Israel – and the pressure from the United States – have forced the Authority to crack down on the Islamist opposition. Thus in recent years the Authority has sought to undermine the social work conducted by the Islamist movement by closing a number of key institutions – including *al-Jam'iyya al-Islâmiyya* – and not least by taking over the Hamas-controlled mosques. Through their co-operation with Israel and the United States on security matters they have also undermined most of Hamas' military infrastructure, i.e. *Kata'ib Izz ad-Din al-Qassam*. Since the late 1990s, under pressure from the Authority, the movement has sought – despite considerable internal opposition – to pursue a more moderate line.

Among other things the proposal has been made for a long-lasting cease-fire, or *hudna*, and parts of the Hamas leadership regarded the movement as a positive opposition to the Palestinian Authority – a clear acknowledgement of the balance of power between the two main actors on the political scene in Palestinian society. More than ten years after the movement embarked on its activist line, Hamas seemed as if it was returning to its starting point, focusing on the (re-) islamisation of Palestinian society.

The Aqsa Intifada that erupted in late 2000 changed this discourse. The Aqsa Intifada was an advantage to Hamas, which changed its position significantly. Armed struggle became the basis of the movement's massive support. Polls showed that Hamas were stronger than Fatah. Yet the new focus on armed struggle had its price. IDF assassinated a number of the leaders of the movement, among them Ismael Abu Shanab and Abdel Aziz Rantisis, as well as the spiritual head Sheikh Ahmad Yasin. The movement lingered on and in the wake of the death of Yasir Arafat the new leadership decided to enter into the political game. They fared well in local elections in 2004 and 2005, but in January 2006 they shocked the world and won a landslide victory in the national elections. Hamas was in power although they faced severe difficulties in executing this newly gained power.

In the following chapters I will present the empirical results of my fieldwork conducted in the Gaza Strip during the late 1990s. The next chapter focuses on the reasons behind taking an active part in Palestinian civil society, as emphasised by the leaders of the Islamist movement.

3

THE ISLAMISTS' UNDERSTANDING OF ISLAM

Their View of History and the Need to Engage
in Civil Society

A central aim of this chapter is to look at the reasons given by Islamist leaders in the Gaza Strip for their participation in civil society in general. This
chapter begins with a brief account of the Hamas movement's understanding of Islam and their view of Islamic history, which constitute the foundation of the movement's *da'wa*: their means of re-islamising Palestinian society. *Da'wa* in the present context can best be translated as a mission or an invi-
tation to Islam.[123] As we saw in Chapter 1, the creation of "*sound Muslims*"
is a precondition for establishing the Islamic state. It follows that it is essential for the movement to become engaged in Palestinian civil society, i.e. in
social work and education.

The Islamists' understanding of Islam

Islam is construed by the Palestinian leaders of Hamas both as an alternative
to other ideologies and as a model for solving the crisis in which not only
Palestinian society, but the whole Islamic world, currently finds itself.[124] Like
other Islamist groups in the Arab world, Hamas sees Islam as an all-embracing system: *dîn wa dawla* (religion and state).

> Islam covers all aspects of life. Islam is human, economic, political, and
> social. It is motherhood and childhood. Islam covers everything ...[125]

According to Francois Burgat Islamism is an anti-colonialist movement and
it is part of what he has termed the 'rocket of de-colonisation'.[126] In the wake

of the secular nationalist, pan-Arabist and socialist-inspired attempts at
obtaining political and then economic independence the Islamists of today
furthermore attempt to gain cultural autonomy. They attempt to rewrite history, and in doing so, they use what is being presented as an 'authentic' language, the language of Islam. Hence, Islam as a political ideology stems from
the failure of Arab nationalism and other secular ideologies to solve the problems of the Arab-Islamic world. Islamists use this argument throughout the
Arab world, including Palestine. Islam is essentially timeless and therefore –
in the view of Islamists – valid for all times. However, it is essential that Islam
be used in the proper way. To be equipped to use it properly, according to
the late Hamas leader Ismael Abu Shanab, one must be:

> A person with knowledge of the Koran and of present-day life and a
> profound acquaintance with the time at which the Koran was revealed.
> When you combine these three elements you become capable of under-
> standing the Koran and its application to present-day life. If you do
> not, you end up imitating earlier generations who understood the
> Koran in their lifetime, but not in ours. They interpreted the Koran in
> a way appropriate to their epoch, but now things have developed.
> Things are developing in our time, and this needs to be taken into
> account. That's why the Koran is appropriate for all times.[127]

Islam needs to be contextualised, and *ijtihâd* (fresh interpretation) is a *sine
qua non*. Muslims should behave as if the prophet had only just received the
revelations from God. This view thus contains an implicit criticism of the
established *ulamâ*, who have largely engaged in *taqlîd* (imitation). Hamas'
view of who is qualified to carry out *ijtihâd* is inspired by the Sudanese
Islamist Hassan al-Turabi, who offers a very broad interpretation of what
ulamâ should mean in the current context. Turabi writes:

> What do I mean by '*ulamâ*'? Historically the word has meant those
> who were well versed in revealed religious knowledge (*'ilm*). But *'ilm*
> does not refer to that alone. It refers to those who know something well
> enough to relate to God. Since all knowledge is divine and religious, a
> chemist, an engineer, an economist or a lawyer are all *'ulamâ*.[128]

Precisely because, in the Islamist understanding, all forms of knowledge are
related to each other and in the final instance to God, it is permissible
for Hamas leaders to make the necessary interpretations themselves. The
majority of the leaders do not have any religious training; many of them in

fact were educated in the natural sciences.[129] Thus religious authority in the Palestinian context has become fragmented, with secular and Western-educated Muslims often competing with the traditional religious establishment and in the process forging a new Islamic discourse.[130] For Hamas, then, the reason for the crisis of Islam lies not within Islam itself, but in the way in which it has been practised hitherto:

> Islam is Islam. There is a rift between Muslims and their religion. They understand their religion in the wrong way. There was a period of ignorance before the establishment of the new Islamic movements, which are reforming Islam with a view to getting people to understand their religion as it is. The fault lies not in Islam, but in Muslims' understanding of it.[131]

The cause of this rift between Islam and Muslims is first and foremost Western imperialism. According to Abu Shanab:

> We are constantly under pressure. This also applies if we go a bit back in history to the time when the countries of the West with their colonial mentality wanted to control our region. Since that time they have controlled everything here. They interfere in the education system; they interfere in the political system. They have also been involved in a great many military coups in the Arab countries, and they give strong support to the intelligence services. We are under pressure. At present the mission (da'wa) of all Islamic organisations is based on wanting to explain the ideas and the thinking of Muslims, who are now under pressure from the other culture ... If I have something valuable and you offer me something less valuable, why should I accept your offer and abandon what I already possess?[132]

Abu Shanab is referring here to what Islamists see as an ideological invasion of the Muslim way of thinking. This is an oft-discussed theme among Islamists, including Palestinians. It is crucial, in their view, for Islamists to understand the historical relationship between the West and Islam, in order to liberate themselves and (re)-create an authentic identity of their own. Islamism in this context can be understood as an anti-colonial uprising. It is one link in the Arab-Muslim attempt to achieve liberation from the West.

The Islamist view of history

In a telling foreword to a book by the Hamas leader Mahmoud Zahhar, *Ishkâliyât – al-Khitâb al-Siyâsî al-Islâmî al-Mu'âsir* (Problems in Propagating the Political, Islamist Message in the Present),[133] Abdel Fattah Dukkhan sums up the factors that Islamists need to take into account in seeking to win people over to Islam.

In poetic language Dukkhan describes the origins of the problems facing the Islamic world today. Dukkhan sees the matter in terms of a struggle between civilisations.[134] In his account, the struggle is between *al-haqq* and *al-bâtil* – truth and falsehood – in which Islam naturally represents the truth and the West *al-bâtil*. These two terms are central to the world picture presented in the Koran and have therefore been adopted by many Islamist movements. The Koran (*Sura* 21: 18) reads:

> Nay, We hurl the Truth against falsehood, and it knocks out its brain, and behold, falsehood doth perish! Ah! Woe be to you for the (false) things ye ascribe (to Us).[135]

The Koran can be read as a holy text that sketches out the history of mankind from the creation to the present as a battle between *al-haqq* and *al-bâtil*. God has sent down prophets through the ages to establish *al-haqq*. Since the prophet Muhammad, according to Islam, is the last in this line of prophets, Islamists see it as their task to ensure that *al-haqq* prevails over *al-bâtil*. They are to fulfil God's mission.

According to Dukkhan, ideological invasion began in the wake of the West's defeat at the hands of Salah ad-Din at the battle of Hattin in 1187: a defeat that opened the way for Muslims to re-conquer Jerusalem. As a result of their defeat, the Europeans realized that they were incapable of conquering the Muslims by military means – "ideological invasion" (*al-ghazw al-fikrî*) was needed as well. The Western leaders therefore embarked on a campaign to educate orientalists who could then translate and interpret the Koran with a view to contaminate Muslim thinking. The project was successful, Dukkhan maintains, proof being that Muslim world leaders no longer command the correct interpretation of Islam. However, this was not of course the fault of orientalists alone. Other forces contributed as well. Thus Christian missionaries, "under the guise of humanism", likewise played a part in the imperialist project. Similarly, the practice of sending Arab scientists to Europe in the late nineteenth and early twentieth centuries helped to corrupt the Arab intelligentsia. Imperialism has also profited from the various sects within Islam, such as Babism and Ahmadiya. Thus the imperialists have succeeded in creating a rift within every house in the Muslim *umma*. Dukkhan also emphasises the key role played by the mass media in this process, and concludes his foreword by saying that it is within this alien milieu that Islamists now have to operate. In their attempts to inculcate *al-haqq*, the truth, they are constantly working against the current.[136]

The Islamist view of history is thus imbued with cultural pessimism. As Emmanuel Sivan (1985) among others has observed, Islam is on the defensive, and has been penetrated by a powerful modernist/westernising element in Arab Muslim society. Thus, far from being on the road to triumph, as some of the academic literature and particularly the media would have us believe, Islam is, and perceives itself to be, defending itself against powerful outside influences.[137]

Hamas' charter, published in summer 1998, emphasises some of the same points touched on by Dukkhan. One paragraph of the charter reads:

> The current Zionist invasion was preceded by many invasions of the crusading West and the Tatars from the East. As the Muslims confronted those invasions and prepared for fighting and defeating them, so they should ready themselves to confront and defeat the Zionist invasion. And this will not be difficult for Allah if intentions are pure and efforts wholehearted, and if Muslims have benefited from previous experiences, have been freed from the effect of the ideological invasion and have followed the way of their predecessors.[138]

As can be seen from Dukkhan's words, the Islamists see the crusades as the first in a series of moves against Islam. In its charter, Hamas also includes Zionism under this category, seeing it as an extension of the Western imperialist project of conquering Islam. It is against this background that we should understand Hamas' attack on Zionism.

The Islamist movement does not distinguish between Judaism, Zionism and Israeli nationality.[139] Zionism – and on occasion Judaism too – is seen as the extended arm of imperialism; thus in Hamas' writings Jews are often considered the representatives of *al-bâtil*. The phobia against Jews that has resulted from this fusion of concepts, together with the Islamist view of history in which Zionism and colonialism are seen as two sides of the same coin, should be understood as a response to the fact that the state of Israel was established on territory that the Palestinian Islamists consider a part of *Dâr al-Islâm*, and hence the Islamic *waqf*, until the Day of Judgement.

Numerous other texts could be cited to illustrate this linkage between

Zionism and colonialism, and in Hamas' 1988 charter in particular there are many examples of the same kind of conspiracy theory thinking sketched above. The charter asserts, among other things, that:

> With presumptuous manoeuvres and well-formulated plans World Zionism and the imperialist powers seek to draw the Arabic nations one by one away from the struggle against Zionism ...[140] There are several reasons for linking imperialism and Zionism with the defeat of the crusaders. First and foremost, Salah ad-Din[141] acted in the context of a divided Muslim world, but he succeeded nevertheless in winning the battle, which in the Islamists' view was a battle on behalf of Islam. By drawing this historic analogy Islamists thus instil hope at a time when internal division likewise weakens Islam. Islam has triumphed before over colonialism, it is argued, and this can happen again (and the state of Israel too can therefore be conquered). The Islamists' conflation of Salah ad-Din's victory with the victory of Islam allows Muslim to draw an important lesson from history. As Dukkhan among others has argued, the Muslims of today have become alienated from their religion. It is important to learn from history; hence the significance of the battle of Hattin in 1187. Salah ad-Din won the battle in Islam's name, which is why the answer to today's problems in Arab-Muslim society is a historical answer, involving a return to Islam. This is why it is essential that Muslims liberate themselves from the ideological invasion that has contaminated their understanding of Islam. Liberation must occur through the conversion or re-islamisation of the individual. It is in this connection that we should understand the Islamists' engagement in civil society, as an ideal platform for this project.

The Hamas charter thus stresses the need to educate Muslims ideologically:

> It [i.e. Hamas] works through ... educating the Islamic people ideologically, morally and culturally with a view to [Islam] playing a role in the struggle for liberation, just as it played a role in vanquishing the crusaders and repelling the Tatars and thereby saving human civilisation, and this is not difficult for Allah.[142]

From the point of view of the leadership, then, the project is to create *sound Muslims*. Before touching upon the reasons given by the leaders for engaging in civil society, I will comment briefly on the way Islamists view history.

The twin heritage

Many of the points made by today's Islamists can be traced back to ideas put forward at an earlier period, albeit under a different rhetorical guise. Already in the early twentieth century Arabic historians had begun to link the crusaders with imperialism. The connection appeared particularly self-evident following the colonial powers' failure to keep the promises made in the Hussein–McMahon correspondence (1915), and the subsequent division of the Middle East in the aftermath of the First World War through the Sykes–Picot agreement and the inclusion of the Balfour declaration in the British mandate over Palestine (1920–48).[143]

It is interesting in this regard that it was the Europeans themselves who encouraged Arabic intellectuals to make the connection between the distant past and the present. The inspiration to do so sprang in part from the French school of history, which regarded the crusaders as having paved the way for the French presence in the Middle East in the early twentieth century. The crusaders were followed by Napoleon and subsequently by modern colonialists. Contemporary Arab historians were likewise inspired to make the connection through the pronouncements made by the British General Edmund Allenby and his French colleague General Henri Gouraud (1920). The two generals were both exponents of the view that they were engaged in re-establishing the crusaders' control over Palestine and Syria: a process that had now been launched, if not concluded.[144] Hamas' charter quotes Gourard: "We have returned, oh Salah ad-Din."[145]

It was against this background that Arab historians in the early twentieth century, and especially after 1945, began to treat Zionism as a symbol of imperialism. This view gained widespread credence after the Tripartite Invasion of Egypt in 1956. Although the connection made between the distant past and the present day may not seem entirely convincing to us, from the point of view of the Middle East the link seemed transparently obvious. Thus it was undeniable that Israel had been founded through the co-operation of the hegemonic Western powers, and that in 1956 a secret pact against Egypt had been forged between Great Britain, France and the state of Israel. The aim of making the historic connection – and this applied alike to pan-Arabists and Islamists – was to teach a lesson. The solution to today's problems, and the prospect of a brighter future for the Arab world, lay in applying the model successfully used in solving the problems of the past.[146]

Thus the ideas put forward by Islamists – i.e. Hamas – are not radically new. To a great extent they are identical with those of the pan-Arab ideology, which they purport to reject. In fact, the same ideas have simply been adduced to further a different project. Islamism thus offers an alternative rhetoric based nevertheless on almost identical reasoning. This can aptly be illustrated by a quotation from the Egyptian National Charter of 1962:

> In the history of Islam the Egyptian people – following the message of Muhammad – have played the leading role in defending civilisation and humanity. Before the whole region was shrouded in darkness through the Ottoman invasion, the Egyptian people with great courage took prime responsibility for protecting the region's interests. The Egyptian people bore the material and military responsibility for resisting the first wave of European colonialism that was carried out under cover of Jesus' cross …[147]

Thus for the pan-Arabists too the crusaders represented the first European colonialists, while the Egyptians were the region's saviours. A direct line is drawn in the charter from the crusaders to today. The lesson to be learned was that in modern times, too, Egypt had to take up the burden of responsibility to withstand modern Western colonialism and liberate the Arabs through uniting them.

While in power Saddam Hussein's Ba'th regime in Iraq employed a similar line of argument. At an Arab summit meeting in Amman in March 2001 the Iraqi representative, Izzat Ibrahim, said on Saddam Hussein's behalf:

> Salah ad-Din would never have liberated Jerusalem from the Crusaders without Arabism ('urûba) and Islam.[148]

Izzat Ibrahim thus signalled to other Arab leaders that the way forward in solving the Palestinian conflict lay in Arab unity and Islam. The Arab people can and should learn from the past.

Conspiratorial thinking is not new, nor is it confined to Islamists. The Palestinian nationalists within the PLO similarly draw on such ideas. In 2001 Walid al-Awad, director general of the PLO's refugee department, was credited in the newspaper *al-Hayât al-Jadîda* with saying:

> Ever since the Balfour declaration the Palestinian people have been the victims of an organised and planned operation backed by Western imperialism and the Zionist movement. The aim has been to uproot the Palestinian people from their homeland, appropriate their property and replace them with Jews … the aim has also been to create a Jewish

state and confirm the Zionist movement's lies that this was a land without people and a people without a land.[149]

Although the PLO representative in this instance traces the conspiracy only as far back as 1917, the mode of reasoning in many respects parallels that of Islamist and pan-Arabist rhetoric.

For Islamists the only way to liberate Palestine is to create *sound Muslims*, and it is therefore important that they make themselves visible in civil society. It is here that they have the opportunity to realize their goal.

Islām(ism) and the social and educational sphere

Islam is perceived as an all-embracing life system (*minhâj al-hayât*). In a speech in Khan Younis to mark the ninth anniversary of the founding of Hamas, the above-mentioned Abdel Fatah Dukkhan made the following introductory remarks:

Who are we, and where are we? We are a *salafiyya* call (*da'wa*) on the path of Sunni Islam, and a true sufi movement with a political life, and a sports society and a movement that has links with science, culture and economic activity, and moreover we have ideas about social life ... We distinguish ourselves from the hegemonic upper classes of society and distance ourselves from the other parties and from those who have gone astray (*zâlim*) ... We exist by working step by step with love for our mission (*da'wa*) and by spreading the message to young people, to cities and villages. We are not a charitable organisation (*Jam'iyya Khairiyya*) nor a political party, nor an objectivist or positivist group that works with limited aims. We are a new spirit at the heart of *al-umma*. The Koran nourishes this spirit, and we are the new light that shines and destroys the darkness of materialism in favour of a meeting with Allah. The clear sound from the calling (*da'wa*). This light and this sound make up the prophet's mission (PBH). If you are asked what your calling consists in, answer: "Our calling is Islam as brought about by the prophet (PBH), and government is a part of that [of Islam], and freedom is a necessity of its necessity. And if you are told that you are calling for revolution, say that we are calling for the truth (*al-haqq*) and for peace, which we believe in. And if you are told that you are receiving help from individual persons and groups, say: We believe only in God. We do not believe in polytheists (*musrikun*) ..."

Who are we, and where are we? Quietly we invoke *al-da'wa* (the calling), but it is stronger than *al-asifa*[150] (the storm). Our *da'wa* is limited, yet it is greater than the earth's diameter. We are carrying out a mission (*da'wa*) without fine wrapping, but with content ... our brothers believe in it, and they are just in their actions ...

Who are you, and where are you? You are the Islamic movement Hamas. It is a radiant movement that lives in friendship with God and whose life project (*minhâj*) is rooted in Islam. It seeks to raise Allah's flag over every little piece of Palestinian soil (*'ala kull shibr Filastîn*). Defenders in the shade of Islam (*fî zill al-islâm*). It is possible to live together with people of other religions in peace and friendliness, with security of soul, property and rights, but in the absence of Islam fighting and oppression will break out and corruption will flourish. Obstinacy and war will break out ...[151]

Dukkhan's introductory words are inspired partly by the Koranic style of address, and partly by the Muslim Brotherhood leader Hassan al-Banna. Dukkhan indeed quotes Banna in his opening lines – albeit without crediting him. In Dukkhan's presentation Hamas, like Islam itself, is an all-embracing system, covering politics, religion, science, sport, culture and so on. The movement embraces all areas and facets of life, and Hamas likewise strives to inculcate the truth (*al-haqq*) and to establish a Palestinian state within the boundaries of the former British mandate Palestine.

In fact, the Palestinian Islamists owe a great to al-Banna and the Muslim Brotherhood in Egypt. Their entire "social infrastructure" is almost identical to the base established by the Muslim Brotherhood in Egypt in the 1930s. By that time the Muslim Brotherhood had already established a network of health clinics, educational institutions and sports clubs and was also engaged in social work.[152] In personal interviews several Hamas leaders have indicated that the ideological inspiration for the movement came first and foremost from Hassan al-Banna.[153] It is clear that the movement has also been inspired by the need to give practical help to the poorest sectors of Palestinian society.[154]

It is important to stress that, formally speaking, the arrays of Islamic institutions and organisations that exist in the Gaza Strip have no connection with Hamas. The connections we refer to here are purely informal. Nevertheless, there is a high degree of ideological and personal overlap between the two. Leaders of the Islamist movement emphasise the distinction between Hamas and the various Islamist institutions mainly because of the political situation in the late 1990s in the Gaza Strip. The Hamas leaders were quite simply afraid that any connection between the two would lead to the closure of these institutions, and three decades' work would thus go to waste. Ahmad Bahr, Head of *al-Jam'iyya al-Islâmiyya*, obviously felt he was under attack when I sought in an interview with him to link the various Islamist institutions. He told me:

> They are different. They are all independent but all of them are charitable institutions ... they are united in carrying out charitable work ... the aim of this institution is to help the poorest people in the community. What is the point of trying to link these institutions?[155]

This feeling or fear of being under attack preceded the establishment of the Palestinian authority. The Islamists regulated their mutual relations while under direct Israeli occupation as well. For example, they established several different social institutions with approximately the same remit, such as *al-Jam'iyya al-Islâmiyya* and *al-Mujamma' al-Islâmi*. As one of the leaders put it in an interview:

> If you have 50 eggs in the same basket and you lose the basket, what do you have left? Whereas if you keep them in different baskets, you don't lose everything. Maybe you just lose one of them.[156]

Whatever the exact truth of the matter, it can be argued that Hamas and the Islamic organisations function as a common framework. They have a common purpose and derive their ideas from the same interpretation of Islam. Their immediate aim is to help the poor, the orphaned, the families of martyrs and so on. But they also have in common the desire to spread the Islamist message and Islamist thinking among a broader section of the population. Whether we speak of *al-Jam'iyya al-Islâmiyya*, the Islamic University of Gaza, *Hizb al-Khalâs* or Hamas, their common goal is the implementation of *shari'a*. And as I have indicated, most of the individuals associated with these institutions either belong, or formerly belonged, to Hamas.

The leaders both of Hamas and of the Islamic institutions consistently account for their engagement in civil society on the grounds that Islam is an all-embracing system, and that it is therefore natural for Islamists to engage in all facets of social life. Another argument that is often put forward for participating in civil society is that Islam is a practical religion, and should therefore be put into practice. The late Ismael Abu Shanab said in this regard:

> It is better that people should judge us on our practice than on what we simply tell them in writing about our ideas and thinking. We believe

that Islam should be practised on earth. The prophet Mohammed (PBH) was once described by his wife as the living embodiment of the Koran on earth. You know that the Koran is a holy book and this holy book should be put into practice, and Mohammed practised the Koran in his life. All of us Muslims have also been asked to practise the Koran in all aspects of life. We should practise Islam. In that sense it isn't political. It's a practice of Islam. It is faith.[157]

The practical aspect of Islam is strongly emphasised here, and is closely bound up with the Islamist notion of role models. The Islamist leaders are required to act as "model Islamists", and to act as role models in their social network, at the university, sports club and so on. This role is crucial to the way that the surrounding society regards Hamas, especially in the context of the corruption that marked Yasir Arafat's secular regime. The more so-called "white sheets" Hamas or the associated Islamic institutions can hold up, the more respect and sympathy they are likely to attract. Their strategy is thus based on the idea of the good example.[158] The Koranic message that you should "enjoin what is right and forbid what is evil"[159] ('*Amr bil-ma'rûf wa nahi an al-munkar*) is interpreted by many Islamists as an injunction to participate actively in the life of the community. The statute of *al-Mujamma' al-Islâmî* incidentally begins with a quotation from the Koran that presents the same message.[160]

The Hamas leadership's strategy for convincing young Palestinians about 'the truth' of Islam, or rather the Islamist message, is thus based on three elements: (a) the leaders' behaviour as role models; (b) participation in all aspects of daily life (as for example sport and education); (c) *da'wa*, i.e. the attempt to create *sound Muslims*.

Summary

The Palestinian Islamists – like Islamists elsewhere in the Middle East – perceive Islam as an all-embracing system that is valid for all times, provided that it is contextualised and subject to constant interpretation. Islam has been put on the defensive by Western civilisation. This applies alike to culture, politics and economics. Islamists see the Islamist project itself as a means of putting an end to the post-colonial power structure. They believe it is essential to know the background of the present balance of power if the Islamist project is to succeed. The shift in the balance of power between Western and Islamic civilisation has deep historical roots, originating, in the Islamists' account of history, from the defeat of the crusaders at the hands of

Salah ad-Din in 1187. In the wake of that defeat the Western world embarked on what the Islamists regard as an ideological invasion directed against the Arab-Muslim world: orientalists were trained to distort the holy scriptures and to contaminate Muslim thinking, the intelligentsia was corrupted by studying in the West, and a rift was thus created within the overall framework of Islam in the *umma* of the colonial Western powers. Zionism is treated as an outgrowth of these forces. In Hamas' view, lessons can be learned from history. Salah ad-Din won the battle in 1187 by virtue of Islam. Thus history teaches that a return to Islam is essential. Through Islam the individual can be liberated from ideological invasion. It is noteworthy that there is in fact nothing new in this theory. Pan-Arabism made use of a parallel reading of history and similarly sought liberation from invasion. The difference lies only in the fact that in the case of pan-Arabism this liberation was to occur through Arab unity.

Palestinian Islamists – like Islamists all over the Middle East – justify their engagement in Palestinian civil society by referring to Islam as an all-embracing system, and they perceive civil society institutions as a tool of creating *sound Muslims*.

In the next chapter I focus on the practical work carried out by Palestinian Islamists and the way in which the "consumers" respond to the services offered by the football club, *Nâdi al-Jam'iyya al-Islâmiyya*.

4

FOOTBALL AND ISLAMISM
IN THE GAZA STRIP

This chapter focuses on the young Palestinian men who had chosen to play football in the Islamist club *Nâdi al-Jam'iyya al-Islâmiyya*. In the introductory section I briefly sketch out the history of the club as well as how the Islamist leaders see sports as *da'wa* to Islam. This is followed by an examination of to which extent the club is a hotbed of indoctrination. I then go on to discuss the participants' motives for joining *Jam'iyya*. In addition, I aim in this chapter to arrive at a deeper understanding of the relationship between the articulation of Islam as a philosophy and the way it is practised in society, and to consider to what extent the young men involved in the club accepted and appropriated the club management's aims and their attempts to create *sound Muslims*. Since the Islamist discourse – like all other such discourses – is also based on exclusion procedures, the chapter will likewise look briefly at the attitudes of the young players towards the Palestinian Authority, as the main institution to which Islamists relate in the local context.

Nâdi al-Jam'iyya al-Islâmiyya – a short history

By the late 1990s *Nâdi al-Jam'iyya al-Islâmiyya* was one of four sports club (out of some 35 official sports clubs in the Gaza Strip) that was regarded as Islamist, both by Islamists themselves and by the local community.[161] The club is part of a larger social organisation, *al-Jam'iyya al-Islâmiyya*, led by Ahmad Bahr, while another prominent Hamas figure (the first Hamas Palestinian Prime Minister), Ismael Haniyya, heads the sports section. The club organises a wide range of sports activities: volleyball, swimming, football, tennis, boxing, basketball and instruction in Karate and mon-cha-ko.[162] Although at first sight it appears to be a large club, at the time of my fieldwork (1997–98) there were relatively few participants in each discipline: for example, there were only four tennis players and fifteen boxers, while the football section, which was the biggest in the club, had only about 100 members.[163] In addition, *al-Jam'iyya al-Islâmiyya* is associated with a number of so-called mosque teams that are not officially registered with the Palestinian Ministry of Sports and Youth. According to its administrators, the club sponsors some of these informal teams, and thus extends its network further. Several of the club's players either play or have played in these mosque teams. Despite its quite limited membership *al-Jam'iyya al-Islâmiyya* is the largest of the Islamic-oriented clubs.

Al-Jam'iyya al-Islâmiyya was established in 1976. The idea came from the leader of the Brotherhood, Sheikh Ahmad Yasin, who at that stage was involved in setting up another organisation, *al-Mujamma' al-Islâmi*. Unlike *Mujamma'*, *al-Jam'iyya al-Islâmiyya* had no problem in gaining official recognition from the Israeli occupying power, since initially the organisation was concerned exclusively with youth activities such as sport. It was only later that *al-Jam'iyya al-Islâmiyya* extended its activities in order – as Abu Shanab puts it – to meet other social needs.[164] The desire to become involved in sports and leisure activities arose quite "naturally". Over the past decade leading Islamists had offered instruction in the Koran and other subjects at various mosques (e.g. *al-masjid al-shamâli*) for young people in the Shati refugee camp. They had learned from experience that many of the young people sought out other institutions during the school summer holidays in order to take part in various leisure activities, such as sport. Abu Shanab explains:

> These institutions encouraged bad habits and behaviour. So we thought: how can we create an entirely Islamic community. The young people needed a club where they could engage in their activities, so we said OK, we should set up such a club ourselves. So we set up *al-Jam'iyya al-Islâmiyya* with a view to offering education and recreation.

The Islamists thus initiated these sports activities to prevent any setback to their existing efforts in other areas. The work of creating *sound Muslims*, if it was to be successful, required an institutional framework, and in ideological terms the initiative was justified by the fact that Islam was an all-embracing system that naturally included sports as well.

> As you can see in our institutions, we encourage sports activities. If you look at Islam as a whole you'll discover that the Koran and *Sunna* encourage us to be "well-trained" in all respects. In science, in sport, in fighting, in prayers and worship, in all ways … the prophet

Muhammad (PBH) enjoins us in his *hadîth*-recommendations to train in the sea (i.e. to swim), to train in archery, etc., and the prophet himself practised wrestling. Our religion therefore challenges us to be strong in our physical training ...[165]

Thus the Islamist leaders have no problem in arguing retrospectively that sport, too, is a part of Islam, and that they are simply following the prophet Muhammad's example.

Within the health sector Islamists make no attempt to reinstate traditional Islamic medical practices, but operate – in the literal sense – according to modern Western principles.[166] The same applies to sports and leisure activities. The sports primarily practised in the Islamist sports clubs are not the traditional Islamic activities such as wrestling, horse-riding and archery but the colonialists' imports: football, volleyball, basketball and boxing – a clear instance of the Islamists' ability to adapt to "modern reality". Their interpretation of Islam makes this unproblematic: Islam is relevant for all times and should thus be interpreted in the context of the present. At first sight, therefore, it is difficult to see in what respect the Islamist sports clubs represent an alternative. The difference however consists in the fact that alongside the sport, or, more accurately, over and above the sport, there is another factor at work – an element of upbringing or discipline aimed at creating *sound Muslims*.

The Head of *al-Jam'iyya al-Islâmiyya*, Sheikh Ahmad Bahr, incidentally came up with an interesting counter-question when asked to what extent there existed a connection between Islam and sport. He answered: "Naturally [sport] is a part of Islam, or would you prefer that all Muslims should be lazy?"[167]

Sport as a *da'wa* to Islam

As we have seen, the Islamist leaders seek to legitimise the movement's involvement in leisure activities within an Islamic framework, but the aim is political in the sense that the purpose of encouraging these activities is to create *sound Muslims* and hence to propagate Islamism as an alternative ideology and as a role model for the surrounding community. *Al-Jam'iyya al-Islâmiyya's* statement of aims reads:

The aim is to lead people to Islam (*al-hanîf*) and to work spiritually with worship, intellectually with science, physically with sport and socially through charitable work.[168]

The intention is clearly that the institution should play a leading role. Thus it should act as a role model worthy of imitation, with the members setting a good example. The creation of *sound Muslims* is closely linked to the idea of healing the alleged rift between Islam and Muslims. The first step in this direction is to teach good morals to young people in the club. For the leaders of the Islamist movements, morality is of central significance. Thus the most important aspect of the sports department, in their view, is not sport as such. Purely in sporting terms, *al-Jam'iyya al-Islâmiyya* is no different from other clubs: "We don't treat sport in itself as a goal, but see it as a means to create morally good young people."[169] It is worth pointing out that *al-Jam'iyya al-Islâmiyya* does not differ significantly in this respect from the tradition represented by, for example, the Danish Gymnastics and Sports Associations (DGI). The founding idea of the DGI, which originated in part from the Danish "folk highschool" tradition, can be captured in the notion of "folk", or popular, sport. For the DGI, just as for the Islamists, sport as such is not the goal, but should rather be understood "as a means of revival and enlightenment, whether in a historical, national-patriotic sense or in a national-democratic sense".[170]

Ideologically the Islamist leaders believe that the Palestinian population has largely abandoned the Islamic virtues, and that this decline has been aggravated by the establishment of the Fatah-led Palestinian Authority. After the Authority was set up, a number of PLO cadres returned from exile abroad. Their presence is evident on the streets of Gaza, where a number of women who have returned from exile go round attired in short skirts and short-sleeved T-shirts. Compared with the period of the *Intifada* (1987–93) this is a marked change in style. At that time all women – including Christians – wore veils, the veil being a symbol of resistance against Israel. The Authority also established a beach club, *Shallihât*, where women at a certain point in the 1990s could bathe in swimsuits and bikinis – a phenomenon unknown in the Gaza Strip since the early 1970s. Moreover a number of clubs have been set up along the coast, in several of which oriental dances are held and alcohol quite frequently consumed. In the view of Islamists such as Ismael Abu Shanab, therefore, Palestinian society is more decadent than it used to be and is now in a state of moral crisis:

> You will find the whole society gradually beginning to change in the direction of Islam. Do you remember 1967? Before the Six-Day War I saw no veiled women in Gaza. After *Mujammâ* and *Jam'iyya* were established women began to wear the veil. You could see it. Day after day … now the opposite is happening. It is one of the ways our socie-

ty is being undermined. Israeli society attacks us on this point. You can imagine how happy (Shimon) Peres was when he came to Gaza and saw all these clubs on the beach. He went back to his party in Tel Aviv and said to them: remember how Gaza looked during the *Intifada*, and see what the town is like now. And he mentioned all the nightclubs. Maybe he saw this as modernisation, but we see it as corruption, because modernisation must happen in our way ...

MICHAEL: But who is responsible for this development?

ABU SHANAB: The Palestinian Authority. We're constantly telling them: you are responsible for these things because it's you who have brought in people with this mentality, and you don't protest or do anything against this development ...[171]

Against this background, then, it is seen as more essential than ever to inculcate good morals in young people.

All the leaders I interviewed emphasised that it was a central part of their job in the club to ensure that young people's morals were improved and that they conducted themselves properly. In this regard they set great store by the proper use of language. Young people should speak nicely: to the leaders, to each other, to the referee, etc. It is of course taboo to use bad language or swear words cursing Allah.[172]

In this context it is paradoxical that the head of the club, Ismael Haniyya, while arguing that Islam is an all-embracing system, aims at the same time to present the Islamists' engagement in the club's activities as apolitical. Of his own association with the club he says:

The main point is that when I'm concerned with the club and work for the club, all my work is concentrated on sports activities and not on Hamas. One proof of this is that throughout my time as leader of the sports club I have never encouraged the players to become involved in Hamas' activities.[173]

One reason for giving such high priority to morals is that morality is seen as a crucial factor in strengthening the Islamist movement and in giving it social and cultural capital.[174] It requires moral strength to overcome life's temptations – those of the flesh as well as material temptations. Moral purity is also completely crucial in the situation in which the Palestinian Islamists currently find themselves, since perceived moral impurity can destroy a person and, worse still, destroy society as a whole. Amorality is thus to be treated as a contagious disease that can spread and ruin the community. This is why good morals are crucial for the political project that the Islamists are committed to carrying out.

In theory the leaders require that the young people who frequent the club should have demonstrated "good behaviour" even before they become members, although in practice this is not always the case. *al-Jam'iyya al-Islâmiyya*'s statutes specify that it is a condition of membership that one should be "a good and well-behaved Muslim".[175] But in practice the club is open to young people who have not yet found the right path. As one of the club's leaders puts it:

> If a person doesn't behave properly, we try to turn him around ... the main purpose or aim of *al-Jam'iyya al-Islâmiyya* is to create good Muslims and to get them to behave well.[176]

One thing is how the leaders perceive the club another is how the 'consumers' consume the goods. I will now turn to the playing ground.

The club: a profile

During the period of my fieldwork the club was in the second division in the Gaza Strip, and until 1996 had been in the first division. Unlike most of the other, mostly secular clubs in the Gaza Strip, *Jam'iyya* had at the time no permanent grounds and therefore played in various places round the city. Once a week the team trained at the Islamic University (IUG), once at al-Boura in the Sheikh Radwan neighbourhood, and now and again they got the opportunity to train at one of the city's larger stadiums, Yarmouk or Filastin. The pitches in all cases were gravel: there was not a single grass pitch in the Gaza Strip. However, there were plans to establish three grass pitches, including one in Gaza City (*mal'ab Filastîn*) and one in Rafah, home to the best team in the Gaza Strip. Because the club had no grounds of its own, *Jam'iyya* owned a minibus and employed a driver (sharing both with *Jam'iyya*'s kindergartens). The young people met at a particular, fixed spot in the Shati camp, where roughly half of them lived, and from there drove to the appointed pitch, often stopping in town to pick up other players. Players from other parts of Gaza City had their transport expenses paid by the club. After the training session most of the players were driven back to their own neighbourhoods.

At the time of fieldwork roughly half the players, as mentioned above, lived in the Shati refugee camp on the outskirts of Gaza City. Slightly fewer lived in the Sheikh Radwan district. Some players came from other neighbourhoods of Gaza City, such as al-Sabra and al-Shajaiyya, while a few others lived outside the city, in Nuseirat refugee camp and in Khan Younis (respectively 15 and 30 km south of Gaza). Thus the great majority of the players came from the immediate vicinity of the northern part of the Shati camp, where *al-Jam'iyya al-Islâmiyya* itself originated and still has its headquarters. The majority of the families living in the Shati camp came originally from towns such as Hammama and Faluja, or the villages near Ashdod and Asqelon that today lie within Israel's borders – or rather lay: over 418 Palestinian villages were razed to the ground by Israel in the years following the *al-Nakba* (catastrophe) of 1948.[177]

The players came from a wide range of backgrounds; they included, for example, a number of students from IUG (and a few from al-Azhar),[178] several tailors, a schoolteacher, a mechanic, a porter, a pharmacist, a building worker and an apprentice electrician.

As a rule the young men who play for *al-Jam'iyya al-Islâmiyya* train for about two hours twice a week. On average during the period of my fieldwork there were around 18–25 players, aged 17–33, engaged in the training. The club employed a semi-professional trainer who earned roughly 200 dollars a month – approximately the same as a police inspector in the Palestinian Authority. The club also had an assistant trainer. At the time I was there, the main trainer had just returned from almost three decades' exile in Libya, where he had also worked for a number of years as a trainer for youth teams. A typical training session began with the players trickling in some 5–20 minutes before training was due to begin. Since there were no changing rooms at the grounds where *al-Jam'iyya al-Islâmiyya* played, many of the players came in their strip, while others changed on the sidelines. They chatted and fooled around in a friendly way, and everyone shook hands. At every training session 3–7 players – different ones on each occasion – prayed before training began. The others had already prayed at home or at work. By their own account all the club's players prayed at least five times a day.

The training itself was extremely rigorous and varied, typically going as follows: the players initially warmed up by running 5–10 times round the pitch. Then they practised tight dribbling with balls and cones. Next they played in threes, doing kick-offs and headers. Then came 25 push-ups and 20 half-metre jumps with both legs, followed by a series of other exercises, and finally a 45-minute training game. Especially at the beginning I found it difficult to follow the training programme; some of the club's permanent players also found it tough and not all were able to do all the exercises.

A hotbed of indoctrination?

Some of the academic literature concerning Hamas embarks from a security policy perspective.[179] This approach is based on the perception of Hamas and Islamism in general as a threat to Israel, the United States and the Palestinian Authority alike. A number of other researchers who base their work on a historical-politological approach take an overwhelmingly negative view of the movement, often using the metaphor "monster" in describing Hamas.[180] There is likewise almost total consensus that Islamic institutions such as *Mujamma'* and *Jam'iyya* are used by Islamists for purposes of propaganda and indoctrination in Islamism and – so at least some academics argue – in terrorism.[181] This tendency however is even more conspicuous in parts of the press and among politicians, especially in the United States and Israel. Interestingly enough some of the players were conscious of their presumed role as disrupters of peace – in other words, terrorists. Umar's spontaneous remarks offer a good example. Umar, a player in his mid-30s, had joined the club mainly for social reasons. He never played in competitive matches and acted more as a kind of moral whip. He worked at a school in Gaza, was married and had half a dozen children. The Israeli army had killed one of his daughters during the Intifada (1987–93). After I had been training with the team for a couple of weeks, he asked me:

> What view does the West take of the Islamist movement? Do you think we're all terrorists? Have YOU ever seen any terrorists? How do people treat you here? Do you know that the only thing *Kata'ib Izz ad-Din al-Qassam* does is to defend our country? What do you think you would have done if someone had taken your country?[182]

And in a subsequent conversation he said:

> Have you heard the news today? Muhi ad-Din al-Sharif was martyred in Ramallah two days ago. He was known as *al-Muhandis al-Thâni.*[183] As you know, [people in] the West call us terrorists. For more than seven months there have been no actions, and now we have this. Maybe you also remember what happened to Khaled Mish'al[184] in Amman, Jordan a couple of months ago. They stole our country. They kill our children. They have raped our women, mothers, wives and sisters. They kill or attempt to kill our leaders. We need someone to react to this. We can't just sit here with our arms folded. We feel the fire burning in our hearts – it's like a volcano – and sometimes it erupts … we aren't terrorists, but what do you want us to do …[185]

Umar thus sought to contextualise the use of violence by the military branch of the Hamas movement. Although he of course knew that I was interested in politics, his statements came as a surprise in view of the fact that I had at no point sought to discuss Hamas' military actions with the players. Such statements suggest that "they" have a clear conception of what "we" think about "them".

After a couple of weeks of training I wrote in my logbook: "No outward signs of Islamism – no institutionally organised common prayers – no nothing. Just tough training."[186] In so far as there was an attempt to influence young people in the club, this took place through the talks on morality given at regular intervals by the club's leaders. These lectures usually focused on the length of the players' shorts, and at first I did not pay much attention to them.

But this moral teaching in regard to the dress code is not without interest, since the whole purpose of the club is not simply to play sport but precisely to create moral human beings. The aim is for the club to set a good example. It is morality that serves as the focal point in the relationship between the Islamist club and the – politically – dominant secular society surrounding it. Through this moral teaching, a crucial distinction is created between "us" and "the others". In Islamic tradition there are a number of prescriptions concerning the way orthodox Muslims should dress, and these apply to men as well as women. As is well known, there is a consensus among Islamists that women should cover themselves so that only their hands and face are visible when they appear in public. The area that women should cover is referred to as their *'awrah*. Men, too, have an *'awrah*, which in their case means that they must be covered from the navel down to the knees. In everyday life this rule is not especially relevant, but it becomes highly relevant for sportsmen, who often wear shorts. Thus Islamists who engage in sports (in principle) wear knee-length shorts. The club's leaders emphasise this to varying degrees when explaining in what respects their club is specifically Islamist. Haniyya says:

First and foremost all the players should fulfil Islamist requirements concerning prayers, fasting, visiting the mosque and so on, whereas other clubs do not demand this. We also differ in our focus. According to Islam we should cover our bodies from the navel to the knees. We feel that those who don't do this, but wear shorts… it is mainly the new players who do this and it doesn't happen often, but we keep an eye on them.[187]

Thus the new young players are under observation to begin with. Not everyone can play for *Jam'iyya*, since the club is a shop window for Islamism. It is therefore necessary that the new players should be closely inspected. Rotten vessels create bad publicity for the club, and mean that *Jam'iyya* would lose a certain amount of the social capital acquired through its engagement in the discourse of morality and good behaviour.

The above quotation incidentally illustrated a point made by Olivier Roy (1993), who observes that, in contrast to radical Islamism, moderate Islamism (neo-fundamentalism in Roy's terminology) is deeply conservative.[188] On the same subject of dress, another of the club's administrators says:

> We don't like the players wearing brief shorts. Although it's not that important, we try to get the players to behave in a thoroughly Islamic fashion. Wearing Islamic shorts is not a command (*fard*), but it is what Islam recommends.[189]

Thus complete consensus does not apparently exist among the club leaders as to whether it is a *sine qua non* that players should follow the Islamic dress code. However, they agree that this is desirable. From my observations during fieldwork it became clear that in practice none of the club's players observed the code. Virtually all the players were dressed in copies of the big international teams' kits – Tottenham Hotspurs, Glasgow Rangers, Ajax Amsterdam and so on. Ironically enough, I was virtually the only one who consistently kept to the code. The club's leaders were concerned about the matter, and touched on it on several occasions during training sessions.[190]

On the ideological and symbolic level the dress code is a crucial factor in profiling the club as a living example of the alternative approach. And this is precisely what the leaders want – that Islam should be made visible in the public realm. The leaders themselves practise *da'wa* for the young people in the club by presenting their own lives and modes of behaviour as examples worthy of imitation. Over and above this, however, they want the club's players themselves to practise *da'wa* by representing Islam on the playing fields. It is therefore important that the young people should be inculcated in the "correct" moral conduct. As the Head of the sports club, Ismael Haniyya, puts it:

> In the sports department it's very important for us to demonstrate good Islamic behaviour and to get the players to set an example of this. It is

therefore important that they reflect the path of Islam in their personal conduct, and that *others* get to see this."[191]

Thus the club makes explicit their wish that *al-Jam'iyya al-Islâmiyya* should set an example (*qudwa*) that is worthy of imitation by other clubs. In this way the Islamic message is spread and standards of public morality improved. Once again, the club's social capital is at stake. The conduct of the players is of the greatest importance in determining whether the club's symbolic capital is increased or reduced.

Hence on the playing ground the leaders' sermons were often prompted by dissatisfaction with the young men's style of clothing. They would frequently emphasise in this connection that:

> You are *shabab Muslim* and *al-Jam'iyya al-Islâmiyya* is an Islamic club. If you have no long shorts, you can apply to the management.

And the moral ticking-off would continue:

> *Al-Jam'iyya al-Islâmiyya* is an Islamic club built on Islamic principles. This means *intimâ* [close association with] Islam and *intimâ* to *Jam'iyya*. *Intimâ* is something you feel in your hearts. You set an example to players in other clubs. That's why high moral standards are essential. That's also why long shorts are necessary. We can't do otherwise.[192]

The players' motives for joining the club

Why play in an Islamist club? Ayman was a player in his mid-20s who had just begun to play in the club. He had recently completed a BA at the University of Amman in Jordan and was unemployed at the time of the interview. Ayman told me:

> I don't know ... I didn't get the chance in the other club, you know ... There's also a certain partisan attitude among the young men there. Many of them are Fatah sympathisers, and there are also some supporters of the PFLP. Although they're my friends, you don't always feel comfortable taking your own position there ... So I changed club. I play forward. There are many good forwards in my former club but none in the Islamist club. Also, I was contacted by the trainer and by one of the members of the *Jam'iyya* administration and asked if I wouldn't play for them ...[193]

Another new player, 21-year-old Ahmad, who worked as a tailor, offered a similar explanation. Ahmad, too, felt that he had a better chance of getting on the team with *Jam'iyya*. In explaining why he had joined the club, he said:

> I didn't get the chance with my previous club ... and I have several friends who play for *al-Jam'iyya al-Islâmiyya* ...[194]

Nabil, aged 27, was one of the more regular players from the Sheikh Radwan neighbourhood. He was unskilled and worked as a porter (*hâris*). Nabil gave a religious explanation for his membership of the club. He told me:

> The prophet be praised! I believe in God, I chose this club primarily from a religious point of view.[195]

In the same interview, however, Nabil also indicated that there were geographic reasons for his choice of club: "The club was near my home and I always played on their grounds." Ibrahim, in his early 30s, was one of the club's oldest players, and lived in Sheikh Radwan where he ran a garage. He had played for 14 years for a secular club before joining *Jam'iyya*, and explained his choice of *Jam'iyya* as follows:

> During the Intifada there was no organised football here in the Gaza Strip, but then teams began to develop in association with the mosques. We played in the yards attached to the mosques. I played for around four years at the Sheikh Radwan mosque. Once organised sport started up again I began playing for *Jam'iyya*. I had made several contacts in the mosque and I chose *Jam'iyya*. The club chose players from the mosques ... I came to this club because of *intimâ'*. Even if it had been based in Rafah I would have chosen it ...[196]

It is thus surprising to see that the players' choice of an Islamist club was by no means based solely on religious or political considerations. On the one hand there are the motives that both Ayman and Ahmad express: they had a better chance of fulfilling their personal ambitions as footballers in this Islamist club. Ayman and Ibrahim both indicate that the fact that they had been invited to play for the club by the club's leaders – i.e. as a result of an active initiative on the latters' part – had been important for them. Only Nabil states directly that he joined the club for religious reasons, but at the same time he also makes clear that as a teenager he had lived in the immediate vicinity of the club's (former) grounds, and that it was therefore natural for him to play there.

It is clear that a number of non-ideological factors contributed to the players' choice, and several of the players in fact had a "consumer's" relationship to the clubs. They switched clubs partly in order to satisfy their own sporting ambitions. The examples also show that the players had mixed motives and were not strictly Islamist. But it is also worth noting Ibrahim's comment that even if the club had been located in Rafah, he would have chosen *Jam'iyya*. Rafah is the southernmost town in the Gaza Strip. It is located about 35 km from Gaza City, and the reason Ibrahim mentions Rafah is that he cannot imagine anywhere further away: a reminder of the lack of freedom of movement that is part of the everyday life of people living in Gaza.

When *Jam'iyya* was demoted to the second division in 1996 it lost a number of its players: altogether ten men left the club. In this instance it is obvious that for the players concerned their personal sporting ambitions overrode their Islamist allegiance. Ziad, in his mid-20s, was one of those who left. Before transferring in 1997 to a first division club, he had played for *Jam'iyya* ever since his teenage years. Ziad gave a succinct and precise account of his reasons for changing clubs:

> When the club moved down from the top to the second division a number of clubs contacted me to see if I was interested in playing for them, so I chose one of them.[197]

Mahmoud, a schoolteacher in his mid-20s, who also decided to switch to a secular first division club after playing for *Jam'iyya* for five years, explained his decision as follows:

> I chose *Jam'iyya* for various reasons, just as I decided to leave the club for several different reasons. You know, most players want to satisfy their personal ambitions. They hope to improve their skills as players in a better … or a good club in order to fulfil their ambitions. That was one reason why I changed club. Another reason was that I had run into various problems in *Jam'iyya* which had to do mainly with the club's fans.

Mahmoud stressed that his problems were principally to do with the spectators. He told me:

I was playing forward and sometimes when we drew or lost they would put the responsibility on me. These problems weren't confined to the football pitch but also affected me at home and at the university. This made me very frustrated, and it also contributed to my decision to change.[198]

There is thus a high turnover in the club. New players join the club to pursue their ambitions while other leave it for the same reason – even though it means joining a secular club. None of those interviewed, incidentally, explained their choice of an Islamist club in terms of material advantages or benefits, such as better training facilities or other fringe benefits such as enhanced job opportunities or better accommodation. There was complete agreement among the interviewees that, if what they were after were better conditions, increased job opportunities and so on, they would be better off moving to one of the big Fatah-dominated clubs, which offered such benefits, rather than staying with the Islamists.[199]

Nabil put it as follows:

I have always had the chance to play in another club and I would get greater benefits from doing so, but I'm not interested in the benefits that would follow. It would be like being away from my own home …

Several of the players in fact complained about the club's poor facilities.[200] This contradicts the view that journalists, in particular, often have of Islamists: namely that they have great economic resources at their disposal. Like the players, I too had the impression that the club was not well-off: judging from the physical facilities and material goods the club was able to offer its members, there was nothing to suggest that the Islamists had any noteworthy economic resources at their disposal.[201] Through the interviews I conducted with both the leaders of the Islamist movement and with secular Palestinian observers, it emerged that the Islamist movement in recent years had been weakened economically, among other things because the United States in the mid-1990s had prohibited the collection of funds for the Islamist movement. Israel, too, had contributed significantly to this development. It is therefore clear that there is a price to pay for being affiliated to *Jam'iyya*. The Islamist club is not in a position to offer its players the same range of material benefits provided by some of the Fatah-controlled clubs.

Does one become Islamist by playing for *al-Jam'iyya al-Islâmiyya?*

If the club is indeed a hotbed of indoctrination, one might expect the young players to relate that they had undergone some religious awakening through their membership of it. In their book on young women in the political Islamist movement, Christiansen and Rasmussen (1994) say that many of the young women they interviewed had stories of conversion to recount; they had undergone an Islamic awakening and "seen the light". The results of my own study of the football club point in a different direction. The young men in the Gaza Strip had gradually become more Islamic, but they had always been believers with a capital B. The men I interviewed were thus unable to identify any particular turning point or awakening. Ibrahim described the beginning of his engagement in Islam as follows:

> It started before I joined *Jam'iyya*. When I played with my previous club I was the only player on the team who prayed ... the milieu in which I grew up also played a role. It has always been Islamic. I grew up in an Islamic milieu. So one could say that it comes from my home, from my own family.

Nabil related:

> I've always been a good Muslim ... I heard about Islam when I started playing at the club, but I learned about religion myself. I also heard the imams at the mosques and on TV.

Most of the others similarly related that they had always been Muslim believers. None of those interviewed saw any change from the past to the present when it came to their degree of religiosity. I believe there may be a gender explanation for the fact that the young (male) Islamists I interviewed had not experienced the kind of awakening that many of the young women in Christiansen and Rasmussen's study describe. For women Islamists, the division between the past and the present is very obvious, since it is associated with wearing *hijâb*, and thus with a marked change in the women's outer appearance. In other words, the woman's relationship to the outside world is changed radically. This applies both to the way others see her, but also to the fact that she now moves in other social circles. Another reason that the (male) players, unlike the women, did not register any particular change relates to the fact that women often start to frequent the mosques only after their "conversion", whereas the mosque represents a social meeting place for men almost throughout their lives.

The fact that the young men had not as a rule undergone any conversion, and that there was no Islamist instruction within the framework of the club, was indeed the subject of sharp criticism by Islamist leaders in the Gaza Strip who were not directly associated with the club. The late Ismael Abu Shanab, who was one of the founders of *Jam'iyya* in 1976, criticised the present leadership in one of the interviews I conducted with him. He emphasised that in the early years *Jam'iyya* had offered a form of education, with lectures in various aspects of Islam and so on. He was irked that this was no longer the case, and told me:

ABU SHANAB: I think it is essential they improve [on this]. They should train their players with a view to maintaining the unique Islamist code of behaviour and Islamist doctrine.

MICHAEL: Do you think they don't do this for fear of the Palestinian Authority's reaction?

ABU SHANAB: No. They're incapable of doing it. The system is about to become obsolete. That happens with other systems too, and we're not ashamed of that. Ahmad Bahr has been the leader of *Jam'iyya* since 1988. He has never been replaced. Why not? Now, moreover, he has become *amîr* for the *shûrâ* Council in *Hizb al-Khalâs*. He should work either in one place or the other. One can't be in two places at the same time, not doing anything [in either]. So if we reflect a little on that and hold new elections and choose new people that may bring in new blood, then I think things will develop. We're considering doing this but not for the time being. I'm talking completely honestly about this problem. *Al-Mujamma' al-Islâmî* also has the same problem; indeed it's even worse. Nowadays *Jam'iyya* is more active than *Mujamma'*, even though historically *Mujamma'* has been significantly larger.[202]

Apart from being a personal attack on Sheikh Ahmad Bahr, Abu Shanab's criticism is also directed on the lack of emphasis on Islamic education in the club. The solution, as he sees it, is to get rid of the present leadership and bring new blood into the institution.

Islamism and the Israeli prisons

Through my many interviews and informal discussions I concluded that, if one is looking for cases of conversion and Islamic awakening, the searchlight needs to be directed elsewhere, namely at the Israeli prisons. Ayman related:

I was very keen on the PLO. I was very keen on Abu Ammer [Yasir Arafat]. During the Intifada [1987–93] we suffered a great deal under the Israelis. They kill us. They shoot us. I wanted to do something to remedy this situation. At that point Hamas was doing something ... and people were turning to religion. They did so rapidly, people turned to religion to pray to God to help us during the Intifada. Children went to the mosques as well. At that point Hamas raised various issues; they said to people: no one but God can help us at this time. And we have high moral standards here. Our habits and traditions tell us that we must go with God. We asked God to do something for us in this dangerous situation. So we followed Hamas. I didn't join Hamas' armed wing. No, I simply followed Hamas in my convictions. I didn't take part in the armed wing because my family needed me. But I threw stones in the name of Hamas and above all in the name of God. Afterwards I was arrested and landed up in prison. You know how in the prisons we were divided up. There were prison blocks for Hamas, Fatah and PFLP prisoners. When I was put in prison the Israelis asked me which block I wanted to be put in. I replied that I wanted to be with the Hamas prisoners. And they became my friends, and that was very nice. I'm sorry; I forgot to say that this was my second time in prison. The first time I had been put with Fatah. [I was there] for four months, and I got to know them quite well, and I found out that there wasn't much to be said for being with them. They were spies, and I was afraid of them. So I didn't want to be put with Fatah a second time. So during my second stay in prison I wanted to be with Hamas. They taught us about religion, about the Koran. They taught us. [203]

As Ayman's statements show, the main reason for his "conversion" was the PLO's inability to remedy his frustration over the behaviour of the Israeli occupying forces. In this sense Ayman offers good evidence of the tendency that Jean Francois Legrain (1994) has pointed out, namely that during the Intifada (1987–93) Hamas was able to attract individuals from within the PLO's ranks. Ayman was the only one of those I interviewed in the club who described some form of awakening. His account shows that his ideas concerning Islam and politics were formed during his second stay in prison, where he was put with prisoners who were all either members of, or sympathisers with, Hamas. In what follows, therefore, I will take a slightly closer look at the conditions in Israeli jails, since certain Palestinians are clearly islamised in these surroundings.

The prisons represented an ideal place to study and develop as a person. After 1989, when the Israeli occupying forces imprisoned a growing number of Hamas leaders and sympathisers, the leaders of the Islamist movement took upon themselves the role of tutors and teachers.

The late Hamas leader Ismael Abu Shanab, who was imprisoned from 1989 to 1997, thus gave the following answer to my question: "Do you agree with the view that imprisonment during the Intifada continues to play a key role for the people who support Hamas?":

> Yes, even though this wasn't part of our methodology, but we came to adopt this method in Hamas. It was a new philosophy. For me, too, it was a new experience – a very fruitful experience. I met prisoners who had been in Israeli prisons since the early 1970s and they explained how they had struggled for everything in the prisons. They told us how at first they had slept on the floor. Later they got beds and mats, and after 30 years' struggle within the prison walls the prisoners had obtained most of their rights. [These rights] weren't just handed to them by the Israelis. They had come about as a result of our struggle. As for Hamas … I think our history in the prisons began in 1985. At that point our people were just a small minority. After the Intifada we became a large minority. Fatah still had most prisoners, but we constituted the next largest group, with around 40 per cent of the total number of prisoners. Life in prison is not very different from life outside the prison walls. At the hours for prayer our cell was transformed into a mosque, and half an hour later into a classroom, and later on in the day into a restaurant. These changes were the result of dedication and good organisation. We work hard at being well-organised people. Not an hour was wasted. Our time was very structured. It's very fruitful when all your time is used for something sensible. When we got up in the morning we had an hour's sport on the programme, and after that we ate breakfast. Then we had lessons. At around midday we had common prayers. In the afternoon there was time for a nap. And in the evening we could either read or watch TV. So it was a very organised system. Some people would perhaps regard it as boring, but we made it very active and lively.[204]

Abu Shanab was one of the main teachers in the prison at Asqelon, where he served most of his eight-year sentence. Rather than teaching engineering, he gave instruction in religion and politics.

Ghazi Hamad, another Islamist leader, earned a MA during his stay in prison through taking a correspondence course at an American university. Hamad, who was imprisoned from 1989 to 1994, described this period as the best time of his life, and told me:

> It was a sort of university. To suffer is to learn. In the last 3–4 years of the Intifada the prisoners themselves could choose whether they want-ed to be put in a Hamas, Fatah or PFLP block. This was due to a num-ber of problems that had arisen between the various fractions. In the prison we had a huge library consisting of around 2,000 books, includ-ing the words of Muhammad Hussein Fadlallah, Sayyid Qutb and Hasan al-Banna. There was no strict censorship; even though certain books had to be smuggled in … In the Israeli prisons we had instruc-tion for 4–5 hours a day. This included lectures in religion and politics. We had an hour's sport every day, after which there were 23 hours left in the day – what else could we do but study and teach? We created people with a different mentality. Perhaps you have also heard about the experiment in South Lebanon – Ibn Taymiyyah University?[205] In the Ansar III prison in Negev there was a university as well, named Yousuf University. There you could even sit an examination. I think we suc-ceeded in creating men who would do good in their society.[206]

Thus it is clear that Israel's policy towards the Palestinian population has played a crucial – albeit indirect – role in islamisation and the creation of *sound Muslims* among the Palestinian population, even if this effect is due first and foremost to the Islamists' own ability to organise themselves. During the Intifada over 100,000 Palestinians were imprisoned in Israel. At least 20,000 of these were in "administrative detention".[207] Abu Shanab esti-mates that approximately 40 per cent of these have served their time in the Hamas blocks of Israeli prisons. This means that around 8–10,000 young men have taken part, for a longer or shorter period, in Hamas' "education system" within the prisons, and thereby undergone Islamist "instruction". A substantial proportion of Palestinian men thus owe a good deal of their knowledge of religion and politics to their time in Israeli jails.

The spread of Islamism via these "educated" former prisoners should not be underestimated, partly because imprisoned Intifada heroes enjoy a certain authority, and not least because the spreading of the Islamist message perhaps occurs to a greater extent through informal networks than previous studies have recognized. Through his own conduct – by acting as "a good example" – the individual Islamist influences those immediately around him, whether his family, friends, fellow-students or neighbours.

The club stands out for its high moral standards

Contrary to my expectations – and those implicit in much of the literature – I found that the football players, apart from Umar, did not talk constantly about Islam and politics. Much of the young people's attention was focused on Egyptian football; indeed, because of the growth in satellite stations and, not least, satellite dishes, many Palestinians, including those in the refugee camps, also knew a good deal about European football. During training sessions the players spent more time teasing one another, for example by poking one another in the shoulders without being caught, than in discussing politics.

But what, then, distinguished this club from others? Even after several months' training in the club I did not get the impression that there was any form of indoctrination, but something else was going on. Nabil told me:

> What distinguishes this club from other clubs in Gaza is first and foremost the players' morality and the way that the team members treat one another.

Ali, aged 20, was a student at the Islamic University from the Sheikh Radwan district. He had played in the club since the age of 14. He expressed a similar view of the club and morality:

> The club is different, it's Islamist, it represents Islamist men. The other clubs often have low moral standards. The players may drink; maybe they don't pray in the other clubs. There's a big difference.[208]

Ismail was 22 years old and likewise a student, in this case at al-Azhar University. He was one of the few players who came from far afield, namely from Nuseirat, 15 km south of Gaza City. Ismail explained the matter in almost identical terms: "[The club] is Islamist … it represents the Islamic men in Gaza", and to a follow-up question as to how this identity was expressed, he answered:

Shabâb Muslim ... Shabâb masâjid ... We pray before training and the leaders of the club are Muslims. Most of the players come from the mosques. [The club] represents Islam. We are good Muslims and the proof of that is the way the club suffers under the Authority and the fact that [the Authority] has closed the [club's grounds].[209]

It was true to a certain extent that the players prayed together, but there was no institutionalised practice involved here. Some of the players prayed together, while the majority prayed beforehand either at home or at work. And it was obvious to an observer that they aimed to get the prayers over and done with quickly (with four *rak'ât*) so that they could get on with the real business at hand: namely football. Ismail's remarks illustrate the difference between theory and social practice. He also suggests that the proof that the Islamists represented *al-haqq* was that the Palestinian Authority had suppressed them. In order to understand Ismail's argument it is important to recall the Islamists' view of history, as sketched in Chapter 3. It is this view of history that Ismail is drawing on when he presents the Palestinian Authority as a part of *al-bâtil,* which is fighting on the side of the West and the Zionists in the struggle against *al-haqq,* i.e. Islam.

The fact that moral standards were indeed higher in *Jam'iyya* was however confirmed by several players who had now left *Jam'iyya* to play for other secular clubs. Mahmoud, who had played in a secular club for two years, said: "There is no doubt at all that moral standards in *al-Jam'iyya al-Islâmiyya* are higher, but that is not sufficient reason to stop playing here [in the new club]." Another former *Jam'iyya* player, Ziad, a man in his late twenties who was employed in one of the Authority's numerous intelligence services, said: "Moral standards among the *Jam'iyya* players are higher ... here [in the new club] you often come across not particularly nice language ...".

Ayman explained how *Jam'iyya*'s identity as an Islamic club was expressed.

Everyone here knows the club, and it's known to be very ... to have high moral standards. The people that play here have high moral standards. Many of the players are keen on religion and want to do everything that God asks of them ... some of them hate the leaders of the Palestinian Authority.

Bourdieu's theory of social and cultural capital is very relevant in understanding why these young footballers found it rewarding to play for *Jam'iyya.* In doing so they gained social capital, since "everyone knows the club, which is distinguished for its high moral standards"; through their association with the club, the players thus enjoyed a high reputation among Muslims. In the context of Gaza, where economic capital is almost impossible to raise, wealth is often associated with the Authority and also therefore with corruption. Economic capital has thus increasingly become an unacceptable form of wealth, since it has come to imply a selfish and corrupt way of life. The fact that the players themselves sought to acquire social capital is evident from Ayman's statements:

> I have high moral standards, and I would like the people around me to say that Ayman is a good man, an Islamic man. For us here it's good to be an Islamic man.[210]

Ali's and Ismail's (and to some extent also Ayman's) statements – "we are Muslims" – make clear moreover how the Islamist discourse is associated with exclusion procedures. Christiansen (1998) describes such procedures as follows:

> As an Islamist one is urged to pay constant critical attention to one's own behaviour and moral standards in order constantly to improve them and thereby practise, i.e. put the spirit and ideas of the religion more and more into practice. This critical gaze is sometimes inevitably turned on other people, and this entails actively distancing oneself from one's immediate surroundings on a moral and spiritual-intellectual level.

Precisely through this discourse on morality and behaviour the players exclude all other Palestinians in the Gaza Strip from belonging to the category of "Muslims". These others are implicitly stamped as deviants and in principle as non-believers. The players' statements thus come close to branding as heretics (*takfir*) all others in the surrounding society.

Articulation vs. social practice

Bourdieu's perceptions are likewise useful in illustrating human complexity in so far as he focuses on the relationship between normativity or articulation and social practice. Through my choice of method I was in a position to cast light on the relationship between these two levels.

As a case in point I will return to the issue of dress code as discussed at the beginning at this chapter. Clothing was a factor to which the players alluded in explaining how their club differed from others. According to Ibrahim:

First and foremost, we wear long shorts when we play. We have high moral standards. We are all Muslims.

Nabil and Ali likewise emphasised the crucial significance of clothing as a sign that the club was Islamic. As already mentioned the great majority of the players were dressed in smart clothes copied from the strip of the major European, and in some cases Egyptian, teams. Thus one could see young men dressed in the team strip of, among others, Tottenham Hotspurs, Glasgow Rangers (whose kit incidentally advertises McEwans Lager), Ajax Amsterdam, the Italian national team, the top-division Egyptian club al-Mansura, and the Cairo teams Zamalek and al-Ahli. Some of the players wore longer shorts under their "smart" shorts and thereby managed to keep to the Islamic dress code.

As mentioned the club's leaders accorded great importance to the Islamic dress code, and on numerous occasions the players were reprimanded for not observing it. On these occasions the players were embarrassed and pulled their shorts down a bit further so that they covered their knees. Nevertheless, some of the players answered back, complaining that their outfits would no longer match if they had to play in long shorts. Ayman made the following comment on this:

AYMAN: You know the press and the spectators laugh at the Islamists and our shorts. We don't like people laughing at us, so therefore we have to be flexible. And ordinary shorts aren't so heavy to play in, and not so ugly either. So we have to bear that in mind. The main thing is that we want God to be satisfied with us.

MICHAEL: But I know the club's leaders aren't too happy about that. They've told you three or four times during training: "You are *Jam'iyya*. You have to play in long shorts ...", yet there are still very few players who do so.

AYMAN: I don't know how to explain it but in the team ... Not everyone has such high moral standards or is Islamic ... some of them are quite ordinary people.

David Chaney's theory throws some light on the reason why it was important for the players to oppose the leadership on this issue. According to Chaney, the practice of sport has a great deal to do with living out a dream, and these dreams can easily be shattered if one proves unable to copy one's idols. Writing about the role of sport, Chaney argues that sport is carried out for an audience and that amateurs either entertain hopes of being accepted among the ranks of professionals, or play out the dream of their mentors.[211]

It would appear that the practitioners here had two colliding dreams: on the one hand the dream of being a good Muslim (Islamist), and on the other the desire to fulfil their ambitions on the football pitch. It seems that in practice the majority of the young players chose the latter dream, while still sticking to Islamic ideals in theory. Foucault's theory of power relations can be applied here to explain why the club's leaders were quite simply unable to make the players conform to their wishes. According to this theory, a negotiation takes place between the leaders and the players. The players are able to negotiate because the club (and in the broader context Islamism) cannot survive unless those involved support the leadership – notwithstanding the fact that it is the leadership that defines what constitutes "correct" Islamic behaviour. In this sense the situation is open to negotiation. And in this concrete instance the players were apparently able to trump their leaders. It would seem that one of the main reasons for this was that they did not want to be laughed at by the surrounding secular society. Thus what we see here is a negotiation, articulated through the discussion of dress codes, concerning the definition of what constitutes "correct" Islam.

Ayman defined being a moral person as follows:

> Being a moral person means praying, not creating problems with other people, not yelling at them or yelling back; not doing anything wrong or anything that goes against God's wishes.[212]

The players in *al-Jam'iyya al-Islâmiyya* were not always able to live up to their own criteria for moral behaviour, as the following story suggests:

Scandalous match in Tuffah[213]

Players and spectators run amok

Tuffah, Gaza City (4 May 1998)
Yesterday Beit Hanoun and *al-Jam'iyya al-Islâmiyya* played one another in the Gaza Strip's second division. The match, who ended in a 2–2 draw, can best be described as a scandal, since it was marked by violent play and unrest among the spectators. Beit Hanoun looked set to take the lead and in the first half kept *Jam'iyya* under heavy pressure. *Jam'iyya*'s defence, however, was irreproachable, and meant that Beit

Hanoun was unable to score in the first 45 minutes. Indeed, by half time the Islamist team was – somewhat undeservedly – 1–0 ahead. Only five minutes into the second half Beit Hanoun equalised, when *Jam'iyya*'s goalie did a spectacular miss. Less than five minutes later *Jam'iyya*'s goalie was once again centre stage when he gave away a completely unnecessary penalty kick. Following a Beit Hanoun attack the ball was played into the field and the goalie went into action. A Hanoun player came running up in an attempt to press back the goalie, who deliberately elbowed the Hanoun player in the face. The referee duly showed the goalie the red card for this, at the same time awarding a penalty kick. The goalie's foul led to fisticuffs on the field between the two teams' players, and the game was interrupted for 15 minutes. The stadium was in uproar. At a certain point one of Beit Hanoun's managers went so far as to draw his gun and fire into the air in the hope of putting a stop to the commotion. At this point the game resumed, with Hanoun deservedly drawing ahead 2–1 with the penalty kick. After Hanoun's second goal *Jam'iyya* got more into the game and towards the end pushed forward to get even. 13 minutes into overtime they equalised with a free kick from midfield that took the otherwise reliable Hanoun goalie completely unawares. At this point uproar broke out again. The *Jam'iyya* players were naturally jubilant over the equaliser and ran (very provocatively) towards the roughly 4–500 Beit Hanoun supporters, turning cartwheels and so on. *Jam'iyya*'s 50–80 supporters yelled at full throttle: *Allâhu Akbar. Allâhu Akbar.* At this the Beit Hanoun fans ran amok. With one accord they grabbed stones and began hurling them around, first at the *Jam'iyya* players and then at their supporters (and yours truly: one stone hit me in the back). After this pause the last two minutes were played and the game ended in a 2–2 draw. Before the last whistle *Jam'iyya*'s captain also lashed out at one of his fellow-players after a misunderstanding within the *Jam'iyya* team. The two had to be separated by their eager fellow players. After the game one of the leaders of *Jam'iyya* commented: "This is the worst game in the club's history." The *Jam'iyya* captain said: "I obviously lost my head. I don't know what I was doing."

As is clear from the above "article", the game in Tuffah in many respects represented the opposite of what the Islamists aim to stand for. For the players, however, the match against Beit Hanoun did not give rise to any great soul-searching, apart from the acknowledgement that "nobody's perfect". In an interview a couple of months after the match, Ayman said:

> Playing and yelling and getting a player sent off doesn't mean that you've abandoned your good moral standards. We're humans and we have a temperament. Nobody's perfect. It's different if you're shown the red card for cursing God or because you insult the referee. Look at Zein ad-Din Zidane,[214] he never gets a yellow card but recently he was shown the red card and had to sit out two matches. He has a temper and couldn't control himself. Which means that even if you've got a red card or come to blows with someone on the field, you haven't stopped being a moral person. That's a different thing, as I see it.[215]

Ayman thus justifies behaviour that ought not to arise in an Islamist club by arguing, "We're all human". He uses the example of Zein ad-Din Zidane, one of the greatest players in the Muslim world (and indeed the world), to justify his fellow-players' actions. The same things had happened to Zidane. The latter, incidentally, is considered by "football experts" to be a nebbian on the pitch.

The club administration did not take quite the same view of the match, regarding it instead as the worst game in *Jam'iyya's* history. Afterwards they therefore felt obliged to punish both the goalie and the captain. It is interesting to note how the club's director, Ismael Haniyya, initially tried – when I interviewed him on 27 June 1998 – to avoid discussing the match with Beit Hanoun. Asked how, as the director of the club, he regarded the match, he answered:

> I didn't see the match, but it ended in a 2–2 draw. We always try to win because we don't like losing. When we meet Beit Hanoun next time I hope we'll win.

His answer did not seem on the face of it very relevant to the events that had taken place during the match with Beit Hanoun. Instead it gave a clear signal: "this is a match that I do not wish to remember, still less to comment on". I therefore asked a follow-up question:

> MICHAEL: I know that the match had consequences for some of the players. You deprived the captain of his captain's armband and the goalie too was punished. Why these sanctions?

> HANIYYA: Because the captain behaved in an inappropriate way by hitting one of the players in public, and *Jam'iyya's* management decided that he should be punished for behaving in an un-Islamic way.

Relations between the captain and the players ought to be good. As far as the goalie was concerned, he deliberately attacked a member of the opposing team, which resulted in our losing a point.

The response to *Jam'iyya*'s game against Beit Hanoun serves as a good illustration of the fact that moral standards are important in practice to the leaders of the club: there are sanctions for bad behaviour, and the players get punished for un-Islamic conduct. Haniyya's statement moreover indicates that it is extremely important to the club management that *Jam'iyya* should win. They obviously want a successful shop window rather than the opposite. Reactions to the punishment among the players were mixed. Ayman, for example, felt that the leaders of the club had taken the right decision:

> From my point of view this was a good plan. We have Islamic morals, and we don't want anyone to say that *Jam'iyya* had a man sent off because of a fight on the pitch, or whatever. So I think this was a good decision.

This however contradicts Ayman's former statement that Islamists, after all, are human beings too. Ahmad, a new player, was by contrast extremely critical of the decision. According to his own statement he had attempted to defend the captain, whom the club management had deprived of his captain's armband and punished furthermore with six playing days' quarantine. Ahmad described what happened:

> I discussed and shouted and was ready to hit one of the administrators, but Samir [one of the other players] dragged me aside and stopped me ... The assistant trainer came to my house the following Monday and told me that the administration had decided that I should no longer play for the club ...[216]

Ahmad's resistance to the decision and his obviously aggressive manner thus led to his being expelled: a consequence that should be understood in the light of the club's moral values. With a player like Ahmad, it would be impossible for *Jam'iyya* to act as an example to other clubs. New players, who are not "100 per cent moral", are on probation. If they adapt after a certain time, fine; if not, they are likely to be expelled. This is of great importance, since otherwise the club would no longer be able to serve as a shop window for the "Islamic alternative", and its symbolic capital would be squandered.

But as the examples show, there is a big difference between articulated theory and social practice.

Why an Islamist football club?

A further interesting question is whether the players' consciousness had been raised as a result of their participation in the club, and whether they had absorbed the management's reasons for becoming involved in sport.

> This [involvement] is quite natural. The Islamist movement should be represented within every aspect of life in our society.

Such was Ali's response to the question: "How do you explain the fact that *Jam'iyya Islâmiyya* has also established a football club?" Ali was not the only exponent of the idea that Islam is an all-embracing system. Nabil gave more or less the same answer to my question:

> *Jam'iyya* is active in all fields. Within health, education, culture and sport. You can get all you wish from *Jam'iyya*.

The players have a clear understanding that Islam should be active in all conceivable social contexts. The aim is to convince more Muslims that Islam, through *da'wa*, offers an alternative to the existing order. It is important to emphasise that *da'wa* in this context is directed towards Muslims. The terms *da'wa* and *tarbiya* (the education or formation of Muslims) are today used synonymously, since *da'wa* also involves preaching, lectures and so on.[217] Ibrahim told me:

> The Koran tells us [translator: 'No, not the Koran'], a *hadith* tells us [translator: 'No, it was Umar ibn al-Khattab'], OK, Umar ibn al-Khattab said: We should teach our children to shoot, swim, ride a horse ... and likewise, if the club attracts lots of young people, they'll come to follow the path of Islam just by playing for the club.[218]

There are two interesting points about Ibrahim's answer. First, Ibrahim was clearly aware of the football club's function as a political space for mobilisation. Second, he knew that there was an Islamic model for explaining the club's involvement in sport. He simply couldn't remember the details. This again indicates that no actual indoctrination took place at the club. Rather, I would suggest that the club offered a form of *schooling*.[219] At any rate, there was certainly no question of learning by rote, for although Ibrahim was familiar with the idea in question; he could not cite the right reference. In the first instance he though it must be from the Koran, and then from the Prophet – the key references within Islam. Finally, it is noteworthy that the interpreter knew the answer. This suggests that the lesson in question was one that everyone learned at some point or other. Whether or not the players had all the right arguments at their fingertips, they were quite conscious of the management's strategy.

The players and the Palestinian Authority during the reign of Fatah

Bourdieu argues that groups acting in a given social space always form themselves in opposition to other groups that they regard as less legitimate. In the final section of this chapter I aim to examine how Islamism is articulated in a political context, focusing on the players' view of a "less legitimate" grouping, namely the Palestinian Authority.

In the previous section I cited a number of statements from players in *Jam'iyya* indicating their strained relationship with the Palestinian Authority. This applied, for example, to Ismail, who straightforwardly placed the Authority on a par with the West and the Zionist enemy. In general the players had little enthusiasm for the Authority.

In answer to the question "What do you think of the Authority and its actions in the last three years?" the experienced player Ibrahim replied:

When the Authority first came on the scene, we greeted them with singing and jubilation. Once they got established, they changed. The people who opposed them are now in jail. The Authority seeks any excuse to stop Muslims and put them in jail. The Authority treats anyone still fighting against Israel as their enemies. The Authority and Israel work together. They have an agreement to combat the Muslim forces.

Ismail was likewise very harsh in his criticisms:

The Authority has been responsible for a number of inhuman actions towards us. I have been arrested several times by the preventive security forces in Deir al-Balah, and they interrogated me in a completely inhuman way. I also found out that these people are totally uncultured.

They haven't even finished school. They control us and they're completely ignorant. Moreover, these people played absolutely no role in the Intifada. We really hope to reform and change the situation for the better. We want the Authority to give Muslims the chance to work for the interests of society.

Ayman, who was one of the few players to have previously supported Fatah and Arafat, described his relationship to the PLO[220] today:

They created peace. They told us they would obtain more land. OK, do that. We're waiting for you – but until now they've done nothing. They haven't even got Khalil [Hebron] back. There are still big settlements in Gaza. The Jews control the area around Khan Younis. Where is the peace? If we're in our country and our area, why are the Jews here controlling the roads? I don't know about this peace ... It's very strange. They've put us in a big prison. It's a joke.

Ayman's metaphor of the Gaza Strip as a prison is very telling. A good deal of the frustration evinced by many of the club's players was bound up with the sense of being shut in. In his book on globalisation, the sociologist Zygmunt Bauman describes the human consequences of this phenomenon for those excluded from its advantages. Bauman's metaphorical account in this respect could have been written about the concrete state of affairs in Gaza:

If your home is locked from the outside, if there are only distant prospects, or no prospects at all, of escape, home becomes a prison. Forced immobility, the condition of being tied to a place and having no possibility of moving elsewhere, appears to be a quite abominable, cruel and ghastly fate; it is the prohibition of free movement, rather than the blocking of a virtual wish to move, that makes this condition especially offensive. The blocking of free movement is a very powerful symbol of powerlessness, exclusion – and pain.[221]

Ayman's criticism of the Authority continued:

If you want to say something or for example write an article for one of the big newspapers in Jerusalem, then [the Authority] will arrest and imprison you. We are back to the old days; they quite simply don't want to budge. They don't want anyone asking them: What are you doing here? What are you doing for your people, for your Palestinians? They don't want us to ask them: Where do you get your money? And these big houses? Have you forgotten the refugee camps? And the people who fought, many of whom died or were wounded or imprisoned? Have you also forgotten them? They don't want anyone at all to pose these questions, so how can we ever get Jerusalem, Acre or Jaffa back?

It is obvious from Ibrahim's, Ismail's and Ayman's utterances that the players were well aware of the abuses of power, corruption and inefficiency that characterised the Authority. They felt these things in their bodies, and to a certain extent they affected their daily lives. The quotations also show that the people interviewed saw the Islamists as a group working and fighting for the interests of the nation and of Palestinian society, while the Authority merely clung to power and worked in its own interests. It was clear that there was a close connection between the players' support for Islamism and their dissatisfaction with the autocratic regime that the Authority represented. Writing about this relationship in a broader Middle Eastern context, Augustus Richard Norton says it is a rule of thumb that any autocratic regime creates opposition, and that Islamism has proved able to tap into this well of dissatisfaction:

> The reciprocal to the failure of the authoritarian state is Islamism. Thus, the pattern of governance in the region has contributed substantially to the comparative advantages of the Islamists ...[222]

The relative success of Islamism in the Palestinian and the broader Arab-Islamist context is thus closely bound up with the inability of autocratic regimes in the Middle East to develop societies governed by transparency, democracy, freedom of expression, observance of human rights, and so on. In other words, the Islamist movements have been partially fuelled by the Authority's numerous mistakes.

It is important in this context to emphasise that, as far as Hamas is concerned, it has only been partially successful in relation to the Authority. Despite its numerous mistakes in the late 1990s, moreover, the pressure put on the Islamists by the Authority has also affected sympathisers to the Islamist movement.

Ayman put it as follows:

> They [Hamas] have nothing to offer. The Authority suppresses them in order to force people to abandon their ideas. If you want to work, if you

want a job, you are forced to think about this peace that we have signed, and you're forced to forget everything about Hamas and religion. Then you can become one of us, and you can get a job and in that way take care of your family. Because of this it's difficult for people – particularly for young men like me who've just started out in life. What can I do if I don't have a job? And you'll see many engineers, doctors, pharmacists who are unemployed just because they're Hamas people. So one has to be flexible in order to be able to cope with the situation …[223]

This quotation makes clear that there is a price to pay for being an Islamist. It also shows that it is impossible to survive merely on the social and cultural capital built up by virtue of one's association with the Islamist movement. There has to be bread on the table too, and in this context it is the Authority that is in a position to provide. Here, too, a form of negotiation takes place between the Authority and Hamas' sympathisers. The latter can get a job and thereby, to a certain extent, gain economic capital, so long as they abandon their Islamist thinking. On a brief follow-up trip to the Gaza Strip in summer 1999 I found that Ayman had given up his involvement in Islamism. He had got a job as a pharmacologist in the Ministry of Health and had also switched football clubs, now playing for one of the secular clubs in the town.

Summary

In the case of the Islamist sports club the Islamist leaders emphasise that the purpose of the club is not primarily sport, but the creation of *sound Muslims*. Good morals and behaviour are essential. The club sets a good example. Every Friday on the football pitch, both leaders and players should show the Islamist flag and demonstrate by their behaviour that they offer an alternative.

Interviews with a number of players in an Islamic football club closely related to Hamas reveal that the young Islamists in the Gaza Strip are not dangerous fanatical terrorists, contrary to the view put forward by a number of researchers, western media and certain western politicians, especially in Israel and the United States. Furthermore, they are not young men with long beards, who are longing for bygone days. On the contrary, they are young men who are able and willing to adapt to the reality of the modern world.

My work in understanding and observing "consumers" of Islamism, i.e.

the players in the *Jam'iyya* team, has led me to de-dramatise earlier research. The literature suggests that the Islamist social institutions are a hotbed of political indoctrination. Although I de-dramatise this aspect, this is not to suggest that the club exerts no influence on those involved – for it does. But I prefer to refer to this influence as "schooling". Schooling is apolitical, in the sense that it does not involve politically incendiary speeches about the role of Islam in political life, about the shortcomings of the Authority, Israel's atrocities and so on. Rather, it is through a discourse on morality and good behaviour that the club's leaders seek to school the players and create *sound Muslims*.

The chapter also shows that to a certain extent the process of islamisation had taken place *before* the young men joined the club. Several of them had been schooled in Israeli prisons. Islamist schooling should not therefore be understood as a political propaganda machine directed from above, but rather as the moral shaping of the population from below. This is entirely in accordance with the Islamists' fundamental idea that one should first raise the consciousness of individuals in order subsequently to be in a position to assume power.

The players had chosen to play for the club for a number of different reasons: in some cases on religious grounds, in others because they had been encouraged by the club management, in yet others because the club was in their neighbourhood. Some players were motivated in their choice by the prospect of being able to fulfil their personal ambitions. It is interesting to note that the club lost 10 of its players when it was demoted to the second division in 1996. It is likewise interesting that none of the players linked the choice of *Jam'iyya* to any material advantages or benefits they might gain from playing for it. According to the players, such benefits could only be gained by playing for one of the Fatah-controlled clubs. Indeed, in some cases there was a price to pay for being associated with *Jam'iyya*. One may therefore conclude that the participants must have had good reasons for choosing *Jam'iyya*, and it is interesting to note that their choice was not always linked to religious motives.

It is important to distinguish between ideals and practice when it comes to being a *sound Muslim*. According to the players, *Jam'iyya* stood out from other secular clubs by virtue of its discourse on morality and good behaviour – a discourse that enabled players to distance themselves from their immediate surroundings. From the interviews conducted it is evident that high moral standards are very attractive to the young "consumers". They seek to separate themselves from their mirror image: the West and the westernised segments of the Palestinian population. By dissociating themselves from decadent westernised Palestinians, the young Islamists are at the same time reaffirming their own cultural heritage: Islam. This dissociation could be seen, for example, in the way that the players set themselves apart from, or *excluded*, other Muslims in the Gaza Strip. The latter quite simply did not belong to the category of Muslims. In my fieldwork I documented that the young men in the club had to a great extent adopted this discourse in their articulation of Islamism. But the interviews also show that the young people did not blindly accept the club administration's notions of the *sound Muslim*. The content of this term was still up for discussion, as was expressed most clearly in connection with the way the players dressed. This would not have been evident had I not combined my interviews with participant observation. The young men were also quite aware of the reasons behind the establishment of an Islamist football club. Islam is seen as an all-embracing system, and the club is meant to serve as a shop window for Islamism in the local context: it is supposed in other words to set a good example.

To a great extent the expression of Islamism in the football club is associated with the *body*. The club, it goes without saying, is a bodily space, but into the bargain a place in which the ideology of Islamism is expressed through bodily action. Discussion within this space revolves around clothing, manner of speech, whether one smokes or drinks, and so on. It is by virtue of these bodily signs that the players distinguish themselves from others through their personal behaviour. In social practice the dress code, for example, is not consistently observed. The young men themselves justified this by saying that a degree of flexibility was needed, and that they didn't wish to be laughed at by outsiders for sticking to the "ugly" Islamist dress code. It was through my fieldwork – and by virtue of the methods I employed – that I discovered that there was a big difference between the articulation of Islamism and actual social practice.

It is likewise telling that the young Islamists to a great extent limited their statements to the local context. This was due to the fact that they represented a shop window for Islamism, and that they played football matches every Friday against secular clubs that represented the hegemonic political, secular discourse on the pitch. For the young people in the club, "the other" was therefore a quite concrete "other" – namely their secular opponents on the field. They articulated their difference from these others via a discourse on morality and good behaviour. In doing so, the young men built up social capital, valued in a context in which economic capital was virtually unobtainable and to a great extent associated, moreover, with what they regarded as the illegitimate and corrupt Authority.

The Islamists were dependent on the misuse of power and corruption evident in the Authority's ranks, in so far as this strengthened the need for an alternative, and thereby created a space in which the Islamists could manoeuvre. At the same time, the young people were critical of Hamas, even though they sympathised with its aims, because the movement had nothing concrete to offer – over and above social and cultural capital. This however was due first and foremost to the Authority's repressive policies towards the Islamist movement during the late 1990s.

5

THE ISLAMIC UNIVERSITY OF GAZA,
THE STUDENTS AND ISLAMISM

In this chapter I will first briefly introduce the history and the ideological orientation of the university and then seek to describe the three central fora in which Islamist schooling takes place within the Islamic University (IUG): namely, the Student Council's activities, the Islamic studies courses, and courses in the English Department. My aim is not only to examine the way in which Islamist schooling is conducted at IUG, but also to look at how the students themselves absorb the Islamists' attempts to create *sound Muslims* through this schooling. The chapter further investigates the way in which students understand and identify themselves via "the other", whether this being "the West", the Jews or the Palestinian Authority.

The Islamic University in Gaza – a short introduction

There are two universities[224] in the Gaza Strip: the Islamic University (IUG), established in 1978, and al-Azhar, founded in 1992. These are the two largest out of a total of eight universities in the Palestinian territories, with respectively 11,500 and 13,000 students (in 2001).[225] Al-Azhar University was established on the initiative of the Fatah movement in the early 1990s, clearly as a counterweight to IUG. IUG on the other hand is an Islamist educational institution, even though the Islamists themselves seek to play down the movement's involvement in the university. The university authorities maintain that it was Fatah, headed by Yasir Arafat, that was responsible for its establishment.

In the early 1970s a number of Palestinian intellectuals had repeatedly proposed that a university be established in the Gaza Strip, but initially nothing concrete came of the idea.[226] It was not until 1978 that the project came to fruition with the establishment of IUG. The university was developed on the basis of the al-Azhar Institute, which until that point had been one of the few higher educational institutions in Gaza. As its name indicates, the al-Azhar Institute was affiliated with the prestigious, religious al-Azhar University in Cairo. Students could obtain a diploma-level education from the institute, corresponding to two years' study beyond high school.[227] The Head of the Institute was a prominent sheikh, Muhammad Awad, who was not associated with the Islamist movement, representing instead the traditional *'ulamâ'*. One of the main reasons why the idea of founding a university was finally put into practice in 1978 was that after 1977 Egypt had begun to limit the number of Palestinian students from the area. Until then the majority of Gaza's educated young people had got their degrees in Egypt. The reason given for the Egyptians' decision at that point to limit the number of Palestinians from Gaza was that a Palestinian group had been responsible for the murder of a prominent Egyptian intellectual. More significant, however, was Anwar Sadat's peace initiative, his visit to the Knesset in November 1977 and the negotiation and signing of the Camp David agreement that followed. The great majority of Palestinians opposed these moves. Hence the Egyptians' decision to close the doors on Palestinian students, which made clear that a Palestinian university in the Gaza Strip was needed. During its first two years (1978–80) the new university was housed in the buildings of the al-Azhar Institute, but in 1980 it moved to a site nearby. Initially there were only three faculties: Arabic language, *Usûl al-dîn* and *sharî'a*: in other words, the classic Islamic disciplines. However, it was seen as important that the university be able to produce graduates capable of developing Palestinian society in directions other than the purely spiritual. Since then it has established a number of more secular disciplines and faculties such as nursing, engineering, journalism, English, business, accountancy and so on.

In 1980–6 the religious orientation of the university led to conflicts between Islamist and secular students. The power struggle that took place on the campus during this period was more than just a struggle for control over the university as such. It was a reflection of the more general political power struggle occurring in the Gaza Strip at that time. In the late 1970s the best-organised political group in Palestine were the communists, who wielded considerable influence in a number of NGOs and other organisations.[228] The Islamists, however, had also begun to organise themselves through establishing institutions such as *al-Mujamma' al-Islâmî* and *al-Jam'iyya al-Islâmiyya*. Fatah, too, as the largest organisation within the framework of the PLO, had begun in the late 1970s to establish a more organised presence in the occupied territories, including the Gaza Strip. Under Abu Jihad's (Khalil al-Wazir's) leadership Fatah established a number of organisations during this period, including women's associations, student organisations, trade unions etc. Thus Fatah, too, aimed to acquire greater control and legitimacy within the occupied territories. Until then the main strength of the organisation had been in the Palestinian diaspora. In connection with the establishment of the Islamic University in Gaza, Fatah entered into an alliance with the Islamists, in an attempt to prevent the communists and the left-wing factions of the PFLP from gaining control over the university.[229] There is no doubt that Fatah aimed in the longer term to take control of the university themselves, which however they never succeeded in doing.

A former leader of the PFLP, who had been employed at IUG for more than a decade (since 1980), told me:

> When I look back at that time, it was an open question whether Arafat was stupid, or rather had made a mistake, or whether he was very clever and hoped that he could turn the situation round.[230]

Around 1980, when the university had established itself as an Islamic institution with some marginal influence from the Palestinian Left, Fatah set about trying to transform it into a more secular educational institution. Riad al-Agha, who represented Fatah, succeeded Sheikh Muhammad Awad as the Head of the University. Over the next few years, however, a number of Islamists were appointed to positions at the university – not only as lecturers but as administrators, caretakers, gardeners and so on. According to the left-wing lecturer cited above, this resulted from the co-operation between Riad al-Agha and Sheikh Ahmad Yasin, who at that point was Head of *al-Mujamma' al-Islâmî*. The lecturer told me:

> I don't know what Arafat was thinking when he appointed Riad al-Agha as president ... al-Agha could be described as a charlatan. A two-faced man, but at the same time attractive. When he met with people from Fatah he would say that he was part of Fatah and that he wanted to do everything for them. The next moment, when he needed new staff, he would go to Ahmad Yasin and then he'd appoint the new people.

In early 1983 an open battle broke out between the Islamists and the nationalists at the university. The background to the conflict lay in a series of power struggles around the leadership of the institution. Riad al-Agha was fired as the Head of the University and a sympathiser of the Islamic movement,

Muhammad al-Saqr, was to be appointed in his stead. Fatah, based in Tunis, refused to accept this change, since their leaders supported Riad al-Agha. After two months of unrest and strikes, the conflict erupted into open battle.[231] But the left-wing lecturer cited above, who himself was involved in the row, took a different view:

> Together with al-Agha, Abdallah Hamdani, who was close to al-Agha and who today is governor of Rafah, was responsible for the clashes and the violence – not the Islamists.

The Islamists came off best in the struggle, and after 1983 won control over the university. However, fresh clashes between Islamists and nationalists continued to occur, for example in 1985 and 1986, but in these cases too the Islamists emerged the winners. One reason for this was that the nationalists had failed to create a united front. In 1985 it was Fatah alone that fought the Islamists, while in 1986 it was the turn of the PFLP. Be that as it may, since 1986 the Islamists have had full control over IUG. One indication that the nationalists had given up attempting to wrest control over the university was that in 1992 the PLO, or more specifically Fatah, established a new university alongside IUG, under the name al-Azhar.[232] This move can be interpreted as an explicit attempt on Fatah's part to establish an institution over which they would have sole control. The date of its founding, in 1992, was related to the ongoing peace negotiations taking place at that time and the consequent prospect – or hope – that the Palestinians would soon have secure control over the Gaza Strip (among other places).

As in many of the other Arab states, the universities in Palestine are among the few places where young people are able to engage in politics, and the establishment of Al-Azhar should be seen in the light of the prevailing hope that a Palestinian state or an autonomous political entity would shortly come into being. Universities are by definition important recruiting grounds for the state apparatus. Since IUG is Islamic-oriented, it was an obvious move for the secular-oriented PLO to establish a competing university in 1992 as a base for recruiting candidates for positions in the forthcoming state administration. It was important for the PLO to prepare for the future. Since its founding in 1992 al-Azhar has developed into by far the largest Palestinian university in the West Bank or the Gaza Strip, with over 15,000 students. In popular parlance the Gaza Strip thus has two universities today: a Hamas university (IUG) and a Fatah university (Al-Azhar).

The ideological discourse of the IUG

The IUG authorities are by no means happy with this categorisation, and do not wish the university to be perceived as a Hamas institution. The Head of the PR department, Ahmad Saa'ti, a Hamas leader who during the late 1990s was a prominent member of Hamas' legal political party, *Hizb al-Khalâs al-Watani al-Islâmî*, says:

IUG is an independent organisation that is not influenced by the attitudes of any one political party. It is open to all human thought and culture and works in accordance with scientific and technical developments. It shows mutual respect towards, and co-operates with, other institutions … it does not adopt the political view of any Palestinian party, whether that party is religious or not.[233]

Clearly, then, the university was not keen on being presented as an Islamic-oriented institution. When I asked why the university practises a policy of total sex segregation, I was told that this was not at the behest of the university authorities, but was demanded by the local community, which was characterised as "conservative". Ahmad Sa'ati explains:

Let me make it clear to you. This is not the only university in the world where the sexes are segregated. In the United States, in Great Britain, in Egypt and Jordan they have [such institutions] … if we had not adopted this policy we would have lost a great number of our women students. I regard this as a form of democracy. Those families that wish to send their girls to a co-ed university can send them to al-Azhar, and the conservatives that don't want their girls to receive this form of education, they send them to IUG.

Thus this policy is presented not as being religiously motivated, but as resulting from an expressed wish on the part of a large sector of the population. When I pressed Ahmad Sa'ati concretely to answer my questions concerning the university's affiliation with the Muslim Brotherhood or Hamas, he vigorously denied that any such relation existed: "No, I'm being completely honest with you. No, no, no. This is not a religious university. It doesn't belong to *Ikhwân Muslimûn*." However, my persistent questioning did lead Sa'ati to state more precisely what the goal of the university was:

We aim for one thing. We aim to produce morally sound graduates. That is what distinguishes us from other institutions. We aim to produce moral graduates. By that I mean graduates who are loyal to their people, to their land, who are upright, who don't cheat, who don't lie. That is what we want. This is what is moral and what can be classified as such internationally. This is the morality of the Islamist schools, such as *Ikhwan* and others. So if we practise that morality and attempt to instil that morality you can classify us as you wish, but we can't say that this is *al-Ikhwan's* university. We aim to produce moral graduates.[234]

It is worth noting, then, that the university authorities do not wish the a-djective "Islamic" to be taken too seriously. According to their pronounce-ments, IUG is a modern and open university. Despite the fact that a central characteristic of the university is the *islamicum*,[235] Sa'ati sought to "nor-malise" and play down this aspect by stressing that the university taught other obligatory subjects, including languages (English), first aid, Palestinian history and so on. However, Sa'ati finally made clear that the university aims for one thing, namely the creation of moral individuals; or, to put it another way, *sound Muslims*. The aim of the education is to create individ-uals who are loyal to their people and their country, who are upright, honest and do not cheat.

The Professor of English was more direct and clear when I asked him about the university's aims and ideology:

IUG's ideology is Islamic. The basic idea is to educate the Palestinian people. The strategy is to protect the basic things in each individual. These basic things are deeply anchored in Islam. We want people to return to the basics (i.e. Islam).[236]

The university's prospectus (*dalîl*) also makes clear that the university should be regarded as Islamic. The project is an attempt to create knowledge on an Islamic foundation with a view to regenerating Islam, and is thus bound up with the Islamists' attempt to re-islamise society. In a section headed "The university and its Goals", the prospectus states:[237]

IUG in Gaza is Palestinian in its construction, identity and *intima'* … its philosophy is based on the following ideas:

– … It is a university that understands Islam as an all-embracing mes-sage (*risala*), philosophy and guide to life (*minhâj al-hayat*) …

- The university differs from other Palestinian universities in having a policy of sex segregation, so the teaching of students takes place in separate buildings (*mabna haram*) to avoid the problem of mixing the sexes. For the same reason we also make sure that women students wear a uniform (*shar'*) within the university campus. This policy is welcomed and appreciated by the population and by those in the Gaza Strip who respect Islamic customs. It has a positive influence on the education of students and on their efforts, as well as nourishing their love and knowledge and [creating] a good atmosphere.
- The purpose of the Islamic University is to serve Arab and Islamic society generally and Palestinian society in particular in accordance with Islamic philosophy, which seeks to create a new form of cultural development that can stand up to the cultural challenge confronting our nation. Furthermore it aims to foster good minds, good thinking (*al-aql al-salim*), a vigilant conscience, awareness, and good conduct, to cover life in all its aspects, to provide a holistic view of life, to establish co-operation with the surrounding community, and to encourage society to return to the original sources of this nation [i.e. Islam].
- In order to realize these goals the Islamic university seeks to extend knowledge and offer opportunities in all fields, both in the technical subjects and in the humanities. We also seek to do our best to understand the needs of society. IUG supports scientific research both materially and spiritually in order to create an independent, academic and cultural atmosphere and to use this to the public benefit in the development of society. At the same time the university's curriculum is planned to ensure that knowledge, development, culture and values are in accordance with Islam.
- IUG has a comprehensive and scientific strategy built on an awareness of the phase of struggle (*marhala Nidaliyya*) that the Palestinian people and the Islamic nation are currently going through. This strategy consists in developing a structured way of thinking (*al-aql al-munazzam*) and self-confidence in order to counter the weak phase we are living through and to start afresh in renewing our history.

The prospectus makes clear that the Islamic education project at IUG is concerned not merely with the individual, but with society as a whole. The task of creating *sound Muslims* is synonymous with instilling in the individual student an organised way of thinking, a vigilant conscience, awareness, good conduct and a holistic (that is to say, Islamic) view of life. It is also made clear, especially in the last paragraph of the section cited above, what purpose this kind of consciousness-raising serves. The aim is to use this kind of education to rewrite history, to make students aware of the creative potential of Islam and thereby to lead the Palestinian people out of the cultural crisis that they, and the rest of the Muslim world, currently find themselves in. The need for this project, as implied by the prospectus, is closely bound up with the perception of history and of Islam described in Chapter 3. Islam has been put on the defensive both economically, culturally, and technologically, and the curriculum offered by the university offers a way out of this crisis: an education that is aimed at raising students' awareness and activating them to be conscious of their situation, as a precondition for changing the status quo. This change, in the view of Islamists, can happen only through a revitalisation of Islam.

Against this background it is impossible to separate the specific educational project of IUG from the more general political life of Gaza. IUG is one of the forums in which *sound Muslims* are to be created, and to a great degree the university is thus an instrument of politicisation, even though the university authorities may not always wish to emphasise this aspect of its work.

Welcome to the campus of the Islamic University in Gaza

The date is 7 March, the year 1998, the place the Islamic University in Gaza (IUG). The occasion is the introductory ceremony for the university's new students. The organisers are the university's Student Council, led by *Kutla Islâmiyya*.

Around 2,000 students gathered for this occasion. First, we listened to a reading from the Koran, lasting 5–10 minutes; thereafter the university choir sang an Islamic hymn (*nashîd islâmi*), the text of which deplores the rift between rich and poor in Palestinian society. After this the microphone was passed to the Chairman of the Student Council, who began with a brief exhortation to the new students to seek wisdom and study hard. He then turned to speak about the conflict with Israel:

> Israel is gathering weapons. [The Israelis] want to destroy us. All the leaders of the Arabic world have stayed silent. We need them to get moving. To wake up. It is essential that we be strong, only then will we be able to get what we want.

Following this speech by the Chairman of the Student Council and another Islamic hymn – this one with an anti-American theme – the microphone was passed to the Hamas leader Ismael Haniyya in his capacity as a member of the IUG administration:

> Scholarship means something different at this university. From the very first day it is practised in the name of Allah. Our university is different, our students are different, and our *minhâj* is different. During the Intifada [1987–93] the students at IUG were both students and *mujâhidûn*, and one of the members of the Student Council was killed by the Jews. We remember Muhammad Dief from *Kata'ib Izz ad-Din al-Qassam* who was a student here ... this university understands its duties towards its students. It is necessary to bring them up on the Koran and *Sunna*. This is our *minhâj*. The majority of all students at the universities of Palestine support *Kutla Islâmiyya*. There is nothing strange about that. The students are on the true path. They know how to tell truth (*al-haqq*) from falsehood (*al-bâtil*).

Ismael Haniyya then turned his attention to the crisis of 1998 between Iraq and the United States, and then to the relationship between Hamas and the Palestinian Authority:

> The Arab governments are sleeping. We believe that they are making a mistake, and that they are failing to govern in accordance with the Koran and with *Sunna*. The United States wants to destroy Iraq, and this carries a message to all Arab leaders: those who oppose the United States' interests will be destroyed. Thus the lesson of the Iraq crisis is that the United States wishes to destroy us all ...
>
> Look at the resistance movement in Lebanon. The resistance movement kills the Israelis, the collaborators. The resistance forces Israel to leave the area and the Lebanese government allow [the movement] to operate ... here the authorities say no to the people in the resistance. We Palestinians ought to be united. That gives us strength. We demand that the authorities allow *Izz ad-Din al-Qassam* to do what they want. Only under pressure will Israel yield.

Haniyya finished his speech with the words: "Hamas is the true way. And we need [Hamas] in our daily lives."

After the speech the best of the recent graduates were presented with a small gift in the presence of members of the university administration (including Ismael Haniyya), and the welcoming ceremony was over.

Islamist schooling in three fora

Schooling at the IUG takes place in three different fora. It is clear that the representatives of the Student Council are responsible for some of the instruction that occurs, and, as mentioned above, it was also the Student Council that had arranged the introductory ceremony. Another obvious place in which schooling occurs are the university's obligatory courses in *islamicum*, in which the study of Islam plays a central role. *Islamicum* is an umbrella term for a number of obligatory courses that students at the Islamic University (with the exception of Christians) are obliged to follow. These include, for example: *Nizâm al-islâmi* (the Islamic system); *Shûrâ* (which deals with *shûrâ* and democracy); *Dirasât al-Sira* (studies of biographies of the prophet Muhammad): *Hadîth Sharîf* (studies of Muhammad's tradition-al legacy); *Dirasât Qurâniyya* (Koranic studies, including exegesis); and the course *Hâdir al-'Alam al-Islâmi* (concerning the current situation in the Islamic world). Finally the courses in English, two of which I followed for the purposes of fieldwork, also offer a forum for Islamist schooling.

Schooling and the Student Council at the IUG

Ever since IUG was established in 1978 *Kutla Islâmiyya* has controlled the Student Council, and the majority of the students have therefore supported the Islamists.[238] Table 1 shows how marked this support was over a period of almost 15 years. However, it is not only the students at IUG who support the Islamists, the lecturers, administrators and service personnel at the university also sympathise with the movement.[239]

The Student Council plays a prominent role at IUG, enthusiastically running a range of activities aimed both at the university's students and at the wider Palestinian community in the Gaza Strip. The Council is divided into a number of committees, each of which has responsibility for a particular field such as sport, culture, PR, voluntary work, art, social relations and economics. Around 10 students are permanently attached to each of these committees.

The cultural committee is one of the most visible within the IUG. It is concerned with organising cultural arrangements such as the annual "Jerusalem day" (*Mahrajân al-Quds al-Fannî*), which focuses on the continuing judaisation and occupation of Arab East Jerusalem. There are speeches, songs and plays, and the performance is open to the public. In 1998 around 3,000 people attended "Jerusalem day". The cultural committee also frequently runs competitions for IUG students. These include games of the

Table 1: Results of the Student Council elections at IUG, selected years (men)[240]

	Hamas	Fatah	Others[241]
1983	51%	N/A	N/A
1987–88	60%	25%	15%
1996–97	75.5%	17.3%	7.2%
1999–2000	74%	19%	7%
2005*	24 seats (all)	0 seats	0 seats

Source: Mishal & Sela, 2000, p. 24; Sullivan, 1998, p. 62; *Kutla Islâmiyya* leaflet, 30 April 1999; Hroub, 2000, p. 219,
http://www.thejerusalemfund.org/
* No data available in percentage, however the tendency is the same as previous years: The *Kutla Islâmiyya* won by a clear majority.

"charades" type in which students have to guess Islamic sayings. There are also competitions for the best essay on developments in Jerusalem or on the Israeli occupation. Finally, the committee holds public meetings where representatives of the Palestinian Authority, Hamas and the Left discuss political developments. The Committee is also responsible for various publications. These include books on the settlements in Gaza (*Mustawtanât fî qitâ' Ghazza*), a tribute to *Kata'ib Izz ad-Din al-Qassam* entitled *Shuhadâ al-Qassâm 'Ushshâq al-Khulûd*, and books on subjects such as the geography of Palestine.

The Student Council is moreover visible in the public spaces of the university through a series of centrally placed notice boards. Here members of the Council pin up selected articles, some taken from the journal *Filastîn al-Muslima* (Muslim Palestine), published in London, some from *al-Sirât* (The Way), which, as the then Student Council Chairman Ayman Taha put it, "develops the spiritual side of the students". *Filastîn al-Muslima* is Hamas' organ and deals primarily with Palestinian politics, but also includes articles on the broader Islamic world. All the articles are written from an Islamic point of view. The journal is in fact prohibited, and IUG is thus one of the few places that its contents can be read. In addition, articles from the PLO journal *Filastîn al-Thawra* (the Palestinian Revolution) are sometimes pinned up on the notice boards.

The spiritual side of the students, which the Student Council also aims to cultivate, is fostered among other ways through articles pinned up on the boards concerning Islam and its alleged opposite, Western materialism: in April 1998, for example, the boards were adorned with a series of articles focusing on the "opposition". The pictures spoke for themselves; there was a drawing of a heart that was filled on one side with peaceful light and the Koran, and on the other stuffed with large cars and other Western consumer goods: a symbolic image of the struggle between civilisations which – so Islamists maintain – is currently being played out between Western capitalism and the Islamic world.

The students moreover perceive globalisation as a part of this "struggle". For the young people at IUG globalisation primarily represents an aggressive attempt on the part of the West to create a global Western culture, if not economy. They likewise focus on the influential works of Samuel Huntington and Francis Fukuyama[242] and see these authors, and their views, as representative of the West. For many of these young Palestinians, Islam constitutes the natural riposte to globalisation.[243]

The final two examples that I will use to illustrate the Student Council's schooling activities are drawn from the *bayâns* (leaflets) distributed by the Council in the spring semester 1998. The first was circulated in connection with the start of the semester and was aimed at the university's new students. The second was distributed immediately before the summer exams and offered good advice on how to achieve the best results.

Kutla Islâmiyya introduces the first *bayân* by bidding the new students welcome to IUG, which is described as a university established to promote the truth (*al-haqq*). The *bayân* goes on to describe the political situation in the area, arguing that through their inhuman actions the occupying power has proved that the enemy does not want peace. What Israel wants, rather, is to normalise its relations with its Arab neighbours and to fleece the Palestinians. In the midst of this hopeless situation, in which the enemy has all conceivable military hardware at its disposal, and in "a world that does not know the truth (*al-haqq*)", the Student Council nevertheless instils some hope. Allah has promised the Islamists victory through *Qanûn al-Istikhlâf*, a concept drawn from the Koran (*Sura al-Nur* 24:55), which states:

> Allah has promised, to those among you who believe and work right-eous deeds, that He will, of a surety, grant them in the land, inheritance (of power), as He granted it to those before them ...

In their exegesis of this verse Palestinian Islamists engage in *ijtihâd* (new interpretation): first, the verse is turned into a law (*qanûn*), and the term "earth" (*al-ard*) is interpreted to mean Palestine. According to this interpretation it is the Islamists who "do good". Thus, in this new interpretation of the verse, it is they who have the prospect of victory (*al-nasr*). In an informal discussion my interpreter, Hassan, explained *Qanûn Istikhlâf* as follows:

It is a law based on the Koran, and its meaning is that Muslims should fight against the Jews and that they will win and live in the land (of Palestine) until the Day of Judgement.

The conclusion of the leaflet addressed to new students was therefore that the future was not against them, but on the contrary lay before them. Islam would again be strong. The students therefore had a mission to reform and change (*Islâh wal-Yaghyîr*) the forces that make scholarship self-serving in a negative sense (i.e. the secular forces). The council's *bayân* in this instance ends with an exhortation to continue with Allah's blessing to be active and clever and to pursue one's work until one's aim is fulfilled: "Allah is with you, and He will not reduce your work."

The other *bayân* circulated by the Council gives good advice on preparing for exams. The leaflet touches on a number of points such as: "The best way of memorising and studying"; "How to overcome boredom"; "How to overcome forgetfulness"; "Studies and the use of medicine"; "Exams and nutrition", and ends with the key point to remember in exam preparation: the *bayân* makes clear that studying – provided one studies for the sake of Allah and not for one's own personal advantage – should be treated like any other form of worship of God. The secret of success lies in relying on God. The Student Council's advice is particularly interesting in the section on "Exams and nutrition". The section begins with a *hadîth*: "We are a people who do not eat before we are hungry and do not fill our stomachs when we eat." This is followed by another *hadîth* with the same message: "A small amount of food is enough for the body to keep strong." The idea in present-ing these two *hadîth* is to demonstrate Islam's superiority, since in this respect Islam is in accordance with modern science. Indeed, further on in the text the leaflet mentions that modern science has proved that too much food transfers blood to the digestive system, which affects both body and soul. People often experience tiredness after they have eaten their fill, the text goes on to say, which naturally reduces their desire to study. Against this back-ground students are encouraged to follow the prophet's *Sunna*, since even before modern science Islam was aware of the consequences of excessive con-sumption of food. The text concludes by emphasising that before embarking on their daily studies students should utter a *Du'â* (prayer): "Oh my God, create a light in my heart and make things easy for me. Loosen my tongue and let me be a good speaker." After preparing for their exams, students are encouraged to make a further *Du'â*, worshipping Allah with a view to ensur-ing that what they had read would stay "in their heads". Yet another *Du'â* was to be uttered just prior to taking the exam, and a further one once the exam was over. The council's *bayân* ends with a *Du'â* that things will go well for all the students, and a wish that all should become strong followers of Islam.

Schooling and *islamicum*

As mentioned above, the *islamicum*, or Islamic studies, offered by the university are one of the tools used by the administration to inculcate in students the "correct" understanding of Islam. The central place that Islamic studies occupy in the curriculum cannot be overestimated. The disciplines taught in connection with these obligatory course are accorded high priority at IUG, on the grounds that the knowledge built up through studying the Koran, *hadîth*, *sira* and so on provide the foundation for all other – in principle secular – teaching. This in turn is connected with the idea that all subjects should be studied from an Islamic perspective.

One of the key Islamic courses is *Hâdir al-'Alam al-Islâmi* (The state of the Islamic world). The textbook for the course was written by a lecturer from IUG, Salah Hussein al-Raqab, and is entitled *Hâdir al-'Alam al-Islâmi wal-Ghazw al-Fikrî* (The state of the Islamic World and the Ideological Invasion). The book is designed for teaching, and contains a series of short chapters that go through various central concepts and themes, all of which have had an influence on developments in the Arab-Islamic world. Thus there are chapters on, for example, the concept of *Jâhiliyya*,[244] on the ideological invasion by the West (*al-Ghazw al-fikrî*), on the Christian mission (*tabshîr*) in the Middle East, on socialism, on the Westernisation of the Islamic world, on nationalism, on women, on harmful and misguided movements (such as Freemasonry or Babism), on the concept of democracy and on the future of Islam and the Islamic reawakening (*al-sahwa al-islâmiyya*).[245]

Before briefly looking at an example of the actual contents of the book, I would like to comment on its front cover, which brilliantly symbolises what the book is about. The top half of the cover is reserved for the Arab-Islamic world. It is here that the words *Hâdir al-'Alam al-Islâmi* are placed. To the left we see a picture of the al-Aqsa Mosque (the symbol of Palestine) and to the right the *Ka'ba* in Mecca. Between these two images there is an open Koran showing a verse that, freely translated, means: "The Jews and the Christians will never be satisfied until you follow their path." On the bottom half we find the words *al-Ghazw al-Fikrî* together with a number of symbols, such as the star of David with a snake running through it, the hammer and sickle, a bomb, a US dollar sign, the Christian cross and so on. The symbolism is unmistakable. There is a struggle going on between civilisations: the Christian and Jewish on the one hand and the Islamic on the other. Nor can we be in any doubt that Islamic civilisation represents *al-haqq*, whereas the other represents *al-bâtil.*

The front cover gives an excellent idea of the book's contents, which again accord with the account given by Abdel Fattah Dukkhan of the development of the Islamic world since the time of the crusades (cf. Chapter 3). Al-Raqab starts with the crusades and continues up to our day, arguing that Islam is the solution to all the problems that have arisen. In my example I will therefore focus on his account of the significance of the Islamist movements. In his section on these movements, Raqab writes as follows:

> Human beings will not achieve a worthy life without turning back to God and to the Koranic programme: in action and conduct …[246]

This sets the tone. Raqab then presents a critical overview of the movements, while at the same time seeking to convince the reader of the necessity of following Islamism. He also aims to inspire hope among Islamists by disqualifying other competing ideologies. Thus he writes:

> A large proportion of young people are turning towards Islam despite the fact that the secular and atheist parties are trying to deter them from [doing so] … some of these parties are suffering from stagnation (*al-kasâd*) in terms of both ideas and influence. Fewer people are knocking on their doors and they are often the subject of ridicule and irony. Many members of the nationalist and socialist parties are therefore switching to the Islamist movements.[247]

Raqab also seeks to instil hope in the prospects for Islamism by describing the fears entertained by the rest of the world – especially the West and Israel – with regard to an Islamic resurgence. He writes as follows:

> The enemies of Islam (*'A'dâ al-Islâm*) are well aware of the danger that an Islamic awakening poses for their stepdaughter Israel and their interests in Islamic regions (*Diâr al-Islâm*) which are associated with their agents (*Umalâ*) in the Islamic world, and they are co-operating in a common effort to wipe out any sign of this Islamic resurgence in a hostile, aggressive Jewish spirit that is directed against Islam and Muslims. The former Israeli Prime Minister [David] Ben Gurion said: "We are not afraid of socialism, nor of revolutions, nor of democracy. The only thing we fear is Islam. This giant that has slumbered so long but is now ready to stir anew."[248]

Raqab's thinking in this passage is based on conspiracy theory. He never says concretely who the enemies of Islam are, but leaves us in no doubt that he is referring to the great powers. Nor, in mentioning "their agents", does he make explicit who is in the firing line. The context, however, makes clear that he is referring here to Arab regimes such as those of Egypt, Saudi Arabia and Jordan, all of which co-operate with the West and have relations with the state of Israel. Al-Raqab's account of Islamism leaves the reader with the impression that this is a rising movement that will be very difficult to suppress. The hope for the establishment of a Palestinian state lies in Islamism, he suggests. Islam is the only ideology that Israel fears. On the basis of this example we may conclude that, through *islamicum*, IUG seeks to create *sound Muslims* who will interpret the world from a distinctly Islamic perspective that is strikingly reminiscent of the view put forward by the Hamas leadership (cf. Chapter 3).

Schooling and the study of English at IUG

Because of IUG's Islamist approach to education, the courses offered to students at the English Department are likewise taught within an Islamist framework. Thus a form of schooling occurred in the teaching of the two English courses at IUG that I took part in: Literary Appreciation and American Literature in the 20th Century. This schooling, which consisted principally in raising students' awareness of the differences between the Islamic world and the West, took several different forms. In what follows I will give a few examples of how teaching was conducted at the Institute. The examples presented below can be characterised as "extreme cases" where the Islamic context is more overt than average, but nonetheless they still illustrate the way in which teaching is being conducted at the English department at IUG.

The first example is taken from the first class of the semester in the course on "literary appreciation", which took place on 1 March 1998. The lecturer, Mr Muhammad, started by outlining the structure of the course and explained that the aim was for students to acquire the ability "to evaluate, understand and criticise literature, as well as to develop skills in interpretation over and above the ability to paraphrase". He also pointed out that the course aimed in addition to improve the students' "language awareness". In order to enhance this aspect of the course, Mr. Muhammad intended from time to time to have us examine a poem in terms of content and linguistic style. This indeed happened at the end of the first double class. The following is taken from a stenographic record of the session:

MR. MUHAMMAD (M): Today I would like to begin with a little language awareness. I will do this with the help of a poem entitled "The Cats' Protection League" … Now I'll read you the whole thing. Look at the grammar and finally consider: How would you as Muslims interpret this text?

[The poem][249]

> Midnight, a knock at the door
> Open it? Better had
> Three heavy cats, mean and bad
> They offer protection. I ask: "What for?"
> The boss cat snarls: "You know the score
> Listen man and listen good
> If you wanna stay in this neighbourhood
> Pay your dues or the toms will call
> And wail each night on the backyard wall
> Mangle the flowers, and as for the lawn
> A smelly minefield awaits you at dawn."
> These guys meant business without doubt
> Three cans of tuna, I handed them out
> Then they disappeared like bats in hell
> Those bad, bad cats from CPL [Cats' Protection League].

M: What do you think of the language?

STUDENT: It's informal language.

M: Yes, it's dialect. Everyday language, even though it's not in a friendly tone. It reminds us of American gangs.

STUDENT: Jewish gangs.

M: Yes, just like during the Intifada.

STUDENT: Jewish as usual.

STUDENT: It reminds me of Fagin in *Oliver Twist*.

M. As you read the text, try to fill in the semantic and linguistic gaps. "Midnight". Why?

STUDENT: It's dark.

M: Yes, it's a very economical way of setting the scene. "A knock at the door. Open it. Better had". Look at the adjectives. Later on they get very sinister. This isn't for fun. It's serious. Did he give away the tuna of his own accord?

STUDENT: No, he was forced to.

M: Look at the linguistic images, for example: "Bats in hell". How would you as Muslims interpret this poem?

STUDENT: Why use cats as symbols? Cats are sweet and soft.

M: Cats constitute a minority. Which is why they've formed a league to protect themselves. Against what?

STUDENT: Maybe they're referring to the race question. "Midnight" could symbolise black people.

STUDENT: I think it refers to the current situation in the Middle East. The West and the United States versus the Arabs. The cats are the West and the man is a symbol of the Arabs.

M: That's a good point. Just like during the Iraq crisis.

STUDENT: I take a similar view. The cats symbolise the Jewish lobby in the States, and the man is an image of the United States.

M: But we need to look at this as Muslims.

STUDENT: It has something to do with Western capitalism.

M: We Muslims willingly pay *zakât* and *sadaqah*. We don't need any league. In capitalist society the rich get richer and the poor poorer, so this is the reaction of the lower classes.

STUDENT: I read this socially and psychologically. All wars are about food and the difference between rich and poor. The only thing that makes people commit crimes is hunger.

STUDENT: I think the cats symbolise Jews whereas the man is a symbol of Muslims and particularly the refugees.

STUDENTS: Cats are fine and peaceful animals. That's to say the cats are an image of Islam, which is friendly and peaceful. But when other governments, both West and Arab, violate Muslim rights we're forced to react. But we're peaceful. Give us back our rights and we'll be peaceful people.

STUDENT: I agree. Like in the present crisis in Algeria.

M: OK, I think that's enough. We read the poem differently. So you see, this is an example of language awareness. Now and then during the course we'll go into this discussion in depth."

With these remarks the class ended. The case demonstrates how the Professor encouraged the students to interpret the text from an Islamic point of view. While being presented initially as 'language awareness', the issue was hardly touched upon, whereas interpretation was in focus. The poem is open for numerous interpretations, which is also evident from the lengthy quote above. The Professor led off with a discussion on language. Soon, however, the class ended up discussing the political content of the poem, and the Professor was very engaged, even leading, in this process. His understanding of the poem was clear: it's about the failure of capitalism in the Western world.[250] He pointed not only to this as the core content, but at the same time stressed that such a development could never take place within the confines of an Islamic state. The argument is that Muslims pay *Zakat* and *Sadaqah*. The students on their part were very keen on participating in the discussion, and most of them read the poem through strong anti-Jewish lenses.[251] It is also characteristic that some of the students read it as a poem about contemporary Middle Eastern politics. Their interpretations were strongly influenced by their political circumstances and hence contained an extremely critical view, not only regarding Jews/Israelis, but also concerning the West at large. It was evident from the discussions that the students were reading the poem in a global context. Also of interest are the students who had severe difficulties in accepting the cats being the 'bad guys', as most

Muslims regard cats as clean animals. Thus, more than a few saw the cats as symbols of Islam which, due to severe pressure, were forced to react against injustice – if necessary by all means. Therefore, if on a number of occasions Muslims act violently, this is not because violence is an integral part of Islam, but rather because the situation in which the believers have been placed by the surrounding society has forced them to react violently. Thereby, an apology for violent Islamism was established.

Another example of how the Islamic point of view in some of the classes is being pursued is taken from the course 'American literature', and presented below. Among the texts we studied was the first novel by Nathaniel Hawthorne (1804–64), *The Scarlet Letter* (1850). The novel is a tale of destiny set in the period when the first pilgrims came to America. The heroine, Hester Prynne, refuses to tell the outside world who is the father of her child, Pearl. Her punishment is to be forced to wear a red "A" as the symbol of her adultery. Thus the turning point of the novel is the stigmatisation of Hester. We discussed the work at IUG over several double classes, and I quote here from a session in which the lecturer, Mr Muhammad, and his students discussed the consequences of Hester's stigmatisation and her subsequent exclusion from the surrounding puritanical society. This class took place on 21 March 1998. At one point in the discussion of Hester Prynne's punishment in the novel Mr Muhammad asked the students:

M: If you were the judge, what would you do?

STUDENT: From an Islamic point of view?

M: Yes, of course. If you were the jury, what would you say to defend her?

STUDENT: Her husband was away … she was young.

STUDENT: She was weak.

M: Women in general are weak.

STUDENT: We can't judge her without knowing [what became of her].

M: In the novel she was doomed to live forever with her shame. In our Islam there's a rule that such a woman should be stoned. This punishment is in line with Islam. Death is better for her. She prefers dying to having to wear the scarlet letter.

STUDENT: From an Islamic point of view then she wouldn't die in shame either. She would go to Paradise. The scarlet letter is also shameful for the child. It would be hard to have to live like that.

STUDENT: But she ought in any case to have two years to rear the child.

M: The Islamic death sentence would have been better for her.

This brief insight into the discussions illustrates yet again how the students are being encouraged to read literature within an Islamist frame of reference. The teacher asks how the heroine of the novel should be punished from an Islamic point of view. And he provides the answer himself: she should be stoned to death. The idea of comparing cultures (i.e. the West and Islam) accords fully with the way in which the students are taught in *islamicum*. Here the students are presented with various Western attitudes, all of which are repudiated. Islam is left as the only answer. In this example, too, it is obvious that the novel is being discussed in a global context. The Islamic response in this instance is highlighted as superior and more humane compared with the Puritans' way of settling Hester's fate. The teaching was designed to inculcate a clear understanding of Islam's moral and ethical superiority to Puritan Christian society. The dialogue between Mr Muhammad and the students created a sense of fellowship in the class based on Islam: a sense that contributed not only to developing social capital but also cultural capital, in so far as the students gained increased insight into Islamic cultural codes. A spirit of community revolving around Islam was being built up.

Another notable aspect of this discussion is the view of women that the teacher puts forward: "Women in general are weak". On several occasions in the course of the term the male students were offered similarly conservative views, for example in an analysis of Emily Dickinson's poem "Not in Vain", which was discussed on 4 March 1998. At one point during the discussion of the poem Mr. Muhammad wanted the students to focus on Dickinson's use of language in order to grasp the point that women write differently, using another, more sensitive kind of vocabulary. Mr. Muhammad commented as follows on the poet's use of language:

Women are partial to repetition. It's as if they do it to confirm themselves. They want to assert themselves. They are very repetitive. Women repeat things to convince themselves ... they are always hesitant, always subjective. This shows that she is not especially confident.

Here it seems appropriate briefly to comment on the teacher's role in these classes. Just as the leaders of the football club were supposed to "set a good example", it was important in this educational project that the teacher, too, should present "a good example". It was not enough that the teacher be professionally competent – he must also have the right moral outlook and view of Islam in order to be able to put across the university's ideology. As the examples above show clearly, Mr Muhammad lived up to the university's aims. Islam was his point of departure for teaching, and it was through his teaching that the students were presented with a holistic Islamic view of the world.

The students and their choice of IUG

In the remaining part of this chapter I turn my attention to the students themselves. First, I look at the background factors that motivated their choice of IUG. Next, I analyse how the students themselves perceived and absorbed the schooling in Islamism that they received at IUG. In an extension of this, I will also examine how they articulated their own identity through the mirror image of "the other", defined as the West, the Jewish people and the Palestinian Authority.

Twenty-one-year-old Salim, who lived in the Shajaiyya district of Gaza City and was a final-year student in English at IUG, explained the background to his choice of IUG as follows:

At that point the Intifada was not yet over and support for IUG was at its highest. There are many people in Palestine who back IUG. Al-Azhar University is not particularly good academically – that is still the fact of the matter today. On the other hand it's generally believed that IUG is a good place academically. It's also a good place from the point of view that the male students are separated from the female. That's really good. Islam leads us to approve of that. As I've told you, I come from a religious family and that has also contributed to my support for IUG, which gives a very complete picture of Islam – very complete. This university supports Islam in general and does many good things for Islam – which makes me support it, because Islam represents perfection in this life. The fact is that this university is better than other universities. The general perception is that it's really good and the best place to study … you can see how my answers are all related to one thing: my affiliation to Islam. It is Islam that led me to study at this university. That is the point.[252]

One of Salim's fellow students was Munir, aged 24. He was from a farming family in the northern part of the Gaza Strip and was likewise in his fourth and last year as a student at the English Department. He had the following to say about his reasons for choosing IUG:

> MUNIR: There is a story behind it. I was compelled to study here. Circumstances forced me to study at this university. I wanted to study in the United States, I was actually accepted by an American university, and I have relatives over there. But I got no chance to leave. At that point conditions were really bad, and I was prevented from leaving Palestine. Even prevented from going to the embassy. This was during the Intifada. I began studying at the English faculty to improve my English and so that I would be able to get into an American university. During the first couple of years I wrote to various universities over there to get a place, but I couldn't leave ... so I was obliged to study here. This was my only possibility.

> MICHAEL: But why did you choose IUG?

> MUNIR: This was the only possibility ...

> MICHAEL: What about al-Azhar University?

> MUNIR: At that point ... you know, IUG has more experience and is thought to be the most progressive in terms of its curriculum. Academically speaking it's better than al-Azhar. Another reason has to do with the fact that I grew up in a Muslim family. You know what al-Azhar is like, and I would prefer to keep away from forbidden things.

> MICHAEL: But there is also sex segregation at al-Azhar.

> MUNIR: But they still have contact with one another in the university grounds ... they talk together ... al-Azhar also strikes me as a bit like a school. It has small buildings, like a school. It's not particularly developed. We regard it as an un-academic place, and the teaching is at an elementary level ...

Later on in the interview Munir explained in more depth what he saw as the difference between students at al-Azhar University and at IUG:

I believe you're familiar with the two universities, and you've seen [the difference] with your own eyes. If we look at the students at IUG and compare them with the students at al-Azhar, we can see a difference in attitude. There's a positive and negative attitude ... there, the girls try to imitate ... look at the way they dress. Look at the way they treat each other. Look at the canteen. The canteen [slightly agitated], that's really out of order. Often you'll see someone trying to attract the girls' attention ... that says something about their personality. That's not all, but there is a difference, and also they neglect [their studies]. I would say about 50 per cent of the students don't care about their studies. They just turn up, and if you look at their grades ... many of them fail. They're not as successful as at this university. Students who want to study go to IUG. I see all of them here, they're always busy. You don't see that there. They're never busy. They're just playing around. That tells you something about the way they think. Sometimes I feel sorry for them. I'm sad about it. Why do they go there and waste money? Why do they turn up, when they don't really care?[253]

Twenty-five-year-old Muhammad, who came from a tradesman's family in Gaza City, wanted to study English in order to open up new business opportunities for his father's firm. It was intended that he should in due course take over the firm. He had not originally planned to study at IUG:

MUHAMMAD: To start with I hadn't intended to study in Gaza. The occupation was still going on, and my father was afraid, so he decided to send me abroad. So I went to Jordan. But I felt I couldn't continue there and I left. When I was back home I regretted having returned. Ultimately it's my future that's at stake, and I decided to study in the United States. I tried to get a passport and all the [necessary] papers but it's difficult getting to the United States. It didn't work, I tried to return to Jordan but that didn't work either because of the Israeli security measures. The Israeli authorities didn't give me permission. So there was nothing for it but to start at IUG.

MICHAEL: You could have chosen al-Azhar?

MUHAMMAD: I'll tell you why I didn't choose al-Azhar. At al-Azhar the English Department is part of the humanities faculty. To begin with I was afraid of studying at the humanities faculty because I'd heard it was very difficult ... not al-Azhar, but the faculty. I started English at IUG.

There you can study English at the teacher training college level, which is easier. So, it wasn't for political reasons. That doesn't matter to me. What interests me is the language … I think education should be kept separate from politics. Education is education and politics is politics."[254]

Most of the students thus chose to enrol at IUG because they considered the university to be more academic, in contrast to the neighbouring university al-Azhar, whose academic standards they doubted. Salim was unambiguous on this score: he had chosen IUG because of its close ties with Islam and for the related reason that it practised sex-segregated education. For Munir, too, this was a contributory factor. Certain students, such as Muhammad, had also chosen IUG for lack of other alternatives. Muhammad had not been able to settle in Jordan, where he began his studies, and subsequently had been quite simply unable to get permission to leave Gaza. The same in fact applied to Munir, who had originally wanted to study in the United States.

Munir draws certain interesting distinctions: al-Azhar is treated as exclusively negative, while IUG stands for the positive. There is "moral corruption" at Azhar, where the sexes are mixed. In addition, according to Munir, only about 50 per cent of the students at Azhar take their studies seriously; they display no seriousness towards their work, they do not appear busy, and their success rate is poor. The opposite can be seen at IUG, where all the students without exception are engaged in their studies and are therefore also much more successful. Munir feels straightforwardly sorry for the poor students at al-Azhar.

It is clear from the interviews that the students were seeking – just like the football players – to accumulate social capital through a discourse on morality and good behaviour. In their account the Islamists, in contrast to the secular students, are presented as conscientious and hard working, which in turn is seen as the Islamist ideal. The picture of IUG as a morally pure university – by virtue of its sex segregation, which the students praised – was likewise placed in sharp contrast with the moral corruption allegedly found at the secular al-Azhar. The distinction, which the young people drew between the two universities, clearly seems to mirror the dichotomy between al-haqq and al-bâtil; it is on this basis that the students are able to exclude "the other", i.e. the secular students at al-Azhar.

The students' view of *islamicum*

It is one thing that *islamicum* is of crucial important to the university administration, but how did the students view the compulsory courses involved?

Did they absorb the ideas promoted? Munir had this to say about the value of *islamicum*:

> It opens your eyes in relation to many things concerning your conduct in life. How to treat other people. How you ought to think. How to do things the right way ... we really have many good things. We've been taught a lot about what is important in our everyday lives ... such as how we ought to treat one another. How we should be tolerant towards others. About modesty. About humility. Try to respect other people, try to respect their attitudes, try to respect the expression of different opinions in a quiet, academic way, try not to raise your voice ... We have also had instruction in how Muslims ought to act and how we ought to think ... not being over-hasty ... concentrating before we act ... co-operating with students and respecting each other ... In fact I can't summarise all of it but there are lots of positive things and all of them are good ... Actually I used to criticise [*islamicum*]. I used to say – why should we study this? But it's a kind of culture, it's our culture. Lately I've become aware that our culture needs a revival and these requirements open your eyes to many things. We look at people in the West ... we study the Western way of thinking and the way that Christians perceive Muslims and how they invaded us with their culture and civilisation. How they – the West – try to tempt us with their culture and change the Muslim people's way of thinking and show Muslims that ... try to change [them] and cast a spell over them with their civilisation ... this civilisation will be corrupted. We know that before long ... we don't know in how many years ...everyone will have their time ... [look at] the United States ... its fate is like Turkey's, the Ottomans', like the Soviet Union's ... the powerful will not be powerful for ever ... sooner or later they'll be brought down.

Ahmad was a 23-year-old student from a small village outside Khan Younis in the southern part of the Gaza Strip. His father was a farmer, and the family moved in 1948 from Bir Sab'a (Beer Sheeva) to Khan Younis. Ahmad said the following about *islamicum*:

> The aim is to turn students into good Muslims. Make them loyal [able to] express their opinions, to reflect Islam. It's for educating or cultivating us in Islam ...[255]

Nabil, aged 21, had lived in Gaza only since the mid-1990s. Previously he had lived with his family on the Egyptian side of the Canada Camp in Rafah. Nabil, whom I interviewed together with his good friend Ahmad, added:

> The lecturers don't tell us this is good, this is bad. Rather, they try to teach us to judge things ... they give us a method for making distinctions. The method is the Koran and *hadîth* and the prophet's customs ... It's also about what we should do in society. Protecting the weak, helping poor families, taking care of other people and not of ourselves. In fact it's this that has motivated me to become a social worker in our local society in Rafah.[256]

Salim described his view of *islamicum*:

> I think we have about 15 subjects that deal with the Islamic dimension. Among other things we have to learn five parts of the Koran off by heart. We also have a course on the Islamic world. From this we learned that all parties – European parties – are bad from an Islamic point of view. Just like communism, nationalism, and patriotism. They're all bad, and it's really dangerous for a country to adopt these courses. They teach us what will happen if they're applied ... [the lecturer] tells us for example about communism and then asks us – what do you think? We understand very well that from our point of view it's very bad. Why choose such a party? It's very dangerous. Finally we're taught more about the subject from a book about the Soviet Union, where this ideology was practised and failed ...
>
> We also have courses in *hadîth* – we learn many *hadîth*, we learn them off by heart and analyse them – and all these *hadîth* have to do with our lives – I mean with our situation ... I think that from this course we get a general idea – a clear idea – about our situation or position in this life and about the position in other countries, and we learn to understand how we should behave towards others – how we should deal with other countries, and how one can understand such things. If these parties or dogma arose here today we would need to understand what's right and wrong. You need to have an analytical approach, and have a clear sense that anything non-Islamic is bad. If these things teach us anything whatsoever about politics – and I think they can, but indirectly – well, they don't give us lectures in politics, but indirectly you understand what you need to understand, and then you can interpret and analyse what you understand ...

The aim of these compulsory courses is to train [us] in a general idea about Islam ... there is a *hadîth* that says that Muslims should know everything in their lives – everything about foreigners, about any country whatsoever – all knowledge – you need to have a computer in your brain – you need to understand everything. This *hadîth* has led us to understand that these courses are very important to us. If I hadn't studied here, how would I be able to understand or know anything at all about communism or patriotism, nationalism?

East, West, Islam is best, the conclusion seems to be. And as these interviews make clear, *islamicum* is an eye-opener for the students. They emerge at the other end with the feeling that they know their own culture – Islamic civilisation: a civilisation that is presented as superior to all others. The students interviewed had a clear sense of the university's entire mission: namely, to revive Islamic civilisation. They had also absorbed the idea that Islam is an all-embracing system that represents *al-haqq*.

The way in which history was taught was based on a non-linear conception of the subject. Cultures and ideologies were shown to bloom and then wither, as happened to the Ottoman Empire and the Soviet Union. The same would happen to the world's only superpower, the United States. History was thus a preparation for the future, and Islam instilled hope for tomorrow. The young people at the university were exhorted to rise above the local context, and their consciousness was raised about the global dimension – the struggle between civilisations that, in the view of Islamists, is being played out all over the world, including the Gaza Strip.

Unlike the football club, then, the university can be defined as a space in which "the other", rather than being merely a local opponent – the secular Palestinians represented by the Authority – is a global "other": Western capitalist civilisation. Implicit in this however is a critique of the local "other": of those who have moved away from the Islamic fundamentals. The westernisation of certain Palestinians is seen as synonymous with their taking the side of the big Western powers, and doubt is thereby cast on their identity as Palestinians. Are they true nationalists? Westernised Palestinians are stigmatised; to be westernised carries connotations of being amoral and a bad Muslim.[257] Conversely, one acquires cultural capital by being Islamist. This is prized by the surrounding society, but it is also seen as a utopian ideal that is hard to live up to. Precisely for this reason those capable of consistently following the Islamist message are admired. It is assumed that, through their studies of *islamicum*, the students build up cultural capital by mastering Islamic cultural codes and forming their worldview accordingly.

The study of English and Islam

Asked to what extent the students felt that they developed their understanding of Islam through their studies of English and American literature, Salim replied:

> You sit with us during the classes, and you know that in our interpretations of the various texts we embark on our analysis from an Islamic perspective ... The first thing we do is to interpret and analyse it from our own tradition, then we go on to analyse it from a Western perspective. In *The Scarlet Letter* for example we try to understand why the author writes as he does. For me, and from an Islamic point of view, a woman such as Hester Prynne should be killed, but in Western culture it's not like that ... I think almost all the students support this kind of punishment [i.e. the Islamic]. Do you know why? We have a sense that it's Islam that sets the punishment ... why is it that we struggle against authorities and governments and say that we need to change the way we handle *hukm* [governance]. It's because the leaders of our society pay no attention to Islam. They pay no attention to Islam.

Nabil replied as follows to the same question:

> With regard to Islam: no, our classes deal with English literature, but it happens that sometimes during class we discuss the text and the various events in the play or the novel from an Islamic point of view ... We discuss the Islamic perspective.

Munir had the following to say:

> I haven't learned about Islam in the literature classes because there's a distinction. We have Islamic requirements [*islamicum*] and English language requirements. So we shouldn't mix the two. But as you yourself have seen on the many occasions when you've been present in the classes, we discuss the texts from an Islamic angle when we study literature ... how would Islam tackle a certain topic ... This helps increase our engagement and stir up discussion, making it more thought-provoking and fruitful.

> MICHAEL: So although English is something different, you still have fruitful discussions about Islam?

MUNIR: Yes, we get insight into two civilisations at one go. We look at
it from a Christian and European point of view and connect ideas from
both here and there. When we mix the two cultures we get a new way
of thinking …

It is telling that in the first instance several of the students rejected the idea
that their classes on English and American literature also developed their
understanding of Islam. Munir at first rejected outright the notion that the
two things should be mixed up, but then went on to mention what the other
two interviewees had also pointed out, namely that the texts in the literature
classes were interpreted from an Islamic perspective. In this way the two cultures – the Western capitalist and the Islamic – were compared. Munir
described the outcome of this as "a new way of thinking". This should not
be understood to mean that the students thereby arrived at some kind of cultural synthesis. Rather, Munir was surely referring to an increased awareness
that Islam was omnipresent and relevant in every context. Through reading
English and American literature the students were made aware of the defi-
ciencies of the Western world, and as Salim points out, their attention was
also drawn to the fact that the leaders of the Arab world were not acting in
according with the prescriptions of Islam.

    Shortly after I carried out my interviews with the students, the English
lecturer, Mr Muhammad, contacted me. He told me that he had heard from
some of the students that I was asking them about the extent to which they
learned about Islam in connection with their English studies. Thereupon he
explained that the only reason he often asked the students to read the text
from an Islamic angle was simply because I was present. He had wanted me
to profit as much as possible, and to come to a greater understanding of how
the students thought and how they viewed Islam. The Islamic angle was thus
emphasised solely in my honour. Moreover, Mr Muhammad informed me
that my presence had had a very positive influence on the students: they were
more active and keen to discuss. The reason for this, according to Mr
Muhammad, was that the students wanted to show a Western researcher that
they were clever, which was associated with the fact that "Arabs like to be perceived as clever and hard-working". In emphasising this point, it was clear
that Mr. Muhammad, on behalf of the students, was combating an orientalist view of Arabs as emotional, irrational and, not least, lazy.[258] It was therefore particularly important for the students to display the qualities he highlighted. This brief meeting with the English lecturer illustrates the not very
surprising point that a researcher can never be just a fly on the wall – my
presence had influenced the surroundings. I am sure that my participation in

the class had indeed affected both the lecturer and the students, but I interpret Mr Muhammad's explanation as a post hoc rationalisation, perhaps due to a desire not to see himself presented as an exponent of an Islamic worldview. None of the students had problems with seeing things from an Islamic perspective, and they gave no impression that this was a new approach. It is possible that the teacher, for my sake, had put particular emphasis on Islamic exposition, but this approach was not alien to the students. In order to illustrate this: in the semester in which I followed the course, the students repeatedly came up with references to former classes in which texts had apparently been discussed from an Islamic angle. On several occasions, for example, reference was made to their discussions of Charles Dickens' *Oliver Twist* and Shakespeare's *Othello*. It was clear from these references that part of the discussion had been about the Jews represented in these works.

On the basis of the foregoing two sections we can conclude that the students had assimilated the worldview presented in *islamicum* and on the English courses – a worldview that was also propagated by the Student Council.

The students and their view of Jews

Further evidence that the schooling they received influenced students and their view of the surrounding world will be presented in the following section, in which I look at how the students understood themselves as a mirror image of "the other". My analysis focuses on their perceptions respectively of Jews, of the PLO's peace discourse and of the Palestinian Authority.

In the above section I gave several examples of the students' view of Jews. In my discussions with them concerning the PLO's agreements with the state of Israel, their mistrust and lack of confidence in Israel and the Jews were repeatedly stressed. Here it is worth noting that Israel – and hence, according to the Islamists' way of thinking, Jews – can be treated both as a local "other" (by virtue of the fact that the students see the Israelis as neighbours and as an occupying force) and as a "global other", since the Islamists regard Zionism as the long arm of imperialism.

The interview with Munir reveals the very negative view the students took of Jews. It also illustrates their rejection of the above-mentioned orientalist view of Arabs as irrational and emotional. Munir, who was extremely sceptical about the agreements entered into by the PLO, told me:

MUNIR: I have often thought about an alternative to peace ... I look at the nature of Jews. I don't think we can live together with them. It's impossible to live together with them. I can describe this quite logically and objectively: the Israeli government is a foreign body that has been placed in this region, and the body – i.e. the Arabic world – is reacting violently to it. Metaphorically speaking one can say that when a foreign element attacks your body, what will your body do? That's the problem. Israel is a foreign body that has been implanted here. In order to achieve peace it has to be removed.

MICHAEL: So you don't accept the state of Israel. Israel shouldn't exist. That's what you're saying.

MUNIR: But that's impossible. But what I conclude from this is that there isn't going to be peace. I don't believe in peace at all. We need to look at this historically, and I think we have to be objective. We need to look at the past. The Jewish people killed the prophets. They cheated and deceived the prophets and broke many agreements. We can't rely on them. That's my experience. That's my attitude. We shouldn't be emotional. We have to use our common sense.

Salim, who like Munir opposed the Authority's agreements with Israel, replied as follows to the question as to whether it was possible to establish peace with Israel:

It's not impossible. It's possible and our religion tells us that we shouldn't wage war. On the other hand our religion also tells us in the Koran that we shouldn't have any dealings with Jews because they're bad people and because they – well – they don't care about [our] holy days. Like Yitzhak Rabin who said that there were no such holy days. Our Koran says many things about Jews. About their bad character and their bad dealings with other people. They think that as a people they rank highest in the world. They are the lords and other people are their servants. That's the Jews' problem. This is … a bad feature of the Jews and I think that these notions come from their manipulated Torah …[259]

Thus, on the question of concluding a peace agreement with Israel, Salim is split between his ideological (i.e. Islamic) viewpoint on the one hand, and the world of "realities" on the other. Asked whether he would be able to accept a peace agreement leading to the establishment of a Palestinian state on the West Bank (including East Jerusalem) and the Gaza Strip, he replied:

SALIM: I'm strongly in favour, that's the agreement we need. A peace agreement with the Gaza Strip and the West Bank. Today I believe no one needs the whole of Palestine.

MICHAEL: That's to say, you accept the existence of the state of Israel?

SALIM: No, but for the majority of Palestinians this idea would be logical. That's life. That's our reality. The Israelis are Israelis. How would we be able to kill six million Israelis? We can't. That's the reality. But personally I can't accept that, because Israel and the Israelis are taboo for this country according to our Koran. The Koran says that after Moses went from Egypt to Sinai, God told him: You and your people take this land [i.e. Palestine]. Moses said OK, but the people said: oh no, there are strong people there and we don't want to go there. People said: you can go there alone with your God and fight and kill alone. We'll stay here and wait and then come later. God became very angry and in the Koran he says as a punishment that this land is a forbidden land. This was the first punishment. The second punishment consists in your having to remain distant from this country and be persecuted for 40 years. This is of course what happened.[260] ... From a religious point of view there is no acceptance of Israel's existence. This is the religious view and anyone who claims the opposite is mistaken. But logically speaking I think I would in fact accept it, but not an agreement like the one that's been concluded. This is a bad agreement.

In the extracts cited both Salim and Munir express their profound mistrust and scepticism towards Jews. Munir presents his point of view as a logical and rational argument, rather than an emotional statement. The rhetoric reflects the medical metaphor often used by Islamists, in which Israel is seen as a foreign body in the Arab world that must be removed in order to restore equilibrium in the region. Salim bases his desire to distance himself from the Jewish state on a religious point of view: an aspect that is also prominent in Munir's argument. Salim's argument is based on a new interpretation of the Koran (*Sura* 5: 20–26).

The rejection of the state of Israel's right to exist was the ideological starting point for several of the young Islamists I interviewed. However, the interviews make clear that the majority would be able to live in peace with Israel. In other words, they were significantly more open when it came to *realpolitik*. Ahmad, for example, put forward the following argument for the possibility of creating peace with Israel:

Because the permanent reality is that Israel exists ... there are around four million [Israelis]. I acknowledge it [the peace agreement] to a certain extent, but this is our country. The whole of Palestine belongs to us, but in the present situation I will accept peace within the framework of *hudna*.

Another student, Adil, was likewise disposed towards – if not enthusiastic about – the establishment of a Palestinian "mini-state" on the West Bank and Gaza Strip:

It wouldn't be bad. In fact I think it would be good, but how is it going to come about? It depends on the Israeli government, but both Likud and the Labour Party stand for the same thing in my view. They have the same priorities.

Several of these young Islamists were thus willing to create peace with Israel on the basis that it is impossible to establish an independent Palestinian state extending throughout the territory of the former British mandate. The kind of peace agreement that they would find acceptable, however, was not the agreement put forward in the PLO's negotiations with Israel. What the Islamist students wanted was not a final and permanent peace accord, but on the contrary a *hudna*, which, as described earlier, is a long-lasting cease-fire amounting to a *de facto* recognition of Israel (cf. Chapter 2).

The students and the PLO's peace discourse

The PLO's peace discourse, which is based on the Oslo process and the – in theory – gradual extension of the Palestinian Authority's powers in the West Bank and the Gaza Strip, with a view to establishing a secular democratic state, was not backed by the Islamists I interviewed. Around the time of the agreement some of the interviewees – for example Ahmad – nevertheless had hopes of a better future.

In response to the question as to how he saw the PLO's agreement with Israel, Ahmad said:

We Palestinians longed and strove for the peace process and we had great hopes that the process would improve our situation, and that in due course we would get our own state and independence. We were glad about the peace. After the Palestinian Authority was established we realized that what we had hoped for was not going to happen.

Everything collapsed. No state. No improvement. The collapse of the economy. Closures. We want peace between partners. If we had the same form of power we would express our views and demand our rights. This agreement doesn't give us what is our right. Israel is the strong party and [the Israelis] are against everything. Look at the confiscations of land. The settlements are being extended everywhere, particularly during the last couple of years. This is a very big problem. I think that if the world … because we can't do anything … but I think that if the world doesn't do something drastic to stop the Israeli settlements, we're going to lose our country. That's why the peace process now stands for something negative … Peace is good if it's implemented in a good way. The Palestinians have many possibilities, and yet still the peace process is the only strategy. But for example we have the option of starting a new Intifada.

A much more common response, however, was the rejection of the PLO's peace discourse on ideological grounds. Muhammad commented as follows on the Oslo agreements:

In reality the Oslo agreement doesn't take into account our rights, so I don't agree with [it]. If they [the Israelis] want peace, why should we ask them for peace … why should we give them our land? This land is ours and we ought to keep it – protect it and sacrifice ourselves for it. If someone or other came to your house and said: "I don't want to share your home with you", would you accept that? I doubt it.

MICHAEL: That's from an ideological point of view, but purely practically …

MUHAMMAD: I think we need to put this ideological perspective at the top of the list. This is our ideology. This is our religion. We can't give it up. We mustn't surrender … we are very, very weak. Israel imposes its conditions on us. We can't object. We can't say no. We're forced to say yes to everything they say. It's a one-sided agreement. Precisely. The Palestinians aren't allowed to say anything – just say yes – just sign [the agreements].

Muhammad's reaction expresses his frustration at the Palestinians' weakness and inability to get the PLO's minimum agreements fulfilled through negotiation. As the weak party the Palestinians were forced to sign the agreements, and according to Muhammad this had not brought any positive results. Muhammad's comments reveal an implicit opposition to giving up the dream of Palestine as a geographical entity: the desire to create a Palestinian state stretching from the coast to the river. For Muhammad, it was Islam that held out the hope of a new future. The mixture of nationalism and Islamism generated by Hamas' ideological position is now presented as the alternative to the PLO's peace-seeking discourse.

In his comments on the agreements undertaken by the PLO Salim was particularly critical of the organisation's abilities:

> I am very reluctant to accept these agreements. There are many reasons I don't like the idea. First, Arafat isn't worthy of the position he occupies. He concluded an agreement that the Palestinians in their hearts are not keen on. They are against it. So my first reason has to do with [Arafat] generally. Arafat is not good enough. Another reason is that if you read the agreement in detail you'll discover [that it means] the collapse of the Palestinian people and of Palestine in general. I think the Gaza-Jericho agreement was about 500 pages long. Why was it so long? That's the question. Arafat, as I say, is not up to his position, and as you know the Jews are very good at manipulating words ...

For Salim the problem with the agreements was closely related to the poor abilities of the Palestinian leadership. The PLO quite simply did not possess the human resources needed to obtain even the minimum legitimate rights of the Palestinians. One of the reasons for this, according to Salim, was that the Jews were not just intelligent, but also willing to manipulate words – i.e. to ensure that the wording of the text was such that the Israeli interpretation would always prevail. The Palestinians were inferior to them as negotiating partners, and this called the legitimacy of the Authority into question. Indeed not only Salim, but virtually all those interviewed regarded the Authority as illegitimate. In the section that follows, therefore, I will look at the students' view of the Authority itself.

The students and their view of the Palestinian Authority

Not surprisingly, the young Islamist sympathisers were critical of the Palestinian Authority, which in their view had not lived up to expectations. Asked to sum up the Authority's work in the period 1994–98, Salim replied:

It's crap. All the progress we've seen is not enough. What have they done? They've surfaced a road here and there. Superficial things that are nice to look at. But fundamentally they haven't achieved anything. In reality the Gaza Strip has collapsed and been destroyed and we need to make use of all the money that the EU and other donors have given us to revive our country. It's not OK to use just 1 per cent of this amount.

Adil was equally severe in his judgement of the Authority. His criticism was directed first and foremost at the Authority's lack of respect for human rights:

The situation is very bad. Today you can be accused without knowing why. Moreover, the Authority's policies are completely lacking in principle and our human rights are not protected. There are quite simply no laws to protect them.

Muhammad put it as follows:

Now and again you feel that individual security has improved, but I believe that's still limited to one group of people, not everybody. There's security above all for those who are members of Fatah and support the PLO, and not for supporters of the Islamist movements. [The latter] are now being imprisoned tortured and killed. They're in the Authority's prisons. So, individual security by no means covers everybody. What benefit do we get from it? In my view everyone in society should benefit from an agreement ... another problem, too, is that the Authority is now trying to play the role of trader. They don't want anyone apart from them to deal in imports, for example the case of flour from Israel. They act as middlemen and of course they have to make a profit from being intermediaries, and so a great many goods have become more expensive for ordinary people. That applies for example to the price of petrol. The population don't find this convincing. They ought to be helping people instead, but still it's obvious that the picture isn't so black and white. There are still some good people employed by the Authority – they aren't all bad.

Ahmad likewise sought to give a nuanced critique of the Authority. He told me:

I think the Authority has both positive and negative sides. One of the positive elements is that individual security has improved. There isn't total security but you feel safer in your own home than before – especially at night. Among the negative sides are the corruption we read about in the newspapers ... It's particularly the corruption that I'm against.

Nabil emphasised as a positive element the increased freedom of movement between Egypt and the Gaza Strip: a point that was personally important to him, since before the Oslo agreements he had lived in the Canada Camp on the Egyptian side of the border and had been unable to visit his family in Gaza (Rafah). Like others, however, he took a critical view of the Authority:

> People who during the [first] Intifada were regarded as criminals and bad people are today the leaders. That's the first thing. Other leaders and generals who are now in power – where were they during the [first] Intifada? They were sitting in comfortable chairs drinking their wine at bars on the beach. That was that. And now it's these people who are to judge you. It's they who say: "you're OK", "you're a criminal", "you have to die", "you have to go to prison". That's the worst thing, and the brave men are arrested and put in prison ...

The students' statements differ only slightly from those made by the *Jam'iyya* footballers. Like the players, the students took the view that the Palestinian Authority did little to take care of the interests of Palestinian society as a whole. The Authority's close ties to Israel and the United States had put paid to the possibility of representing everyone, since under the agreements the Islamists were to be suppressed: a condition criticised by those interviewed. The latter also accused the Authority of economic and moral corruption and lack of respect for the human rights of Palestinians. The Authority's corrupt form of leadership gave rise, in their view, to a problem of legitimacy, and this made it easier for the Islamists to argue in favour of another kind of social structure. The question, then, is whether the opposition (the Islamists) had any alternative to offer.

What does Hamas have to offer?

Asked about Hamas' contribution to Palestinian society since the establishment of the Palestinian Authority in May 1994, Muhammad replied:

They have not done anything, simply because of the Authority. [The Authority] has prevented them. As you know the social institutions have been closed down: *Mujamma' Islâmi, al-Jam'iyya al-Islâmiyya* and *al-Jam'iyyat al-Salâh al-Islamiyya*. They have closed them down. How can the Islamic movement act without these institutions? And if they work in secret they'll be arrested. So there are great restrictions on the Islamist movement. Regardless of whether we're talking of Islamic Jihad or Hamas.

MICHAEL: What does that mean for those who support the Islamic movement?

MUHAMMAD: I take the view that there are two types of supporters. Some are strong supporters just as they were during the first Intifada [1987–93], while others, who are also strong supporters, don't show this in public. They're afraid of being arrested ...

MICHAEL: So can't we say that the movement is ineffective? How can one put faith in such a movement?

MUHAMMAD: People know who [is involved in] the Islamic movement and they depend on it despite this. They knew [these people] during the Intifada. They know what they did during the Intifada. They know how they helped the poorest, and now it's the Islamists who are being arrested. What has the Authority done? I think I'm a quite ordinary person, and when I see people being arrested for saying this is right and that is wrong – why does it happen? There is no doubt that I should support the man who's been arrested. When the population see that the Authority is arresting people who support the Islamic movement ... yes, people aren't stupid – not at all – they understand but they're afraid to express themselves. We don't live in a democratic society here ... Where's the democracy they talk about?"

Ahmad had an interesting argument concerning Hamas' role during the period in question:

The Islamist opposition has played a very positive role. If the whole world had had the impression that all Palestinians supported the agreements, they wouldn't have realized how we suffer under the agreements. The role of the opposition has been to make the outside world aware of this. Make them aware that we can't accept the agreements, and that we have been forced to accept them. They [the opposition] make our case against the Israelis clear and force them to go further than they otherwise would have done, so in that sense they play a positive role ... they also play a positive role in the sense of encouraging Muslims and Arabs throughout the world to help the Palestinian people ...

According to Adil, Hamas' effectiveness was limited:

All their activities are limited and have little effect. The only exception is the Islamic University. This is quite obviously where they are most effective. I had expected more ... and then there are the military actions. Politically Israel is afraid of these actions, so in this sense they are more effective than the Palestinian Authority. And indirectly these actions help the Palestinian leadership. Terrorism is the only effective way of stopping the Israelis' policies. They don't even listen to the United States.

There appeared to be a consensus that because of the repressive measures to which it had been subjected, Hamas had not been very effective in the area of domestic policy. However, Hamas still enjoys support as a result of the movement's activities in connection with the Intifada (1987–93). Adil emphasises that IUG is one of the few areas in which, despite everything, Hamas has continued to be effective. In terms of foreign policy, albeit with some domestic policy undertones, most of those interviewed emphasised that Hamas, and particularly the military wing of the movement, had played an important role, in the sense that Hamas' actions had attracted the world's attention to the population's dissatisfaction with the political agreements contracted with Israel. In addition, the students argued that this would force Israel to go further in the negotiation process – in other words, that Hamas' actions underpinned the PLO's negotiating position. Despite this, the conclusion must be that in actual fact Hamas had little concretely to offer the Palestinian population.

Summary

IUG defines its purpose in terms of creating *sound Muslims*, even though the university authorities may choose not to emphasise this. The university aims to create moral individuals. The university's prospectus makes it very plain that this is the goal. It also makes clear that its purpose is to lead Muslim society out of the crisis that it currently finds itself in, by creating, through education, an awareness of the current situation, and an understanding that change can be achieved only through a revitalisation of Islam. IUG plays a central role in the Islamists' efforts to re-islamise society. Thus both the sports club *Nâdi al-Jam'iyya al-Islâmiyya* and IUG are engaged in an effort to create *sound Muslims*.

It is not surprising therefore that Islamist schooling takes place at IUG. There are three main ways in which this occurs: through the activities of the Student Council, through obligatory courses in *islamicum*, and through teaching in specific subjects – such as, in this instance, English. *Islamicum* plays a central role in the sense that it involves the specific teaching of Islam, which is the foundation for all other studies at IUG. Knowledge of English and American literature is communicated at IUG within an Islamic framework.

We see the West represented as "the other" alike in the work of the Student Council, in the teaching of *islamicum* and in the context of English studies. The students' statements make clear that they had to a great extent assimilated the leadership's goals and *minhâj*. This is most evident in their references to *islamicum*, but through their studies of English and American literature, too, their attention was drawn to the failings of the West and the splendours of Islam.

At IUG it was first and foremost a "global other" that the university and the students used as a mirror image of themselves. In Chapter 4 I described how Islamism was expressed in the context of the football club *Nâdi al-Jam'iyya al-Islâmiyya*. I argued there that the club could be seen as a physical space in which Islamism was expressed primarily through bodily action. In this context "the other" was above all the secular Palestinians represented by the Palestinian Authority. Whereas the Islamists in the club operated quite concretely in a local context in which they had to set a good example and were up against a hegemonic secular discourse, the situation at IUG was different. At the university the Islamists were the hegemonic group, and it was therefore to a greater extent the global order – the West – that came to represent "the other": the Islamists' mirror image. Thus in the present chapter we can see that the global context was brought into the discussion to a greater extent, and that it was largely the Western capitalist social order or civilisation that represented "the other" in these discussions. As mentioned above, this does not mean that the local element was entirely absent, but merely that the global "other" was more often presented as the opposition. Thus Islamism is expressed in different ways, depending on the particular sphere in which it emerges.

As we saw in Chapter 4, there were various reasons why the young men interviewed had wanted to join an Islamist football club. Similarly, the students at IUG had chosen the Islamic University for a variety of reasons. Several students said that they had opted for IUG because it had a higher academic reputation than the neighbouring university, al-Azhar. Some of those interviewed explained their choice on the basis that IUG was an Islamic university – i.e. their motives were religious. Finally, several students said that their choice was due purely to the lack of alternatives – they could not leave the Gaza Strip and study abroad.

The results of my fieldwork lead to the conclusion that, through their participation in *islamicum* and their studies of English, the students to a great extent had absorbed the administration's discourse. The *islamicum* courses "open[ed] their eyes to their own culture and civilisation". They were also made aware of the superiority of this civilisation in relation to the West. Their English studies similarly raised the students' awareness of Islam as an all-embracing system that was superior to the Western world in almost every respect. Islam instilled hopes of a better future. Through their studies at IUG the students absorbed a holistic view of existence revolving around Islam. Islam was seen as all embracing and as representing the solution to the problems facing not only the Palestinians but also the entire Arab world. Through their studies the students accumulated both social and cultural capital. This occurred in several different fora, but was particularly marked in connection with their studies of *islamicum*.

However, the "local other" was not entirely absent at IUG; it was merely less prominent than at the club. Although the Islamists' student organisation, *Kutla Islâmiyya*, had total control of the Student Council – and IUG was regarded as a hegemonic Islamist space – there was clearly, nevertheless, strong rivalry with *shabîba*, Fatah's student organisation. This was due among other things to the fact that the two universities on the Gaza Strip are located close to one another. Opposition to the "local other" was also expressed in terms of the students' distanced attitude to the PLO's peace discourse and the Authority's ability – or lack of ability – to lead the Palestinian people. In this context it is worth noting that, like the Hamas leadership, the students were willing to accept a *hudna* as a solution to the conflict with Israel. The students also identified themselves in opposition to Jews, as is evident in their clearly phobic attitude towards them. Jews were seen as eternally evil, first and foremost because of their "manipulated Torah", as one of the students expressed it. The students' view of Jews appears to be constructed on the concept of *tahrîf*, i.e. on the notion that Jews have deliberately falsified God's word and are therefore not be trusted.

Despite the students' rejection of the PLO's peace discourse and the Authority, it is clear from the interviews that Hamas had little concrete to offer back in the late 1990s. Like the football players in the club, the students argued that this was mainly due to the fact that the Palestinian Authority had repressed the Islamist movement.

6

CONCLUSION

As argued by Francois Burgat (2003) Islamism is to a large extent a reaction not only to the political and economic domination of the West, but also to Western cultural hegemony. Hence, Islamism can be seen as a continuation of the anti-colonialist movement launched decades ago with an Islamic mantle. Furthermore, the Islamists are reacting against the pro-western and corrupt Middle Eastern regimes, i.e. as stated by Richard Augustus Norton "The reciprocal to the failure of the authoritarian state is Islamism."[261]

In the Palestinian context Islamism has primarily been linked to the Muslim Brotherhood, and since late 1987 with the 'new' Islamic resistance movement Hamas. Contextually Hamas differs from most other Islamist movements due to the fact that the movement is operating in occupied territory. Because of its actions towards Israel(ies) Hamas is perceived by many in the West as a terrorist organization, and their social organizations are seen as a place for indoctrination and even as recruiting ground for terrorist activities. All too often when dealing with movements using political violence the political, economic and social context in which they operate is omitted. This is clearly the case in regard to Hamas. This omission has led to the conclusion, by some researchers, that Hamas is one of the least understood social movements in the region.[262] With Hamas in power (in the Gaza Strip) the time is ripe for a broader perspective on the movement. In order to comprehend the movement and its actions it is important to grasp their activities within the context of civil society, as this will help us gain a deeper understanding of Hamas and give us an idea of where it is travelling.

The case studies: Hamas in civil society

Like most Islamists movements Hamas leaders perceive Islam as an all-embracing system. Islam is essentially timeless and therefore – in the view of

Islamists – valid for all times. However, Islam needs to be contextualised, and *ijtihâd* is essential. According to Hamas there is a rift between Muslims and their religion, since, according to Hamas leaders, many Muslims misunderstand their own religion. For Hamas the reason for the crisis lies not within Islam itself, but in the way in which it has been practised hitherto, and this in turn is closely related to Western imperialism and to what is known among Islamists as the ideological invasion (*al-ghazw al-fikrî*) (cf. Chapter 3). In the eyes of the Islamists this "invasion" has distorted the view of Islam taken by most Muslims. Through a new interpretation of Islam the individual can be liberated. Hence, the way out of the crisis lies in the (re-)conversion of Muslims to 'true' Islam. Here civil society comes into play. It is through the Islamists' active presence within civil society that history can be rewritten. It is within this space that they seek to create *sound Muslims*, i.e. a Muslim who regards Islam as a body of ideas, values, beliefs and practices, encompassing all spheres of life including personal and social relations, as well as economy and politics.

The Muslim Brotherhood/Hamas has since the mid 1970s created a comprehensive network of civil society institutions in the Gaza Strip (as well as on the West Bank). A significant number of Palestinians are frequenting one or more of these institutions on a daily basis. Most kindergartens are controlled by the movement, many of the poorest Palestinians receive food donations, others spend their leisure time doing sports in the Hamas affiliated sports clubs or study at educational institutions affiliated with the movement. Others again wait in the reception rooms of the numerous health clinics run by the movement. Orphans get a new chance in life while a number of elderly people are being taken care of. In other words: Hamas offers cradle to grave services to the Palestinians.

Participant observations combined with numerous interviews with players in an Islamic football club closely linked to Hamas and university students at the most important Islamist institution in the Gaza Strip (the Islamic University of Gaza), reveal that the young Islamists in Gaza do not fit the image of dangerous, fanatical, and evil terrorists. They are not longing for bygone days. On the contrary, they are young men and women who are able and willing to adapt to the realities of the modern world.

Within the context of the two examined Islamist institutions the discourse revolves around morality and good behaviour. In the *Nadi Jami'iyya al-islamiyya* it was evident that the Islamist leaders do not perceive sport as the primary aim of the club, but rather the creation of sound Muslims. Despite of this no political indoctrination took place in the club. The leaders of Hamas were irked that *Jam'iyya* did not offer a form of education, focusing on various aspects of Islam and so on. From the point of view of Ismael Abu Shanab, "They [leaders of *Jam'iyya*] should teach their players to maintain a unique Islamist code of behaviour and Islamist doctrine." However, from the fieldwork in the club it is evident that high moral standards were valued highly among the young players and they often sought to separate themselves from their mirror image: the West and the westernised segments of the Palestinian population. By doing so the young Islamists were reaffirming their own cultural heritage, Islam, thus building up the social capital of the players. At the same time the players wanted to live out their dreams on the playing field and to dress like their heroes, even though, as in the case of dress code, this went against the leaders notion of true Islamic behaviour. The young men were primarily interested in football and living out their dreams. This was a clear conclusion from the numerous interviews made with the young players. And the (pragmatic) leadership accepted this. Football itself was the most important aspect, as clearly illustrated by the fact that ten players left the club after *Jam'iyya* was delegated to the second division. This raises the question of whether the leisure time activities offered by Hamas should be seen as the beginning of a secularisation process rather than an islamisation process. In Denmark, for example, the YMCA established a large number of sports clubs in the early twentieth century. Today, one century later, few playing in these clubs are aware the clubs stem from a Christian missionary tradition.

Education is at the heart of the philosophy of the Palestinian Islamists. Most of the "political men" engaged in the Islamist project make use of education in order to rewrite history, and break Western hegemony. Not surprisingly therefore the Islamist movement in Palestine fought for the control of the Islamic University in Gaza (IUG) – and won. From the directory of the IUG it becomes clear that the purpose of the IUG is to create *sound Muslims*. Indeed, the general aim of IUG is to offer a form of education that will lead Palestinian youth out of the crisis currently facing both Islam and the Palestinian society partly by revitalising Islam and partly by recreating a space for Islamic cultural and political autonomy. This helps to explain the presence of Islamism at IUG. A kind of schooling took place in three spheres at the university: a) the Student Council, b) the Islamic Studies courses (*Islamicum*) and c) the students' specific fields of study – here represented by the courses at the English Department. The results of my fieldwork illustrate the way in which the students gained social and cultural capital – in Bourdieu's sense – through studying Islam and thereby learning Islamic cultural codes and forming their world-view on this basis. This process is also manifest in the English classes at the university. It was evident from my

fieldwork that the students adopted the world-view presented by their teachers. The sense of "joint enterprise" at IUG gave the students a reassuring feeling of belonging and strengthened their Islamic identity. It is also worth
noticing that the IUG and its students first and foremost used a "global
other" as a mirror image of themselves, whereas in the context of the football
club "the other" was above all the secular Palestinians represented by the
Fatah-led Palestinian Authority. The Islamists in the club operated concretely
in a local context in which they had to set a good example and were up
against a hegemonic secular discourse. The situation at IUG was different. At
the university the Islamists were the hegemonic group, and it was therefore
to a greater extent the global order – the Western capitalist social order or
civilization – that came to represent "the other". Thus Islamism is used in
different ways, depending on the particular context in which it emerges.
Therefore, more anthropological fieldwork focusing on the socialisation
processes taking place in the numerous Islamist-controlled kindergartens, the
role of health clinics, computer centres or Islamists' activism within the
sphere of syndicates and unions is needed. Such studies would help provide
a much needed insight into how the Islamists are organizing and arguing for
the need of a political alternative, and how this is being perceived by their
"consumers".

National politics: Adjusting to new realities

These forms of "enterprise" at IUG and in the sports club represent only
some of the many activities the Hamas movement has initiated within
Palestinian society – albeit these are among the most important on an
ideological and cultural level. However, many Palestinians consider the social
aid of the various Hamas-related NGOs as being of even greater importance
in their daily lives. This is especially true in the wake of the Aqsa Intifada
that began in September 2000. No doubt Hamas has gained legitimacy and
widespread political support through its engagement in civil society institutions.

Moving from the micro-level of politics to national politics it is evident
that the leadership of Hamas by the mid 1990s became uneasy about the
actions of Fatah. At this point the Palestinian Authority (PA) not only
cracked down on Hamas' armed wing Izz ad-din al-Qassam, but also began
closing their civil society institutions like, for example, *al-Jam'iyya al-
Islâmiyya*. The response from the leadership of the Islamist movement was a
new line of moderation. Most noteworthy was that the leadership began
arguing for the possibility of a long-term *hudna* with Israel as a solution to

the conflict. The *hudna* solution is based on a *de facto* recognition of Israel as a reality. As Ismael Abu Shanab stated in an interview conducted in 1998:

> The state exists [Israel]. De facto it [Israel] is there, and we would not create problems for our neighbors and ourselves if we had a *hudna*. The concept of *hudna* is completely legitimate within the framework of Islam and would hold for at least this generation. Despite the fact that it does not give us all our rights, we hope for God's forgiveness. This takes us to the limits of what we can do. We have fought. We have fought up to this point. So we will keep to a *hudna* and live in peace and let others live in peace...[263]

The leaders of Hamas today continue to accept Israel as a reality. In early 2007 Hamas leader in exile Khaled Mish'al stated: "there will remain a state called Israel, this is a matter of fact"[264] and added:

> The problem is not that there is an entity called Israel. The problem is that the Palestinian state does not exist.[265]

Also the rank and file of Hamas is ready for a two-state solution. Through the interviews conducted at the Islamic University of Gaza it was evident that the Gazan youth supporting Hamas were ready for peace, even though they did not approve of the conditions on which peace was being negotiated. One student expressed it in these terms: "Peace is good if it's implemented in a good way" while another stated: "I'm strongly in favour... that's the agreement we need... today I believe no one needs the whole of Palestine."[266] This tendency is backed by numerous polls.[267]

This line of moderation was born out of need as the Hamas leadership feared they were about to loose the civil society institutions they had established and developed since the mid-1970s. Hence, a pragmatic approach to the conflict with more focus on islamisation of Palestinian society and less on armed resistance was seen as the best to opt for. Basically, Hamas focused on survival during these years. The eruption of the Aqsa Intifada in late 2000 changed the discourse of Hamas. Rather than discussing resistance vs. survival it became a discussion revolving around resistance vs. participation.

Initially resistance dominated. In 2004, after a couple of years of intense military conflict with Israel, which was getting increasingly unpopular and increasingly costly for Hamas, the movement opted for participation. With the coming of local council elections in 2004 and 2005 the leadership of Hamas decided to enter into the political process.[268] Under the name of

'Change and Reform' they participated in the first municipal elections held
among the Palestinians in the West Bank since 1976 and the first ever in the
Gaza Strip. Participation was the new order of the day. Hamas candidates
fared very well and won the majority in a number of councils in important
West Bank cities such as Nablus, Jenin and Qalqilya as well as in cities like
Deir al-Balah and Beit Hanoun in the Gaza Strip. A significant part of their
popularity was based on its extensive social welfare organisations. A number
of the elected candidates have a background in the Hamas affiliated civil
society institutions. A case in point is Ahmad al-Kurd, former Director of
Jamiyyat al-Salâh al-Islâmiyya in Deir al-Balah in the Gaza Strip, who became
mayor after the elections in 2005.[269]

Although hardly any research has been conducted so far, the preliminary
conclusion after the first period of local councils run by Hamas candidates
"has been almost boringly similar to its predecessor".[270] The candidates have
according to a recent International Crises Group (ICG) report emphasised
themes such as "good governance, economic development, and personal and
social security leaving specifically religious issues".[271]

Examples exist, however, of how Hamas has been trying to impose their
Islamist vision on Palestinian society through their newly gained influence.
One example comes from Qalqilya. In summer 2005 a major cultural festival was to take place in the city. Yet the newly elected city council, consisting
of 15 Hamas members, decided to cancel the festival on the grounds that the
festival was endangering the prevailing "values" of Palestinians in Qalqilya.
According to council spokesman Mustafa Sabri:

> We were elected by a segment of people that wants us to preserve the
> conservative values of the city ... the prevailing values reject mixing of
> the sexes ...[272]

This example of guarding Palestinian public morale is an indication on how
a Hamas-governed society could be tempted to control cultural life. As we
have seen in the football club and at the university the movement has, over
the years, attempted to carry out a process of islamisation from below. The
example from Qalqilya is a new tendency where the movement through its
control over local councils attempts to islamise from above.

Another example illustrating this tendency took place in early March
2007 when a book on Palestinian folklore written by Professor Sharif Kanaana
and Ibrahim Muhawi was banned. According to Sheikh Yazid Khader,
Director-general of the Palestinian Ministry of Education:

The book was withdrawn because of the problems with offensive language which contradicts our beliefs and morals.[273]

Despite these attempts to impose islamisation from above Hamas will most likely go about this process gradually and primarily stick to islamisation from below, as the ideology of the movement is based on patience (*sabr*) and constitutes a key concept in their thinking providing hope for Islam and Palestine, despite its current weakness. Therefore the leadership will probably refrain from this temptation, as their newly won power could be brought into jeopardy, since most Palestinians do not want an Islamic state.[274] Therefore, they are not likely to create an Islamic state from one day to the next. Nonetheless, the events of Qalqilya and the book ban are undoubtedly only the first of a number of cases related to different world-views that Palestinians will have to deal with while Hamas is in power.

The way Hamas is travelling: towards greater pragmatism and moderation

As already indicated, in the broader political context Hamas has shown pragmatism and moderation during the past years and this tendency has been crystal clear since the movement opted for political participation. This tendency culminated during the 2006 election campaign and in the negotiations with Fatah and other Palestinian secular forces that followed.

According to Khaled Hroub, who analysed in depth the electoral platform for "Change and Reform", the election program as such constitutes "the broadest vision that Hamas has ever presented concerning all aspects of Palestinian life".[275] Hroub argues that the program presented by Hamas "was designed to carry out exactly the kinds of reform that had been demanded by the international community".[276] Hence, the document stresses the need for a fight against all forms of corruption, it calls for a separation of the legislative, executive and judicial powers, for equality before the law, and in the document Hamas argues for a political system based on political freedom, pluralism, and on peaceful rotation of power.[277] Also of great significance vis-à-vis Hamas' relationship with Israel is the paragraph in the program in which it becomes evident that Hamas is about to abandon the armed struggle and pave the way for negotiations. The document reads:

Our Palestinian people are still living in a phase of national liberation, and thus have the right to strive to recover their own rights and end the occupation using all means, including armed struggle.[278]

Compared to the charter of Hamas from 1988 this is a different tone. In article 13 of the Charter it is stated: "There is no solution to the Palestine problem except through struggle (*Jihad*)."[279] Two decades later Hamas is ready to use '*all* means' to find a solution. Interestingly, the *de facto* recognition of Israel and the path away from armed struggle as the only means to obtain a solution are – as it have been argued by Beverley Milton-Edwards and Alister Crooke – "analogous to the political evolution that occurred at an earlier stage within Fatah".[280] PLO wrote in its 1968 edition of its charter (article 9): "Armed struggle is the only way to liberate Palestine."[281] In the ten-point program of 1974, produced in the wake of the October 1973 War, these words were turned into:

> The PLO will struggle by every means, the foremost of which is armed struggle, to liberate Palestinian land.[282]

Hence, the resemblance to the route taken by the PLO in the 1970s is unmistakable. It is interesting, bearing in mind that at the time the PLO embarked on the route towards negotiations it was regarded a terrorist organization by United States and Israel. It was not until 1993, just before the signing of the Oslo agreement, that the PLO got rid of this predicate and officially became *salonfähige*. Hamas is following the same path and the continued insistence on *hudna*, which is not only to be understood as a temporary truce, but rather as a binding contract that "obliges the parties to use the period to seek a permanent, non-violent resolution to their differences"[283] is a clear sign of this. However, recognition will not occur until a Palestinian state has been established within the 1967 borders. Ahmad Yousuf, who is a senior aide to Ismael Haniyya, explains it in these terms:

> Israel is there, it is part of the United Nations and we do not deny its existence. But we still have rights and land there which have been usurped and until these matters are dealt with we will withhold our recognition.[284] Like Fatah before them Hamas is capable of a transition moving from armed struggle to negotiator of peace. However, while being transformed Hamas insists on changing the discourse of the Palestinian–Israel conflict by insisting that the core of the conflict is related to Israel's illegal occupation of Palestinian lands and that an occupied people has the right to resist occupation.

The widespread activities within civil society, the perceived non-corruption – in Hamas parlance, 'White sheets' – inside the civil society institutions linked to the movement's steadfast rejection of the failed Oslo process and their continued struggle against the Israeli occupation no doubt helped to create the political earthquake in January 2006. The elections signalled the most radical political shift in Palestinian history since Yasir Arafat and his Fatah movement took control of PLO following the defeat in 1967. Hamas' victory was also reaction against the inefficiency, corruption and internal fighting characterising the PLO (and Palestinian Authority), as well as their inability to realise the movement's political agenda during the almost four decades of nationalist-controlled Palestinian politics. Hamas made history in January 2006, sweeping away Fatah's monopoly of power in free and fair democratic elections. These parliamentary elections were a historic step forward in Palestinian democratic politics as voters turned out in unprecedented numbers, for the first time taking part in fiercely competitive multi-party elections. A new phase in Palestinian politics dominated by Islamist political culture could begin.

Though Hamas won political power in January 2006 they had severe difficulties exercising it. Hamas immediately came under massive pressure after their electoral victory, as the United States and EU insisted that Hamas recognise Israel, renounce violence and adhere to past agreements before they would allow any economic assistance to the new government. Meanwhile, Israel withheld huge amounts of tax revenues supposed to be transferred to the Palestinian government. As a result the Hamas government has been unable to pay public employees during most of the first period they held power:

> This did not mean the donor community stopped aid to the Palestinians, but it was disbursed through a new mechanism called Temporary International Mechanism (TIM)[285] or directly through the office of the Palestinian President, Mahmoud Abbas. In fact, the international donor community distributed more aid than ever. Despite of this UN special rapporteur John Dugard noted in his 2007 report that "the Palestinian people have been subject to economic sanctions – the first time occupied people have been so treated."[286]

The aim of this policy was to squeeze Hamas out of power before they were able to exercise it. After more than a year of intense negotiations, and the Palestinians on the brink of a civil war, Hamas and Fatah and a large number of other secular forces created the first ever fragile Palestinian National Unity Government in March 2007. Also this event indicates the level of pragmatism shown by the leadership of Hamas. Not only did they insist on the need of national unity immediately after the election, they also showed willingness of inclusion. Although some secularists in Palestine indicate that they are nervous that Hamas will use its power to islamise society from above (like the case in Qalqilya and the case of the book ban), Hamas is showing clear signs that they are genuinely pragmatic and ready to compromise and include even atheists. A case in point is the appointment of the Minister of Culture, Bassam al-Salehi, in the unity government. Bassem al-Salehi comes from the Palestinian Peoples Party formerly known as the Palestinian Communist Party. The mere fact that the Islamists accepted a communist in government in the role of Minister of Culture, which in Islamist circles is an office of high importance due to culture's influence on public morale, is proof of the movement's readiness to take responsibility for the interests of the nation.

Breakdown of the National Unity Government

However, the National Unity Government did not last for long. Power sharing proved to be more difficult than anticipated, especially within the field of security. The Palestinian conflict between Fatah and Hamas culminated in June 2007, with scenes in Gaza resembling a civil war, causing at least 300 deaths and more than 700 wounded in the Gaza Strip. The Palestinian civil strife in Gaza led to a political division of the Palestinian territories divided in a West Bank controlled by Mahmoud Abbas and Salam Fayyad and a Gaza Strip controlled by the democratically elected Hamas movement.

Most observers in the West have blamed Hamas for the internal conflict. However, according to Palestinian intellectuals from all walks of life the USA and Israel forced President Mahmoud Abbas not to work with Hamas. They argue that pressure, and in particular American support and the donor community's decision to cut aid to the Hamas-led PA, helped fuel the internal fighting.[287] Deputy National Security Advisor Elliot Abrams for example championed the building up of Fatah forces in order to take on Hamas. Many Palestinians, such as the respected Dr Iyad Sarraj, are convinced that the USA deliberately worked to topple Hamas.[288]

After the internal Palestinian fighting a new international US-led strategy for solving not only the intra-Palestinian conflict, but also the Palestinian–Israeli conflict was conceived: the West Bank First strategy. With the new West Bank First strategy, the Quartet and the donor community clearly sided with the secular caretaker government in Ramallah. The underlying assumption behind this strategy is to make the West Bank move in a more positive direction politically and economically. Hence, the disbursal of previously banned aid has been resumed and Israel is paying the Palestinian tax and customs money to the Palestinian caretaker government led by Fayyad. In theory this should lead to a surge in both private and public investment. Ease in restrictions of movement is also part of the assumption. Therefore, more jobs and stability will be created, raising not only living standards but also generating hope for the future – a better one that is. The early impact on the West Bank is felt due to the restoration of foreign aid and tax and customs money from Israel. This at least means that the PA, now controlled by Mahmoud Abbas and the Salam Fayyad government, can pay the civil servants and in that way create some stability. However, the consequences for the Gaza Strip are serious. Gaza is completely sealed off from the outside world, and the prolonged closure has already had disastrous consequences. According to Mohammed Samhouri:

> No exports of any kind have been allowed out of Gaza since Hamas took over in mid-June [2007], and no imported non-humanitarian commercial commodities – from Israel, the West Bank or other countries – have been allowed in.[289]

In the wake of the total closure and the declaration by Israel that Gaza is "an enemy entity" (in mid-September 2007) Gaza's population has become a welfare case. Somewhere between 80 and 90 per cent of the population in Gaza is dependent on external aid in order to survive.

It is therefore evident that the consequences of bypassing the Hamas controlled Gaza Strip have been devastating for the civilian population. It is also evident that for Hamas the political victory in 2006 and its aftermath has been more of a curse than a blessing. The moderate faction has clearly lost ground as they have been unable to create any progress in the circumstances described. The isolation and lack of progress has furthermore created splits in the movement and weakened the moderate wing lead by Ismael Haniyya. Therefore, recent developments have led to a radicalisation of the Islamists, with the armed faction Izz ad-Din al-Qassam setting much of the agenda. The huge increase in poverty as a result of the total closure and lack of resources has furthermore created a situation where Hamas is no longer free from accusations of corruption, as many within the movement tend to first and foremost care about Hamas loyalists. The sheets are no longer as clean as they used to be.

In more general terms the Palestinian population today is dissatisfied with not only Fatah but also Hamas. Palestinian society in both the West Bank and in the Gaza Strip is fragmented and in disarray. The director of

Development Studies at Bir Zeit University, Samia al-Botmeh, described this fragmentation during a personal interview in late 2007:

> We are now a society fragmented by Israeli brutality. Brutality reflects all aspects of society, social, economic, labour market, safety etc. People here do not want to hear about Nablus or hear about Gaza. It is so fragile. We have been dispossessed of all human and economic capabilities. Brutality is a good word to describe the situation…Everybody is in need apart from a small class in Ramallah. The majority is desperate. No prospect of hope. Hope is being brutalised. This is the difference. Before, there was always a hope. It is gone; there is apathy and disrespect for everything.[290]

Hamas is here to stay

Whether one likes it or not Hamas is an integral part of the Palestinian social fabric. Throughout the past three decades the movement has worked patiently on building the structures of civil society. For two decades they have fought against the ongoing Israeli occupation, and they have won the hearts and minds of a large number of Palestinians.

With hopes brutalised and a Palestinian society split in two the prospect for a Palestinian peace offensive along the lines of the Arab Peace Initiative[291] in which the Palestinians can put forward their legitimate rights and claims does no longer exist. Presently, the desperate US-initiated Annapolis track is the order of the day (combined with the collective punishment vis-à-vis the civilian population in Gaza). This will only lead to more radicalisation in the ranks of the Palestinian Islamists, of which most are ready for moderation and pragmatism if only given the chance. Reconciliation is not only a precondition for alleviation of poverty in the Gaza Strip, but also for a possible breakthrough on the political track.

It is time to realise that lasting peace must be inclusive and that there can be no peace without Hamas, which for more than a decade has realised the reality of Israel and hence prepared the Palestinians for the necessity of accepting a two-state solution based on the principles of international law, rather than a solution based upon the current balance of power between occupier and occupied.

APPENDIX

Notes on the Fieldwork
and Methodology

In this appendix I present a brief background of why the selected institutions were chosen. Furthermore I present how I was admitted to the institutions, which back in the late 1990s was something many colleagues doubted would be possible. Finally, I discuss the fieldwork in practice both in the football club as well as at the IUG.

Choosing civil society institutions

The data presented in this book were collected through extensive fieldwork in the Gaza Strip during the late 1990s. I decided at an early point to conduct my fieldwork within civil society institutions of prime importance to the Islamists. By choosing an institutional approach I was given the opportunity to deal both with the leadership level and the level of grass-roots sympathisers as can be seen from the preceding pages. Fieldwork was conducted in *Nâdi al-Jam'iyya al-Islâmiyya* as well as on the Islamic University in Gaza (IUG).

My choice of these particular institutions was motivated in general by the idea that, through studying them, I would be able to sound out the extent to which the Islamist movement has made an impact on the socio-political arena, and to gain insight into the reasons that sympathisers give for their involvement in the movement. My aim was thus to cast light on Islamist activities in various spheres in which the Islamists are engaged in creating *sound Muslims*.

One reason for choosing a sports club, moreover, was that sport is extremely popular in the Middle East. If football was not already the most popular sport in the area before 1982, it certainly became so after Algeria's sensational 2–1 victory over former West Germany during the World Cup in

Spain. It is clear that the dramatic rise in the number of satellite dishes, even in the Palestinian refugee camp in the Gaza Strip, and the growing number of international sports channels on television, have helped whet the appetite for soccer among Palestinian youth.

At the same time I chose to examine the Islamic University (IUG) because over recent decades it has been the arena for an internal Palestinian power struggle between nationalists and Islamists, and because throughout the six-year uprising, *al-Intifada*, of 1987–93, the university was at the forefront of resistance in the Gaza Strip against the Israeli occupation. Moreover, IUG is interesting in the sense that Islamists form the overwhelming majority among both faculty and students. The institution has been seen in the scholarly literature as one of the most important bastions of Islamism, and is also recognized as being academically the better of the two universities in the Gaza Strip, which is the reason many of its students give for studying there. Education offers one of the few opportunities for social mobility in Palestinian society.

The two institutions selected are primarily used by young Palestinians, who because of the demographic structure of the Gaza Strip represent one of the most interesting groups in society. In the early 1990s people under the age of 24 constituted no less than 70 per cent of the population of the Gaza Strip.[292] Finally it is worth noting that neither of these institutions has previously been studied in detail.

Admission to the field

During my first short period of fieldwork, carried out between 5 December 1996 and 25 January 1997, I set out in the first instance to contact a number of secular scholars, journalists and officials in the Gaza Strip and on the West Bank to seek information from them on the political situation at the time and to discuss the Islamists' involvement in civil society. Around mid-December I then made contact with one of the most crucial gatekeepers in relation to my project, namely Sheikh Ahmad Bahr, head of *al-Jam'iyya al-Islâmiyya*. The Islamist sports club that I had selected constitutes a central part of *al-Jam'iyya al-Islâmiyya's* activities. Through my discussions with informants outside the Islamist milieu I had moreover discovered that around the time of my fieldwork *al-Jam'iyya al-Islâmiyya* was also the largest of the Islamist NGOs. The meeting with Sheikh Bahr was a success in the sense that he promised to help me gather information on the institution's activities, and also invited me to a get-together a few days later where I would have the opportunity to meet some of the young men who used the club.

The *al-Jam'iyya al-Islâmiyya* meeting four days later in the Rashad Shawwa Cultural Centre in the centre of Gaza City led to an encounter with another vital gatekeeper, namely the administrative head of the sports department, Saad. Later, Saad introduced me to *Jam'iyya*'s activities and, even more important, to the players, trainers and other key people associated with *Nâdi al-Jam'iyya al-Islâmiyya*'s football team. Thus, within a mere two weeks I had secured permission to carry out fieldwork in an Islamic football club.

Immediately afterwards I began to work on the possibility of conducting another part of my fieldwork at the Islamic University in Gaza. The university is often referred to in the literature as the most important Islamist-controlled institution in Gaza.[293] My first official meeting at IUG was with the Professor and head of the university's English Department, Walid Amr. The latter was extremely obliging, and in the course of the interview promised that I could enrol as a student at IUG during my forthcoming long-term fieldwork. This meeting with the English Professor led me to consider a new idea. Originally I had planned to enrol on one of the university's *islamicum* courses, which are obligatory for all students regardless of their main subject. But instead I decided to carry out my fieldwork at the university's English Department. Since IUG is an Islamic educational institution, in which all subjects are supposed to be studied from an Islamic perspective, the English courses would presumably take an Islamist approach as well. And since Islamists regard Islam as an all-embracing system and a vital point of reference in all contexts, it would be interesting to see how the postulated connection between Islam and English literature would be expressed.

During this first, relatively short period of fieldwork moreover I began conducting my first semi-structured, qualitative interviews (as well as a number of informal conversations), both with various of the football players on *al-Jam'iyya al-Islâmiyya*'s team, and with students at both al-Azhar University and the Islamic University in Gaza (IUG). One of the students whom I got to know at IUG also subsequently became my interpreter.

This first visit to the Gaza Strip thus ensured that the project could be carried out. In addition it enabled me to gain access to my two cases.

On 15 January 1998 I set off once again to the Gaza Strip, together with my family (my partner and two children, then respectively five years and three months old) for a six-month period of fieldwork. Whereas on my first visit the previous year I had stayed in the Sheikh Radwan district,[294] an ordinary neighbourhood in the northern outskirts of Gaza City, on this occasion we settled in one of the city's finest districts, close to the late President Arafat's residence and the headquarters of Force 17 at *Ansâr*. We had a view over the Mediterranean and our landlord came from one of the traditional large land-owning families in the Gaza Strip. I had had some misgivings about this posh address, but it turned out to have a very positive effect. Rather than living among the people I was studying in an area seldom visited by foreigners, we now enjoyed a standard of accommodation that the people around us evidently considered appropriate for us.

Since I had already established contact with some of the people who formed the object of my fieldwork, my return to the Gaza Strip was easier than expected. On 21 January 1998 I contacted my new gatekeeper at IUG, Walid Amr, and officially applied for permission to enrol for a semester at IUG's English Department. I received an affirmative answer three days later. The semester began on 29 February, as did my fieldwork. At the same time I sought permission to take specific courses from the relevant lecturer, Mr Muhammad, whose response was friendly, though he explained that many of the students would probably be wary of me, since they would be bound to take me for an Israeli agent. I opted to join the fourth (and penultimate) year of the course.

As mentioned above, I had also already established contact with *Nâdi al-Jam'iyya al-Islâmiyya*. As an extra precaution I decided to get in touch again with the head of *al-Jam'iyya al-Islâmiyya*, Ahmad Bahr, who confirmed his permission to carry out the planned fieldwork in the club.

The fieldwork in practice

It is important to note that there were methodological differences in my approach to the two different levels involved. At the leadership level[295] I conducted only qualitative interviews, whereas at the sympathiser/grass-roots level I combined participant observation with semi-structured qualitative interviews. The advantage of combining participant observation and qualitative interviews is that participant observation by itself does not provide any opportunity to arrive at a greater understanding of others' actions. The same can be said of the interviews. The two methods combined complement one another in the sense that the interview is aimed primarily at discovering how a given subject is articulated, whereas participant observation is able to tell us something about actual social practice.

I started each interview by explaining the aims of the project clearly to the interviewee. Thus, all those interviewed were aware of why I was in the Gaza Strip and what the purpose of the project was. I also explained why this type of research was important.

Since my study is based on several settings and two different levels –

respectively the level of the leaders and that of grass-roots sympathisers – I aim in what follows to explain my method of collecting data in these various contexts.

The Islamic football club: *Nâdi al-Jam'iyya al-Islâmiyya*

My fieldwork in *Nâdi al-Jam'iyya al-Islâmiyya* took place over two periods, partly in December 1996–January 1997, when I conducted the first qualitative interviews with both leaders and players, and partly in the period February–July 1998. During the first period I was not part of the club. I usually sat on the sidelines with my gatekeeper, Saad. In spring and summer 1998 on the other hand I was a player on the team. I went to training sessions with the rest of the players twice a week for roughly 2–3 hours. In addition I watched a number of the club's weekend matches against other teams. I did not play in these matches myself. My main reasons for choosing to carry out fieldwork are explained above, but it is worth mentioning that I am also a former amateur football player and still take an interest in the game. This meant that my interviewees and I had a common point of reference in advance: namely, the pleasure of playing football. I must admit that it was hard work doing my fieldwork in the club, especially physically: in the course of the six months I lost around 10 kilos. Most of the club's players were between 17 and 25 years old, while in 1998 I was 34. The young men were in top condition and highly motivated, so it took a couple of months before I was able to take part in the training at the same high tempo as the rest. I saw this as a definite advantage as far as winning the trust of my new fellow players was concerned. It was I who had to struggle.

It is evident from my field notes that I was given a warm welcome. The young men greeted me cordially and many were naturally curious. Nevertheless I was often left with the feeling that many of them were still distrustful of my presence in the club. Moreover, I had come as a privileged westerner who in their eyes was materially very well off. Against this background it was a great advantage to me that I was not exceptionally good at football as well. Here was a field that belonged to them, and where they had something to teach me.

When the field is found and the various gatekeepers passed, the next question is: who should be interviewed? As mentioned above I began by interviewing the leader of *al-Jam'iyya al-Islâmiyya*, Ahmad Bahr. Thus I embarked from the leadership level in order to gain access to the field. In addition I carried out a number of qualitative interviews with another central gatekeeper in the institution, Saad. Saad, the administrative leader of the sports department, is a former member of the student council at the Islamic University, where he represented *al-Kutla al-Islâmiyya*. In addition I interviewed Ismael Haniyya, the manager of *Nâdi al-Jam'iyya al-Islâmiyya*. Haniyya is also a high-profile member of Hamas who usually chairs mass meetings of the movement and eventually became Prime Minister in the wake of the January 2006 elections.[296] He is also a former leader of the student council of IUG, where he earned a BA in *sharî'a* (Islamic law). Until early summer 1999 Haniyya was employed in the administration of IUG. Since Hamas' electoral victory in January 2006 he has been the Palestinian Prime Minister. Finally I conducted an interview with Abu Uthman, who is a member of the administration of *Jam'iyya's* sports department. On numerous occasions I attempted to secure an interview with the club's trainer, but despite repeatedly expressing his consent, he never turned up to our meetings.

In the club I also carried out a number of qualitative interviews with the players.[297] In all I conducted eight semi-structured interviews with club players and two interviews with former players who had switched to secular clubs. I interviewed some of the players several times. In addition I had a great many informal conversations with most of the other team members. The club had some 20–25 players altogether. The members ranged widely in age, the youngest being 17 and the eldest 38. The majority, however, were between 17 and 25 years old. Almost all of them came from the Shati camp or the Sheikh Radwan neighbourhood near the camp. As far as I know, all of these were registered UNRWA refugees. A few of the players however came from other parts of Gaza City, such as al-Sabra and Shajaiyyah. Still others came from Khan Younis or Nuseirat in the southern part of the Gaza Strip. The players differed a good deal in terms of education. In my selection of the interviewees I aimed to include players of different ages, from different parts of Gaza and with varying occupations. In addition, I bore in mind the respective players' position in the club, aiming to interview both more and less dominant players.[298]

The Islamic University in Gaza

With the permission of the university administration I began my fieldwork at the Islamic University in the Gaza Strip at the end of February 1998. As mentioned above, I was enrolled at the English Department, and followed courses in "Literary Appreciation" and "American Literature in the 20th Century". During my fieldwork, which continued until June, I was on campus 4–5 days a week. There were approximately twenty students in the class, all of who were in the penultimate year of their BA course. In addition to attending classes I also usually ate lunch or had tea with the students in the university canteen, which helped build confidence.

At leadership level I conducted interviews with, among others, the university's Public Relations Director, Ahmad Sa'ati, and the above-mentioned Walid Amr, who is Head of the English Department. In addition I interviewed Muhammad Hassan Shamma', who is a member of *majlis al-umanâ'*, the university's administrative organ. Shamma' is also *nâ'ib al-ra'îs* (Vice-President) of *al-Mujamma' al-Islâmî* and was one of the founders of Hamas in December 1987. I also carried out a couple of interviews with both former and present employees at the university. In addition I had a number of informal conversations with several other members of the university administration.

Among the approximately 20 students in my class I conducted eight semistructured qualitative interviews. I chose the interviewees on criteria similar to those applied in the football club: i.e. according to age and place of residence. However, the most important criterion was the individual's position within the group. Thus, in order to get a fuller picture I interviewed both the most academically and socially dominant members of the class and the more anonymous students. In addition to the more structured interviews I had a great many informal conversations with virtually all the students in the class. All of them were curious and eager to have contact with me, but at the same time they were suspicious. Who was I? An Israeli spy? An agent from another country? Why had I suddenly turned up in their midst? I am convinced that virtually all the students initially assumed that I was an Israeli agent. I was prepared for this suspicion, having previously spent some time in the occupied territories and having also read a number of reports concerning the widespread use of spies. My strategy in countering the students' mistrust was to state my intentions as honestly as possible. Thus I discussed my project openly with the students and explained the purpose of it to them. I also took part in endless discussions with them concerning the peace process, the role of Islam in Palestinian society, the role of women, the Western view of Islam, and what it means to be a good Muslim. Through these constant discussions a relationship of trust was established. It was also a help that the first people I interviewed reported positively on the experience to their fellow students. This inclined the other students to agree to be interviewed. This leads me to conclude that participant observation not only gave me insight into social practice, but was also of key significance in creating the necessary degree of trust. Another factor that contributed to building trust, not only among the students but also among the football players and other Islamists, was that I was not alone. With me in the field were my partner and two children. In addition, the fact that we remained in the Gaza Strip throughout the six months meant that they always knew where we were, which helped foster their confidence.

It should be added that during classes I almost stenographically recorded everything that was said, so that I have detailed notes from each class. Naturally I have also drawn on these notes in my material presented above.

NOTES

1 Quoted from *Haaretz,* 4 December 2001, internet edition.
2 Essay by the author in the Danish daily *Politiken,* August 2003.
3 *Journal of Palestine Studies,* vol. XXVII, no. 2, Winter 1998, p.158.
4 There has been a tendency in the media to depict Islamism generally, and Hamas in particular, as menacing, terroristic, irrational and so on. An article in the Danish daily newspaper *Information,* written by the paper's then correspondent in the Middle East, Lisbeth Davidsen, on 2 October 1997, stated: "The wholesome description [of Ahmad Yasin] is ill suited to the uncontested spiritual leader of one of the *most rabid fundamentalist movements in the world,* Hamas ... The movement opposes the state of Israel and PLO leader Yasser Arafat's policy of reconciliation with Israel by *any* means available. Its aims are *to kill the Jews* and create a Palestinian state from the Mediterranean to the River Jordan" (my italics). This example is only one of many that have contributed to the demonisation of the movement in the public eye. It offers a remarkable illustration of the public's view and understanding – or rather, lack of understanding – of the movement.
5 Robinson, 1997.
6 Roald, 1994, p. 13.
7 A number of academics have divided the various Islamist political groups into a number of different categories. See for example Dekmejian, 1995, 5–11. See also Mousalli, 1995.
8 See, for example, Krämer 1993, 1994 and 1995. Also Nomani & Rahnema, 1994, Stenberg, 1996 and Vogt & Heger, 2002.
9 There is by no means a consensus on the view that Hamas can be regarded as a moderate movement, and it may seem surprising that I categorise it as such, notwithstanding its militant opposition towards Israel's continued occupation of the West Bank and the Gaza Strip. This categorisation depends on what yardstick you use. My judgement is based on the Islamists' own attitude and relationship to their rivals, and particularly towards the Palestinian Authority – thus I embark from the point of view of internal politics.
10 Norton, 1995, p. 7. It should be noted, however, that not all researchers take the view that Islamist movements constitute a part of civil society. My argu-

ment for treating Islamic institutions as part of civil society is based on the consideration that moderate Islamists display a certain form of tolerance: i.e. despite the fact that there is only one truth, there are several ways of reaching it (pluralism). It is also worth noting, as both Krämer, 1992 and Mousalli, 1995, have done, that the milieu in which Islamists operate is neither tolerant nor democratic, which also applies to the Palestinian context. A fundamental thesis is that the moderate wing of Islamism will be strengthened at the cost of the more radical parts of the movement in so far as they are included in civil society and the political process. Were this to happen, moderate Islamists would become more pragmatic and oriented towards *realpolitik* as opposed to big – unattainable – ideals. The development of Hizballah in Lebanon in the 1990s tends to confirm the validity of this thesis. Norton, 1997. The same goes moreover for Islamists in, for example, Jordan and Kuwait. See Norton, 1995a.

11 Sahliyeh, 1995, p. 142.

12 Lewitt, 2004.

13 In recent years however a few individual studies within the field have focused on the way in which Islamists operate in a concrete historic context. See Sullivan, 1994, Clark, 1995 & 2004 and Wiktorowicz 2004. These authors have examined this question in the context of Egypt, Jordan and Yemen. Their accounts may be taken as a further contribution to research within this special area of Islamist studies.

14 Norton, 1995a, p.8.

15 When researchers such as the above-cited Sahliyeh, 1995, use the term indoctrination, they do not define it. There is no doubt, however, that the term is pejorative. I define indoctrination here as: "inculcating particular opinions and attitudes in other people". The concept covers not only the content of what is inculcated – in this instance a politico-religious message – but also the method: persuasion, violence and group pressure. Indoctrination is considered synonymous with deliberately one-sided influence, the assumption being that it is important to oppose this. The process of influencing people that is carried out in connection with indoctrination has, or at least can have, great social significance, because it can have a crucial effect on people's ways of acting and thinking. The concept is closely related to other negatively-laden concepts such as propaganda and brainwashing. Hegemonic state powers, it is worth noting, often argue that rival political ideologies make use of indoctrination, while using positively-laden terms such as enlightenment, information or education to describe their own efforts to influence the population's ways of acting and thinking. *Leksikon fra det 21. århundrede* (Encyclopaedia for the 21st Century), www.leksikon.org.

16 Outside academia, the Islamist part of civil society in Palestine is described in the prevailing Western political discourse not as a part of civil society, but as the "terrorist infrastructure". It is this "terrorist infrastructure" that the then leader Arafat and the Palestinian Authority pledged to clamp down on, among

other things through the Hebron Protocol (January 1997) and the Wye River Memorandum (September 1998).

17 For a more elaborate discussion of the reasons behind the selection of these institutions and the way the fieldwork was conducted please see Appendix A. Notes on fieldwork and methodology.

18 Since the purpose of this chapter is to provide an analytical summary that will serve to contextualise the empirical presentation that follows, its structure closely resembles that used in most of the already-existing literature. This applies particularly to the first part of the account. Events after the 2006 victory are discussed in the conclusion.

19 See Mitchell, 1969 and Lia, 1998 on the background to and development of the movement in the first decades.

20 According to Thomas Mayer, 1982, p. 103, the first branch was established in Jerusalem in October 1945. The following year further branches were set up in several other places, including Jaffa, Lydda, Haifa and Nablus. See Cohen, 1982, pp. 144–5.

21 Mayer, 1982, p. 103.

22 In the event, there were never that many "brothers" in Palestine. According to Ziad Abu Amr only around 500 participated in the war. Abu Amr, 1994, p. 2. See also al-Awaisi, 1998. However, according to Ilan Pappe of the 10,000 Egyptian troops, participating in the war almost 50 per cent were Muslim Brotherhood volunteers. Pappe, 2006, p. 128.

23 Mayaer, 1982, pp 110–11.

24 Abu Amr, 1994, p. 4.

25 Ibid. p. 5

26 Ibid. p. 6.

27 See Mitchell, 1969, for an overview of relations between the Muslim Brotherhood, the Farouk regime and the Free Officers, who took power through a coup d'état in 1952.

28 Abu Amr, 1994, p.7. See also Mitchell, 1969, pp 105 ff.

29 In 1956 Britain, France and Israel initiated the so-called Tripartite Invasion of Egypt. The reason for the direct involvement of the British and French in the Middle East conflict was that, immediately prior to this, Egypt's President Nasser had nationalised the Suez Canal, in which both Britain and France had strong financial interests. As a result of the attack the Gaza Strip was occupied by the state of Israel. The Israelis withdrew under pressure a year later. See, for example, Yapp 1991, p. 402ff.

30 Abu Amr, 1994, p. 10.

31 See for example Cobban, 1984. See also Sayiegh, 1997.

32 On the Islamist movements in Egypt, see for example Kepel, 1985.

33 Ibid. p. 45.

34 Khalil Quqa resides in the Gulf and has no formal ties with Hamas. Other prominent Islamists from the Gaza Strip to be deported in 1991 were Imad

Alami, Mustafa Qanu'a, Moustafa Liddawi and Fadl Zahhar. All four occupy key posts in Hamas' leadership in exile. Interview with a former high-ranking member of Hamas and subsequently *Hizb al-Khalas al-Watani al-Islâmi*, who wishes to remain anonymous, Gaza City, April, 1998. The person in question was interviewed in his home in Gaza on 30 June 1998.

35 See UNSCO, 1997. The Islamist NGOs are discussed in more detail in Chapter 4.

36 I will return to the circumstances surrounding the establishment of the IUG in Chapter 5.

37 By 1982 the Brotherhood had founded *al-mujahidun al-filastîniyûn* as the movement's military wing, but it was not very active. Legrain, 1994b, p. 420.

38 PFLP, 1992, p.14.

39 Cohen, 1980. Not surprisingly the Islamists themselves give a different account of the attack on the Red Crescent in 1980. According to a former high-ranking member of Hamas, who wishes to remain anonymous, this is what happened: "At that point, i.e. in 1980, the Communists controlled all information in Palestine, and this was also the period when the Islamists were beginning to attract attention. The Communists also controlled many syndicates, but the Islamists started participating in the elections to these. The Communists sought to prevent the Islamists from turning up, and the PLO helped them in this. Accusations were hurled from both sides, and there were demonstrations that developed into fights. The Red Crescent's offices were burned down, but no one knows who was behind this. Most likely the people responsible were working as spies for Israel." Interview conducted in Gaza City, 30 June 1998.

40 Lesch and Tesller, 1987, p. 238.

41 This development, incidentally, was typical of what happened in most of the Arab states. In Egypt, for example, several groupings similarly rejected the moderate policies of the Muslim Brotherhood in the 1970s. Many of these groups were strongly inspired by the Islamic revolution in Iran.

42 It is worth noting that Islamic Jihad in Palestine is divided into two fractions – Shaqaqi and Tamimi. See Legrain, 1994b, p. 419. For a thorough and reliable account of Islamic Jihad in Egypt, see Jansen, 1986. The Muslim Brotherhood's radical ideologue, Sayyid Qutb, in particular, has inspired Islamic Jihad and other similar revolutionary Islamist groups that seek to islamise society from above. See for example Qutb, 1978.

43 See Legrain, 1991b.

44 Among those present at this meeting, apart from Sheikh Ahmad Yasin, were Ibrahim al-Yazuri, Abd al-Aziz Rantisi, Abd al-Fattah Dukkhan, Hasan Shamma, Salah Shahada and Isa al-Nashshar. Legrain, 1991c, p. 15a.

45 Legrain, 1991c, p.50c.

46 Hamas means "eagerness" or "enthusiasm".

47 Legrain, 1994b, p. 420.

48 For an account of the Hamas movement's ideology, see for example Nüsse, 1998, Jensen & Laursen, 2000, and Hamas, 1988. The Hamas charter has been translated into both French and English. For the English translation, see Hamas, 1993. The French translation can be found in Legrain, 1991.

49 See for example Hawes, 1991.

50 The Madrid Conference arose in the wake of the 1991 Gulf War. It represented part of the United States' strategy to initiate a new world order. Despite reluctance to link Iraq's invasion of Kuwait with Israel's occupation of the West Bank and the Gaza Strip, the United States (together with the much weakened USSR) invited all the parties to the Arab–Israeli conflict to a peace conference. The PLO was not directly represented, but prominent figures from the West Bank and Gaza Strip, all of whom were approved by Israel (Haidar Abdel Shafi, Saeb Eraqat, Hannan Ashrawi et al.), represented Palestinian interests and formed a separate unit within the Jordanian negotiating team.

51 See Hamas, 1988.

52 The premises for the negotiations in Madrid and the follow-up in Washington were in clear violation of the preconditions hitherto set by the PLO for negotiating with Israel. For a discussion of the premises, see for example Jensen & Laursen, 2000, Chapter 1.

53 Nüsse, 1998, p.129.

54 Ibid.

55 Hamas, 1988, Article 13.

56 According to a former high-ranking member of Hamas, the Muslim Brotherhood acquired its first modern martyrs in the Gaza Strip in 1982, and the Brotherhood made moves thereafter to establish a military wing. However, it was not until Sheikh Ahmad Yasin's release from an Israeli jail in 1985 that this finally came into being. Al-Majd (Munazzama al-Jihâd wal Da'wa) was established in 1985. Its task was to identify spies, monitor the IDF (Israeli Defence Forces) and draw up lists of people to be liquidated. It was not Al-Majd's job to carry out the killings. Another wing of the organisation was set up for this purpose, namely al-Mujahidûn al-Filastîniûn. This wing was active from 1985 to 1989. It was not until 1990 that preparations were made to establish Kata'ib Izz ad-din al-Qassam, whose focus gradually shifted more and more from targeting spies and collaborators to directly combating the Israeli occupying forces. Izz ad-Din was created around 1992. Hamas' armed wing incidentally took its name from the Syrian-born Sheikh Izz ad-Din al-Qassam, who backed the first armed uprising against Zionism and British imperialism in Palestine in the mid-1930s. Interview with a former high-ranking member of Hamas in his home in Gaza City, 30 June 1998.

57 Personal interview with Ibrahim Ghawsha, Amman, 1 July 1999. Ibrahim Ghawsha and several other leading members of Hamas' political bureau in Jordan were incidentally deported from Jordan in autumn 1999, despite having Jordanian citizenship. After just over two years in Qatar Ghawsha returned

to Jordan in summer 2001. He was permitted to stay in Jordan on condition that he ceases his activities for Hamas.

58 The Likud leader, Yitzhak Shamir, who led the negotiations in the first phase, has subsequently said that the aim on the Israeli side was to drag out the negotiations as long as possible and at the same time to create as many "facts on the ground" as they could, so that there was no longer anything to negotiate about.

59 Thus Oslo I was not a result of the negotiations introduced in Madrid. The agreement on the contrary was negotiated by representatives of the PLO, first and foremost Abu Ala (Ahmad Qurai). Oslo I involved recognition on the part of the PLO of Israel's right to exist in peace and security, while Israel for its part recognised the PLO as the legitimate representative of the Palestinian people. According to the wording of the declaration of principles, "The aim of the Israeli–Palestinian negotiations within the current Middle East peace process is, among other things, to establish a Palestinian Interim Self-Government Authority, the elected Council (the "Council"), for the Palestinian people in the West Bank and the Gaza Strip, for a transitional period not exceeding five years, leading to a permanent settlement based on Security Council Resolutions 242 and 338." Cited from DoP, 1993.

The difficult questions concerning the right of refugees to return, the future of the settlers, the future of Jerusalem and the final settlement of borders were postponed and were to be discussed only two years after the agreement had been entered into. The background for the signing of the Oslo I agreement was that both Israel and the PLO had begun to regard the radicals on both sides, respectively Hamas and the Israeli right wing, as a threat to the possibility of creating a more peaceful Middle East. It was thus a coincidence of interests that brought the two parties together. It should be added, however, that another important reason why Yasir Arafat and the PLO chose to sign Oslo I was that after the Gulf War of 1990–1, in which the PLO had indirectly supported Saddam Hussein, the organisation found itself isolated both in the West and in most of the Arab world, with the result that it was now on the brink of economic ruin. The signing of Oslo I represented a political and economic comeback for the PLO – but on Israel's terms. See also Jensen & Laursen, 2000.

60 The reason that Hamas was able to issue its criticism of Oslo I before the signing of the actual agreement was that the content of the agreement had been publicised in the press at the end of August 1993.

61 Hamas leaflet No. 102, issued 5 September 1993 in the occupied Palestinian territories.

62 Shortly after the signing of the Gaza–Jericho agreement in May 1994 parts of the Palestinian army in exile, the Palestinian Liberation Army (PLA), returned to the territories under Palestinian control. They had hitherto been located in Algeria, Egypt, Iraq, Sudan, Jordan and Yemen. They were to form the kernel of the new Palestinian police force, a force that has been one of the most marked features of the Palestinian authority in recent years. The Oslo I agree-

ment states: "In order to guarantee public order and internal security for the Palestinians of the West Bank and the Gaza Strip, the Council will establish a strong police force" (DoP, 1993). In connection with the signing of Oslo II in September 1995 the point concerning the Palestinian police force was dealt with in some detail. The tasks assigned to the police included countering terrorism and violence and preventing incitements to violence, as well as carrying out other policing functions. The police force was therefore supposed (among other things) to ensure Israel's security. Oslo II also states that the size of the police force, under the agreement, should not exceed 30,000 people. Of these 30,000 police a maximum of 12,000 could be recruited from the Palestinian Diaspora, or in other words from the Palestinian Liberation Army. In the summer of 1998 around 40,000 men were employed in the police force, which – entirely in accordance with Oslo II – also included an extensive and effective security apparatus.

63 FBIS, 7 September 1993.

64 Ibid.

65 Interview with Abdel Aziz Rantisi at his home in Khan Younis, 17 February 1998.

66 Interview with Ghazi Hamad, conducted in Gaza City on 19 February 1998.

67 Hebron Protocol, 1997, see http://www.usembassy-israel.org.il/publish/peace/ note_ record.htm

68 See the Wye River Memorandum, particularly the section on security. Hamas regards the Authority's commitment to the Wye River Memorandum as merely a continuation of their previous policy. Interview with Ismael Abu Shanab, conducted in Gaza City, 5 July 1999.

69 The same went for the liquidation – also carried out by Mossad – of Fathi Shaqaqi, leader of Islamic Jihad, who was assassinated in Malta in autumn 1995.

70 On 24 February 1994 the Israeli soldier and settler Baruch Goldstein ran amok in the Ibrahim Mosque in Hebron. During prayers in the month of Ramadan he shot and killed 29 praying Muslims. It was after this massacre that Hamas began to use suicide attacks and to increasingly regard civil Israelis as legitimate targets.

71 Kristiansen, 1999, pp. 29–30.

72 Sharm al-Sheikh declaration, 13 March 1996. Cited in the *Journal of Palestine Studies*, No. 4, 1996, p. 137ff.

73 A press release from the secular Palestinian Centre for Human Rights in Gaza (PCHR) on 28 September 1997 announced the Centre's indignation over the closures of Palestinian welfare organisations in the Gaza Strip. The PCHR referred to these as "draconian measures" and argued that the closure of the institutions was a direct result of the pressure put on the Palestinian Authority by Israel and the US government, which had demanded "the break-up of the so-called Islamic 'infrastructure'". PCHR furthermore argued that these measures violated human rights, reduced the hope of Palestinian democracy and destroyed Palestinian civil society and the "rule of law".

74 In the aftermath of the international anti-terrorism campaign that followed the 11 September terror attacks on the USA, Arafat likewise re-closed a great many of the Islamic NGOs operating within the territories controlled by the Palestinian Authority. This applied for example to *al-Jam'iyya al-Islamîyya* – including the sports club examined in this book. *(Information,* 21.02.2002)

75 PCHR, 1995; see Articles 5, 7 and 20. The draft included, among other things, a demand that NGOs should seek a license from the Minister of Social Affairs. The latter would consult the Minister of Internal Affairs before taking a decision as to whether to issue the license. If the applicant NGO worked within a different area from that governed by the Minister of Social Affairs, e.g. within the field of health, approval from the relevant ministry (e.g. the Ministry of Health) should also be obtained. Without the approval of the Minister of Social Affairs, moreover, NGOs were not allowed to receive donations from areas outside the Authority's jurisdiction.

76 Sullivan, 1996, p. 98.

77 Ibid. pp. 93–100.

78 Palestine Report 6, December 1996.

79 For a more detailed account of the circumstances surrounding the passing of this legislation, see Jensen & Laursen, 2000.

80 Ibid. See also Iyad Sarraj's article "The battle goes on", www.gemhp.net/eyad/thebattle goeson, in which Sarraj wrote that a battle appeared to have broken out, and that the Authority had apparently decided to ruin civil society. Many see this article as the reason why Iyad Sarraj was again summoned for questioning by the Palestinian police on 5 August 1999; see Palestinian Centre for Human Rights, Press Release, 5 and 7 August 1999.

81 Interview with Sheikh Ahmad Bahr at his home in Sheikh Radwan in Gaza, 16 April 1998.

82 *Al-Risâla,* 4 December 1997. The reason that the newspaper did not discuss the closures until several months after they had taken place was that by August 1997 the Authority had temporarily closed the newspaper as well. However, *Al-Risâla* was permitted to re-open in December that year.

83 Interview with Sheikh Ahmad Bahr, 16 April 1998, Sheikh Radwan, Gaza.

84 Ibid.

85 The first of these institutions was closed by Shimon Peres in early 1996, while the two others were closed down in December 1996 *(Jerusalem Post,* 10 December 1996). According to Imad Falouji, a former editor of the Hamas weekly *al-Watan,* who in 1996 was expelled from Hamas because of standing independently in the Palestinian elections, 50 per cent of the funding to the Islamist NGOs in the occupied territories comes from Israel, 25 per cent comes from the Gulf states, 15 per cent from Palestinians in the occupied territories and only about 10 per cent from the West *(New York Times,* 16 August 1995). Falouji, who served for a number of years as Minister of Telecommunications,

claims that he was responsible for fundraising at the time of this interview with the *New York Times*.

86 *Haaretz*, 21 May 1997.

87 U.S. News, 7 August 1996, "Who funds Hamas? A helping hand from Saudi Arabia", http://www.usnews.com/ usnews/ issue/8saudb.htm

88 Ibid.

89 Ibid.

90 *The Times* (London), 3 September 1996, "Charity cash helps Hamas suicide bombers", http://www.nando.net/newsroom/nt/309charity.html

91 This was part of the USA's so-called anti-terror package. Great Britain has also since then introduced anti-terrorist legislation. This was passed in 2000 without attracting any great attention. On the consequences of the legislation, see Ghada Karmis's comments, "We're all terrorists now" in *Middle East International*, no. 646, 23 March 2001. Post 11 September anti-terror laws became part of the new agenda in all western countries.

92 *Journal of Palestine Studies*, No.3, 1995, p. 153.

93 See for example the Danish daily *Politiken*, 6 February 1993.

94 *Washington Post*, 31 August 1998. The Islamic Association of Palestine (IAP) has also been accused by Israel of supporting Hamas, and several members of the IAP have been questioned by the FBI.

95 *Haaretz*, 4 December 2001, internet edition.

96 See for example Schmidt, 1998, pp. 47–8.

97 Interview with Ismael Abu Shanab in Gaza, 12 April 1998.

98 Personal interview with Ghazi Hamad, Gaza City, 19 February 1998.

99 *Journal of Palestine Studies*, 1998, No.2, p.153.

100 Interview with Ismael Abu Shanab in Gaza City, 12 April 1998.

101 For a brief résumé of the key UN resolutions in this area, see the introduction to Jensen, 2001.

102 Interview with Mahmoud Zahhar in Gaza City, 5 July 1999.

103 Interview with Ismael Abu Shanab, Gaza City, 5 July 1999.

104 See Usher, 2005a.

105 *Tanzim* originated in the period before the first Intifada (1987–1993), and was established on the initiative of Khalil al-Wazir (Abu Jihad). During the first Intifada, *Tanzim* consisted of local Fatah leaders and played a central role in the Intifada. See Usher, 2000. Tanzim was also responsible for a number of suicide attacks against Israeli civilians in Israel itself. Tanzim's leader, Marvan Barghouti, was arrested by the IDF (Israeli Defence Forces) in April 2002.

106 See article by Graham Usher in the Danish daily *Information*, 23 August 2001.

107 See Strindberg & Wärn, 2005.

108 Ibid.

109 As early as 23 September 2001, the US Department of State published a "terror list" including 27 organisations and individuals under "executive order" 13224, which freezes assets belonging to terrorist organisations and individuals

connected with these. New names have been added to the list several times, and in connection with the 3rd revised edition of 2 November 2001 Hamas was included together with other Palestinian organisations such as Islamic Jihad, the PFLP, the PFLP-GC, and the PLF (Palestinian Liberation Front). Some of the Muslim NGOs in the US have been added to the list, including the Holy Land Foundation, which raises funds for Palestinian social institutions affiliated with Hamas. See US State Department, www.state.gov/s/ rls/fs/2001/6531.htm. See also *Ha'aretz* 4 December 2001 for a discussion of the freezing of e.g. the funds of the Holy Land Foundation. See also *De Europæiske Fællesskabers tidende* L 344/93, 28 December 2001 (in Danish).

110 Interview with EU officials, September 2006 in Copenhagen.

111 International Crises Group, 2003, p. 16.

123 International Crises Group, 2003, p. 17.

113 See International Crises Group, 2003, p. 14. The poverty line is defined as $ 2.1 per capita per day. See UNSCO, 2001, 12: "The Impact on the Palestinian Economy of Confrontations, Mobility Restrictions and Border Closures 1.10.00–31.01.01". Besides, it is evident from the UNSCO report that the demand for food and cash is increasing and that demand far exceeds supply. Naturally, this situation has become worse since the closing of Islamic institutions, such as *Jam'iyya Islamiyya*, in December 2001. Things have developed even worse after Hamas' victory in the elections January 2006. According to the World Food Programme (WFP) poverty in 2006/07 affects 46 per cent of the population on the West Bank and 80 per cent in the Gaza Strip. 34 per cent of the Palestinians suffer from food insecurity. See www.wfp.org.

114 Interview with Mahmoud Zahhar published in the Danish daily *Information*, 21 January 2002.

115 Nepp, 2004.

116 Report in the Israeli newspaper *Ha'aretz* 22 January 2003. Wolfowitz' statements were harshly criticised by pro-Israeli lobbyists. See for example the swift reaction of the Zionist Organisation of America (http://www.zoa.org/press-rel/20030123a.htm). At the Azores summit shortly before the beginning of the US-led war on Iraq, close links were made in official statements between the war and the Palestine question. It was understood that the so-called "Road Map" should be made public in the wake of the war. As the then Spanish Prime Minister Aznar declared at a common press conference after the Azores summit: "We've agreed on launching, on boosting the Middle East peace process, and on our vision that that peace process has to culminate with all necessary security guarantees and putting an end to terrorism. And this should end with the peaceful coexistence of two states, an independent Palestinian state and the Israeli state." See http://www.chron.com/cs/CDA/ story.hts/side/1821063.

117 See for example the statements made by the Danish Prime Minister, Anders Fogh Rasmussen, on 18 March 2003: "The government emphasises in its support for the United States that Bush has declared his clear support for a Road

Map leading to a solution to the conflict between Israel and the Palestinians. Without such a solution peace and calm will never prevail in the Middle East." http://www.stm.dk/Index/dokumenter.asp?o=3&n=0&h=3&t=13&d=1434 &s=1.

118 Nepp, 2004.

119 Later it became known that Ismael Haniyya was to become the new leader of Hamas in the Gaza Strip and eventually Prime Minister.

120 PICCR Report on Local Elections, 05/01/2005, http://www.palestine-pmc.com/details. asp?cat=3&id=478.

121 Usher, 2006.

122 There is no single authoritative source for the global number of Palestinian refugee. According to UNWRA in 2002 there were 3,973,360 registered refugees. On top of this number there were more 1,500,000 non-registered refugees. See Badil, 2002, p. 33.

123 The Danish Middle East scholar Jørgen Bæk Simonsen writes of the concept da'wa: "[It] actually means 'a shout, a call', namely for God's help. Today it is a technical term for the work of enlightenment that various Muslim organisations carry out to spread knowledge of Islam ... The Islamic da'wa is often interpreted in the West as a form of mission ...". Simonsen, 1994a.

124 The crisis has its origin in the shift of balance of power between the Islamic world and the West that became seriously apparent in the late nineteenth century. In the concrete context of Palestine the expulsion of the majority of the Palestinian people from their homeland in 1947–9 also plays a central role.

125 Personal interview with the late Sheikh Ahmad Yasin, spiritual leader and founder of Hamas, Gaza, 7 July 1998.

126 Burgat 2003, p. 49.

127 Personal interview with Ismael Abu Shanab, Gaza, 27 June 1998.

128 Turabi, 1983. See also Smilianov, 2000, for an account of Turabi's main ideas. Hamas leaders have stated that they are indebted to Hassan al-Turabi, among others. Interview with Abu Shanab, Gaza City, 12 April 1998.

129 For example, Mahmoud Zahhar is a doctor and so was Abdel Aziz Rantisi, while Ismael Abu Shanab was an engineer and Ibrahim Yazouri is pharmacist. A few of the leaders, such as Ahmad Bahr, were, however, trained as 'alim.

130 In this respect Islamism in the Palestinian context resembles Islamism more generally. On the fragmentation of religious authority, see Eickelman & Picatori, 1996.

131 Personal interview with Abdel Aziz Rantisi, Khan Younis, 17 February 1998.

132 Interview with Ismael Abu Shanab, Gaza City, 27 June 1998.

133 Mahmoud Zahhar's book was published by the Islamist press Dâr al-Mustaqbal based in Hebron (Khalil) on the West Bank. Abdel Fattah Dukkhan, who wrote the foreword to the book, is a prominent Islamist leader in Nuseirat, Gaza Strip, and was one of the co-founders of Hamas in 1987. The publishers, Dâr al-Mustaqbal, have published a series of important Islamist works since the

late 1990s, among them Dr Salah al-Khalidi's *Haqâ'iq Qur'âniya hawla al-qadîya al-Filastiniyya* (the Koranic Truth on the Palestinian Question).

134 In this sense there is a close affinity between Islamists and traditional orientalists. See, for example, Bernard Lewis, *The Middle East and the West*, 1964, in which Lewis argues that the relationship between the Arab-Islamic world and the West should be treated as a struggle between civilisations. This conception has since found favour with many American and other Western political scientists – not least since the publication of Samuel Huntington's (1993) article "Clash of Civilizations?" (and the book *Clash of Civilizations and the Remaking of World Order* which followed it).

135 All quotations from the Koran are taken from the translation of Yusuf Ali.

136 Zahhar, 1997, pp. 11–16.

137 Islamists also feel the strong impact of globalisation, which can be seen as a longing for westernisation. The tendency that Islamists represent is not unique. In his book *Jihad vs. Mcworld* (1995), the political scientist Benjamin Barber argues that this is a global phenomenon: we are witness both to growing globalisation and to a concomitant weakening of ethnic, national or religious modes of belonging. In reacting to this tendency towards "contraction", Islam is therefore closely linked with globalisation – and vice versa. The late Hamas leader Ismael Abu Shanab also became a spokesman for the view that Islamism should be seen as a reaction against globalisation. Interview conducted on 27 June 1998.

138 Hamas, 1988, Article 35. See also Hamas, 1988, Art. 15, which offers arguments similar to those put forward by Dukkhan.

139 In this connection it is important to recognise that most Israelis themselves make no distinction between these concepts, in the sense that Zionism in official Israeli historiography is understood as the culmination of Jewish history. See for example former Prime Minister Ehud Barak's speech to the Council of Foreign Relations on 8 January 2001. On this occasion Barak argued that the Jewish historical tradition incorporates strong ties to the land of Israel and for the Jewish people the establishment of the State of Israel represents the triumph of an age-old dream of independence after centuries of victimisation.

140 Hamas, 1988, Article 32.

141 Hamas seldom misses an opportunity to link the movement with Salah ad-Din's victory. They allude to this victory, for example, in their charter, in their *bayans* (leaflets), in the leaders' speeches at mass meetings and not least on the banners used for festive occasions.

142 Hamas, 1988, Article 29.

143 For the full text of the above-mentioned documents, see Laqueur, 1969.

144 On this point, see Sivan, 1985b, p. 9.

145 Hamas, 1988, Article 15.

146 Ibid. Articles 12–13.

147 United Arab Republic, 1962, p. 23.

148 CNN, live coverage from the Arab summit meeting in Amman, Jordan, 27 March 2001.

149 *Al-Hayât al-Jadîda,* 16 January 2001.

150 *Al-Asifa* is also a reference to the group within Fatah that carried out Fatah's first guerrilla attack against the State of Israel on 1 January 1963.

151 Speech delivered by Abdel Fattah Dukkhan on 13 December 1996 to mark the celebration of the ninth anniversary of the founding of Hamas and to commemorate the movement's martyrs, Yahya Ayash and Imad al-Aql. The "festivities" were held at the football stadium in Khan Younis, and were attended by approximately 20,000 sympathisers.

152 Not much research has so far been carried out into the Egyptian brotherhood's activities in the sphere of welfare, social work, education and economics. See however Lia, 1998, Clark, 1994 & 1995, and Sullivan, 1994.

153 This was the view expressed by Abdel Aziz Rantisi and Ismael Abu Shanab. There is no doubt that al-Banna's text *Nahw al-Nûr* (Towards the Light) inspired the Muslim Brotherhood in Palestine and, later on, influenced Hamas, among other things encouraging its engagement in civil society. See Banna in Wendell, 1978.

154 A number of verses of the Koran describe the welfare tasks that it is incumbent on Muslims to perform. These tasks, which are regarded as fundamental duties, include providing food for the poorest members of the community (69:34; 90:11; 107:1–3) and looking after orphans (17:34; 76:8; 89:17; 90:15; 93:9 and 107:2).

155 Interview with Sheikh Ahmad Bahr in his home in Sheikh Radwan, Gaza, 16 April 1998.

156 Interview with the head of one of the Islamist organisations in the Gaza Strip, who wished to remain anonymous. 14 May 1998.

157 Personal interview with Ismael Abu Shanab, Gaza, 12 April 1998.

158 Rasmussen, 1999, argues that women Islamists in Egypt also make use of the strategy of "the good example" in their efforts to demonstrate that Muslim women have the moral capacity needed for islamisation.

159 These words are used repeatedly throughout the Koran, for example in 3:110; 3:104; 3:114; 9:112 and 22:41.

160 *Al-Mujamma' al-Islâmi,* n.d., 1.

161 The three other clubs are *Nâdi Mujamma' Islâmi, Nâdi al-Jam'iyyat al-Salâh al-Islâmiyya* and finally *Nâdi al-Hilâl.* Like *Jam'iyya Islâmiyya* the first two are associated with Hamas, while the Hilâl club is associated with a small, pro-Arafat party that is nevertheless Islamist-oriented.

162 These kinds of martial sports are very popular, as the following episode illustrates: in mid-December 1996 *Jam'iyya Islâmiyya* held a celebratory party for the club's volleyball team, which had just returned from an international tournament in Saudi Arabia where they had represented Palestine. Around 500 people attended, mainly young men in their twenties, together with a number

of influential Islamist leaders (including Ahmad Bahr, Ismael Haniyya, Hassan Shamma' and Imad Falouji). The programme for the evening included a demonstration of karate and mon-cha-ko. After the demonstration approximately half the guests wandered off, despite the fact that they were only halfway through the programme. The explanation was obvious: a great many of those present had come not to hear the numerous speeches by Islamists, but to be entertained – that is, to see the martial sports demonstration. Doubtless one of the reasons why so many young Palestinians are attracted to these Asian martial sports is that they associate them with their struggle against the Israeli occupation.

163 These figures were given by an administrative employee of *Jam'iyya Islâmiyya*, 22 December 1996. While in terms of numbers football is the club's main sport, the volleyball team is undoubtedly the club's pride and joy. In 1996 the club won the Palestinian volleyball championships and subsequently took part in the Arab Championships in Riyadh, Saudi Arabia. It is noteworthy that the leader of the club, Ismael Haniyya, was also granted permission to travel by the Israeli occupying authorities, despite his prominent position in Hamas. It was incidentally Yassir Arafat who paid for the team's air tickets (Cairo–Riyadh return), while the Saudi hosts paid for the costs of the team's stay in Saudi Arabia.

164 Personal interview with Ismael Abu Shanab, 12 April 1998, Gaza City.

165 Personal interview with Hamas leader Abdel Aziz Rantisi, Khan Younis, 17 February 1998. In this interview Rantisi is referring to a *hadith* that says "*al-mu'min al-qawi khayrun wa-ahabbu lil-Allâh min al-mu'min al-da'if*", which translates as: "The physically strong Muslim is better and more beloved by Allah than the physically weak believer."

166 Morsy, 1988.

167 Personal interview with the Head of *Jam'iyya*, Sheikh Ahmad Bahr, Sheikh Radwan, Gaza, 16 April 1998.

168 *Jam'iyya Islâmiyya*, n.d., p.1.

169 Interview with Ahmad Bahr, Sheikh Radwan, Gaza, 16 April 1998.

170 The quotation is taken from *Den Store Danske Encyklopædi*, vol. 9, p. 242.

171 Personal interview with Ismael Abu Shanab, Gaza, 12 April 1998.

172 This focus is completely in line with the concept of *ihsân*. In Islam *ihsân* is understood as a type of charity, and there are several references to the concept in the Koran, where Muslims are enjoined to speak nicely (*Sura* 2:83 & *Sura* 4:8).

173 Interview with Ismael Haniyya, Gaza, 7 July 1998.

174 My understanding of the role of morality is inspired by Lakoff & Johnson, 1999. Although I do not share their biological and – in my opinion – overdetermined view of morality, I am nevertheless indebted to their interpretation of the role of morality in political life, and many of the metaphors they propose make good sense in relation to Islamism in the Gaza Strip.

175 *Jam'iyya Islâmiyya*, n.d, p. 3.

176 Interview with Abu Uthman, administrator in *Jam'iyya Islâmiyya*, Gaza, IUG,
     1 July 1998.
177 Of the population of the Gaza Strip, 63 per cent are registered refugees, Heiberg
     & Øvensen, 1994, p. 23. Immediately after the first Arab–Israeli war of
     1948–9 the population of the Gaza Strip rose from 50,000 to around 250,000.
178 Most of these were studying business (*tijâra*) or *sharî'a*.
179 This applies, for example, to Pelletiere, 1994; Kurz & Tal, 1997 and Lewitt,
     2004 & 2006.
180 See for example Robinson, 1997, and Usher, 1999.
181 See for example Lewitt 2004 & 2006. Lewitt (2004) argues that "the suicide
     soccer teams exemplify a crucial point about the Hamas network of social insti-
     tutions: They provide an ideal logistical support network."
182 Logbook, 16 February 1998. Informal talk with Umar just before the training
     session.
183 Muhi ad-Din al-Sharif, alias *al-Muhandis al-Thâni* (the other engineer) was
     one of the top leaders of Hamas' armed wing, *Izz ad-Din al-Qassam*, on the
     West Bank. He was killed in mysterious circumstances in Ramallah on 29
     March 1998. The reason for his nickname, *al-Muhan-dis al-Thâni*, is that he is
     regarded by Islamists as Yahya Ayash's successor as a bomb-maker in *Izz ad-Din
     al-Qassam*. Ayash was killed in Gaza by Mossad at the beginning of January
     1996. For an account of the circumstances surrounding Muhi ad-din's death,
     see for example Efrat & Mardi, 1998. For an "insider's" view of Yahya Ayash's
     life and career, see Du'ar, 1997.
184 Khaled Mish'al is the head of Hamas' political bureau in exile. Mossad made
     an unsuccessful attempt to liquidate him in autumn 1997. This failed attempt
     incidentally led to the release of Hamas' spiritual leader, Ahmad Yasin, from an
     Israeli prison. Khaled Mish'al took over the post of head of Hamas' political
     bureau in Amman after Musa Abu Marzuq. Abu Marzuq was imprisoned in
     the USA in the mid-1990s. On this affair see Rashad, 1995.
185 Logbook, 1 April 1998. Another informal talk with Umar in connection with
     a training session.
186 Logbook, 16 February 1998.
187 Interview with Ismael Haniyya, IUG, Gaza, 7 July 1988.
188 See Roy, 1993, pp. 105–6.
189 Interview with Abu Uthman, Gaza, 1 July 1998.
190 The discussions between players and the club's managers concerning the
     Islamic dress code will be examined in more depth in Chapter 5.
191 Interview with Ismael Haniyya, Gaza, 7 July 1998.
192 This is presented as a quotation even though it is not a direct citation. Since I
     myself took part in the training and the ticking-off took place in the middle of
     the grounds, I was not able to write down what had been said until after the
     training session was over. Training grounds at IUG, 28 May 1998.
193 Personal interview with Ayman at his home in the Shati camp, December 1996.

194 Interview conducted in my home in Sheikh Ajleen in Gaza, May 1998.

195 Interview conducted in my home in Sheikh Radwan in Gaza, January 1997.

196 The imam at Sheikh Radwan mosque at this point was Abu Ahmad Jadallah. Jadallah is known to be a "Hamas preacher". Three of his sons are martyrs who were killed in the struggle against the Israeli occupying force. Ibrahim was interviewed immediately after training at al-Boura, January 1997.

The word *intimâ*, which Ibrahim uses, is frequently used by Islamists. The people I interviewed for example often spoke of *intimâ* in relation to the club, Islam, etc. The word implies an extremely close relationship of an almost familial nature.

197 Interview with Ziad at Yarmouk Stadium in Gaza, July 1998.

198 Interview with Mahmoud at Yarmouk Stadium in Gaza, July 1998.

199 However, it should be pointed out that not all the Fatah-dominated clubs are able to offer the same benefits. The best-off clubs are the large ones such as *Nâdi Filastîn* (which at the time of fieldwork was controlled by *mukhabarat*, i.e. the secret service). Moreover, only the most talented players reap these advantages, since these clubs headhunt only the best players from other clubs, in order to make Fatah the dominant force on the football pitch as well.

200 Apropos of this, Ali said in an interview in January 1997: "The worst thing about the club are the results we sometimes get and the fact that we don't have enough equipment."

201 One of the club's more prominent players, who was in his thirties at the time, worked as a schoolteacher and had a minor post in the administration of *Jam'iyya Islâmiyya*, asked me in spring 1998, after a training session, to obtain funds so that *Jam'iyya Islâmiyya* would be able to complete the building of the club's new grounds. This was a further indication of the institution's poor financial position.

202 Personal interview with Ismael Abu Shanab in Gaza City, 27 June 1998.

203 On the role of Palestinian prisoners in Israeli jails and politics see for example the documentary *Hothouse* (2006) by Israeli filmmaker Shimon Dotan.

204 Interview with Ismael Abu Shanab in Gaza City, 15 May 1998.

205 Ibn Taymiyyah (1263-1328), an Islamic jurist (*hanbali*) who has inspired many modern Islamist thinkers. On Ibn Taymiyyah's influence on the modern Islamist movement, see for example Sivan, 1985.

206 Interview with Ghazi Hamad in Gaza City, 3 February 1998.

207 In the period from December 1987 to June 1991 alone over 95,000 Palestinians were imprisoned by Israel.

208 Ali was interviewed in my home in Sheikh Radwan in January 1997.

209 Ismail was interviewed at a peaceful café outside al-Azhar and IUG, April 1998

210 Interview with Ayman on the beach near Sheikh Ajleen, June 1998.

211 Chaney, 1987.

212 Interview with Ayman, carried out in June 1998.

213 I have written this account in the form of a newspaper article merely for the

sake of variation. All the information in the text is from the 4 May 1998 entry in my logbook. The quotations, too, were noted down immediately after the game. I did not take part in all *Jam'iyya's* tournament matches, and these impressions are from a spectator's perspective.

214 Zein ad-Din Zidane was on the French national team that won the World Cup in 1998 and the European championships in 2000. He is a Muslim with roots in Algeria. He was voted the world's best football player, and he finished his long carrier during the World Cup final 2006 in Germany.

215 Interview with Ayman, Shati camp, 21 June 1998.

216 This happened during an evening training immediately after the match in Tuffah against Beit Hanoun. I took part in the training that day, but had to leave 20 minutes earlier than usual to go to another appointment. Immediately after I left, Ismael Haniyya and another member of the administration arrived and informed the players of the consequences of the match in Tuffah. The interview with Ahmad was carried out at his own home in Gaza City, 23 May 1998.

217 See Rasmussen, 1999, p.17.

218 Interview with Ibrahim, January 1997. The interview lasted approximately one hour and was carried out immediately after a training session in al-Boura. It was carried out in Arabic with a translator.

219 I have chosen the term "schooling" because I think it is less negatively laden than "indoctrination". The process of schooling exerts an influence, but does not entail the same degree of pressure that is implied by the term "indoctrination"; my understanding of "schooling" moreover suggests that it leaves room for dissent.

220 In the territories governed by the Authority few people made any distinction between the Authority itself and the PLO, even though legally speaking the two entities are completely separate. The problem was simply that it was the Arafat-led Fatah that controlled both. Formally it was the PLO that negotiated with the state of Israel, and the Authority that administered those areas of responsibility, which, through negotiation, had been transferred to the PLO from the occupying power. The Authority alone thus bore responsibility for those areas that came under Palestinian control, while the PLO in principle continued to take care of all Palestinian interests, including those of the Diaspora.

221 Bauman, 1999, p. 117 (translated into English from the Danish edition).

222 Norton, 1995a, p. 4.

223 Interview carried out in June 1998 on the beach near Sheikh Ajleen.

224 A third university was established in the early part of this century when the Teachers Training College in Gaza was turned into a university as well.

225 Passia, 2002, pp. 54–56.

226 The first Palestinian universities had been founded on the West Bank in the early 1970s (Hebron in 1971, Bir Zeit in 1972 and Bethlehem in 1973).

227 Interview with Muhammad Abu Jarad, General Director, Ministry of Education, Gaza, 20 May 1988.

228 For an account of the communists' role in Palestinian society, see for example Sahliyeh, 1988, especially pp. 87–115. See also Ziad Abu Amr, 1994.

229 The strategy employed by Fatah is also familiar from other Arab states. For example, the former Egyptian president Anwar Sadat used the Muslim Brotherhood in the power struggle against the Left in the early 1970s. In the short term this was a successful strategy, but Sadat paid a high price for it, as he was subsequently killed by radical Islamists (*Jihâd Islâmî*).

230 Interview with a former lecturer at IUG who wished to remain anonymous in view of the quotation presented here. Gaza, 2 June 1998.

231 See for example Milton-Edwards, 1996, p. 110ff.

232 Fatah no doubt chose to use the name al-Azhar because of the legitimacy conferred by its association with the famous university of the same name in Cairo.

233 Interview with Ahmad Sa'ati, IUG, 15 April 1998.

234 Ibid.

235 The concept of *islamicum* covers a number of courses that students at the Islamic university are obliged to follow. These Islamic studies include, among other things: *Nizâm al-islâmi* (the Islamic system), *Shûrâ* (dealing with the debate on *shûrâ* and democracy), *Dirasât al-Sira* (the study of biographies of the Prophet Muhammad), *Hadîth Sharîf* (studies of the tradition bequeathed by Muhammad), *Dirasât Qurâniyya* (Koranic studies, including exegesis) and the course *Hâdir al-'Alam al-islâmi* (the current situation in the Islamic world). This information stems from informal discussions with IUG students in January 1997.

236 Interview with Walid Amr, Professor of English at IUG, Gaza, 23 December 1996.

237 IUG, 1995, pp. 2–3.

238 The Student Council consists of nine members. Elections are run on the principle of "winner takes all", which meant at the time of my fieldwork that *Kutla Islâmiyya* occupied all nine seats. According to a spokesman for the Student Council, the Islamists are opposed in principle to this electoral system and would like instead a more representative system that would give some room to the opposition. The reason why such a system has not been introduced, according to the Islamists in *Kutla Islâmiyya*, is that "Fatah rejects it, because if we had another electoral system, Fatah would lose many of its seats in other institutions. Thus the Authority wishes to maintain the [present] electoral system." Interview with members of *Kutla Islâmiyya* at IUG, 14 January 1997.

239 Since there is total sex segregation at IUG, there are also two Student Councils. It is noteworthy that *Kutla Islâmiyya* has an even greater majority among the female students. Thus at the 1987 election 75 per cent of women students voted for the Islamists, and by 1999–2000 the figure had risen to 91 per cent. This accords, incidentally, with the results that Heiberg & Øvensen (1994) arrived at on the basis of their quantitative data, which showed that women were more inclined to support the Islamist movements.

240 The category "others" includes *Jihâd Islâmî*, the PFLP, the DFLP and the Palestinian Communist Party, PPP. In 1987 *Jihâd Islâmî* accounted for all 15 per cent in this category.

241 Of the 400 alleged leaders of Hamas and Islamic Jihad whom Israel deported on 17 December 1992, in contravention of the 4th Geneva Convention, 155 were from the Gaza Strip, and 86 of these were under 30 years old. If we look at the background of the deported people from the Gaza Strip, 39 were students, 22 had some form of higher education, and 12 were office workers; altogether the overwhelming majority were employed at IUG.

242 See Francis Fukuyama, *The End of History and the Last Man* (London: Hamish Hamilton). For a criticism of both Huntington and Fukuyama, see for example Hylland Eriksen, 2001.

243 Discussion with a number of IUG students at the English Department, in connection with an informal seminar on globalisation and its consequences run by the British Council in Gaza, 8 May 1998.

244 Historically the term *jâhiliyya* has been used to refer to the time before Islam, meaning the time of ignorance. More recently Islamist thinkers such as Maulana Mawdudi and Sayyid Qutb have also applied the term to the present day. This extension of the concept was prompted by these thinkers' view that the Arab-Muslim world was not living in accordance with the Koran's message: a view that, not surprisingly, has been opposed by *ulamâ*. In explaining the concept of *jâhiliyya* Raqab writes that it does not belong to the past, but that "it is a mental state in which God's guidance is rejected, as well as an organisational [state in which the leaders] refuse to abide by what is sent down by God [i.e. the Koran]".

245 Raqab, 1998.

246 Ibid. 1998.

247 Ibid. p. 297.

248 Ibid. p. 299.

249 At no point in the lesson did Mr Muhammad explain when the poem was written, or who had composed it. The poem is part of an anthology called "Bad, bad cats", written for children aged 9+ by Roger McGough – a popular *British* poet.

250 On several other occasions it became clear that Mr Muhammad was convinced of the imminent collapse of the Western world. In connection with a lecture I gave to IUG's female students concerning the West's and Islam's stereotypes of each other, Mr Muhammad commented as follows: "The West at the moment is desperate. [Westerners] have no hope, and they're looking for alternatives. The alternative is Islam. Arabic will become the main language in Europe within the next 50 to 100 years." 19 May 1998, IUG.

251 It might be more correct to see this as anti-Israeli lenses. Student 2, quoted above, stated that it reminded him of 'Jewish gangs'. By and large, Palestinians in the Gaza Strip refer to Israeli soldiers as 'the Jews'. Most have not seen any

other Jews to modify their terminology. Hence taking the student's comment about the 'Jewish gangs' to mean a general anti-Jewish sentiment is somewhat inaccurate as it rather indicates anti-Israeli sentiment. In Gaza, it often means Israeli army squads that used to knock on doors during the First Intifada in the middle of the night as those 'bad cats' did in the poem.

252   Interview with Salim conducted at IUG on 29 and 30 March 1998. The interview lasted approximately 3 hours.

253   The reason that Munir was able to give a view of the situation at al-Azhar University was that the two universities are located close to one another, and that some students have friends at the neighbouring university. Munir was interviewed at IUG on 1 April 1998.

254   Muhammad was interviewed at a café outside IUG on 22 April 1998.

255   Ahmad was interviewed at IUG together with his good friend Nabil over two sessions, respectively on 12 and 14 April 1998.

256   Ibid.

257   See Nour, 1998, p. 53 for a similar point in the Egyptian context.

258   See Said, 1978, p. 40.

259   These views incidentally accord entirely with the Koranic concept *tahrif*, which Munir and Salim are perhaps drawing on here. It is probable that through their *islamicum* studies the students were familiar with and had absorbed this concept. It can be found in the Koran, *Sura* 4:46, which states: "Of the Jews there are those who displace words from their (right) places, and say: 'We hear and we disobey'; and 'Hear what is not Heard'; and 'Ra'ina'; with a twist of their tongues and a slander to Faith. If only they had said: 'What hear and we obey'; and 'Do hear'; and 'Do look at us'; it would have been better for them, and more proper; but Allah hath cursed them for their Unbelief; and but few of them will believe."

260   Salim is referring here to the Koran, *Sura* 5.20-26. In the English translation of the Koran by Yusuf Ali the text reads as follows: "Remember Moses said to his people: 'O my people! Call in remembrance the favour of Allah unto you, when He produced prophets among you, made you kings, and gave you what He had not given to any other among the peoples. O my people! Enter the holy land which Allah hath assigned unto you, and turn not back ignominiously, for then will ye be overthrown, to your own ruin.' They said: 'O Moses! In this land are a people of exceeding strength: Never shall we enter it until they leave it: if (once) they leave, then shall we enter.' (But) among (their) Allah-fearing men were two on whom Allah had bestowed His grace: They said: 'Assault them at the (proper) Gate: when once ye are in, victory will be yours; But on Allah put your trust if ye have faith.' They said: 'O Moses! While they remain there, never shall we be able to enter, to the end of time. Go thou, and thy Lord, and fight ye two, while we sit here (and watch).' He said: 'O my Lord! I have power only over myself and my brother: so separate us from this rebellious people!' Allah said: 'Therefore will the land be out of their reach for forty years:

In distraction will they wander through the land: But sorrow thou not over
these rebellious people.'"
261 Norton, 1995a, p. 4.
262 This has been argued by Robinson, 1997.
263 Interview, Ismael Abu Shanab, Gaza City, 12 April 1998.
264 *The Guardian*, 10 January 2007.
265 Ibid.
266 See chapter 5 for more student views on the possibility of peace with Israel.
267 See for example Near East Consulting. http://www.neareastconsulting.com/
surveys/all/p23/out_ct_trust_q18.php
      In March 2007 a poll showed that more than 67 per cent of the Palestinians
supported a peace settlement with Israel. Some 50 per cent of the people vot-
ing for Hamas supported peace and almost 60 per cent of the supporters of
Islamic Jihad were in favour of peace with Israel.
268 The discussion of participation actually began in the early 1990s and the movement had numerous discussions on this matter in relation to the 1996 elections, which they boycotted. For a more elaborate discussion on Hamas and
political participation see Mishal and Sela, 200, pp. 113–46.
269 Ahmad al-Kurd was appointed Mayor in Deir al-Balah after Hamas' list
(Change and Reform) and won 13 of the 15 seats in the elections in early 2005.
270 International Crisis Group, 2006.
271 Ibid.
272 BBC http://news.bbc.co.uk/1/hi/world/middle_east/4641765.stm.
273 http://www.csmonitor.com/2007/0309/p06s01-wome.html.
274 The January elections 2006 might be interpreted as a signal to Hamas. In the
city of Qalqilya where Hamas' list Reform and Change in 2005 won 15 out of
15 seats in the local council elections no Hamas candidates were elected for the
PLC Council despite Hamas' grand victory. Naturally this can be explained by
numerous factors, but one has to do with the fact that the new local rulers have
disappointed many Palestinians in this area.
275 Hroub, 2006, p. 9.
276 Ibid. p. 11.
277 Ibid. pp 7–15.
278 Ibid. p. 9.
279 Hamas, 1988, Article 13.
280 Milton-Edwards and Crooke, 2004, p. 49. See also Cobban, 1982.
281 Jensen and Laursen, 2000, p.16.
282 ibid. p.18.
283 Ahmad Yousuf: Pause for Peace. *New York Times*, 1 November 2006. Ahmad
Yousuf is a senior adviser to Ismael Haniyya. Yousuf is in his op-ed inviting the
Israelis to negotiate peace with Hamas on the basis that Israel withdrew to the
1967 borders. The mere fact that a senior Hamas aide was allocated space in
the *New York Times* created a great stir in the United States.

284 *The Guardian*, 10 January 2007.
285 While the TIM was capable of providing much needed assistance to some of the poorest Palestinians, it has been unable to prevent the decline in the humanitarian situation.
286 UNGA, 2007
287 Based on a large number of interviews conducted on the West Bank with a number of Palestinian intellectuals, NGO leaders and PA officials during November 2007.
288 See also Alexander, 2007, p. 17
289 Samhouri, 2007, p. 10
290 Personal interview, Ramallah, November 2007
291 The Saudi–inspired plan originally presented at a meeting of the Arab League in Beirut 2002, but ignored the "international community" until 2006–7. The Arab countries re-launched the plan in Saudi Arabia in March 2007. Basically all the Arab countries are offering Israel peace if they withdraw to the 1967 borders. See for example http://www.jordanembassyus.org/arab_initiative.htm for the content of the plan.
292 Heiberg and Øvensen, 1994, p. 44.
293 See for example Shalev, 1991, Milton-Edwards, 1996 and Abu Amr, 1994.
294 One of my interviewees referred to this neighbourhood as *hay al-mujâhidûn* (the Mujahidin's neighbourhood) and it is generally regarded as a Hamas "stronghold".
295 The leadership level in this context includes both the leaders of the institutions selected and prominent leaders of the Hamas movement who are not necessarily involved in the day-to-day management of these institutions.
296 In connection with my fieldwork I also took part in a number of these mass meetings, for example one held on 16 December 1996 in Khan Younis to celebrate the founding of the Hamas movement nine years earlier, and another in Gaza City in spring 1998 to commemorate the movement's latest martyrs at that point, Muhi ad-Din al-Sharif and the Awadallah brothers. Haniyya chaired the meeting on both occasions.
297 As a starting point I have chosen to define the players in *Nâdi al-Jam'iyya al-Islâmiyya* as Hamas sympathisers. The reason for this is simply that the leaders of the institution *Jam'iyya Islamiyya* are all present or former leaders of Hamas.
298 Dominant in the sense that they set the tone in relation to trainers, leaders and the other players. Thus, I chose to interview both more and less dedicated players.

BIBLIOGRAPHY

Abu-Amr, Ziad (1989): *Al-Harakât al-Islâmiya fi al-Diffah al-Gharbiyya wa Qitâ' Ghazzah* (Akka: Dar al-Aswar)

Abu-Amr, Ziad (1993): "HAMAS: a historical and political background" in *Journal of Palestine Studies*, vol. 22, no. 4

Abu-Amr, Ziad (1994): *Islamic Fundamentalism in the West Bank and Gaza – Muslim Brotherhood and Islamic Jihad* (Bloomington and Indiana: Indiana University Press)

Abu-Amr, Ziad (1995): "Report from Palestine" in *Journal of Palestine Studies*, vol. 24, no. 2, Winter

Abu-Amr, Ziad (1997a): "The Palestinian Legislative Council: A Critical Assessment", *Journal of Palestine Studies*, vol. XXVI, no. 4

Abu-Amr, Ziad (1997b): "Shaykh Ahmad Yasin and the Origins of Hamas" in Scott Appleby, R. (ed.) *Spokesmen for the Despised: Fundamentalist Leaders of the Middle East* (Chicago: University of Chicago Press)

Abu Rabi, Ibrahim (1996): *Intellectual Underpinnings of Islamic Resurgence* (New York: SUNY Press)

Aburish, Said K. (1998): *Arafat – From Defender to Dictator* (London: Bloomsbury)

Adwan, Atef (1991): *Ahmad Yâsîn – Hayâtuhu wa Jihâduhu* (IUG: Gaza)

El-Affendi, Abdelwahab (1991): *Turabi's Revolution: Islam and Power in Sudan* (London: Grey Seal)

Ahmad, Hisham (1994): *Hamas – From Religious Salvation to Political Transformation: The Rise of Hamas in Palestinian Society* (Jerusalem: Passia)

AI (1995): *Human Rights: A Year of Shattered Hopes. Israel and the Occupied Territories Including the Area Under the Jurisdiction of the Palestinian Authority*, Amnesty International

AI (1996): *Palestinian Authority: Prolonged Political Detention, Torture and Unfair Trials*, Amnesty International

AI (1998): *Israel/Occupied Territories and the Palestinian Authority: Five Years After the Oslo Agreement – Human Rights Sacrificed for "Security"*, Amnesty International

AI (1999): *Palestinian Authority Defying the Rule of Law: Political Detainees*, Amnesty International

Alexander, Justin (2007): *Conflict, Economic Closure and Human Security in Gaza*, Oxford Research Group

Andoni, Lamis (1991): "The PLO at the crossroads" in *Journal of Palestine Studies*, vol. 21, no. 1

Ashrawi, Hannan (1995): *Freden – En personlig beretning* (Rosinante:København)

Al-Awaisi, Abd al-Fattah Muhammad (1998): *The Muslim Brothers and the Palestine Question 1928-47* (London: I.B.Tauris)

Ayubi, Nazih (1980): "The Political Revival of Islam: The Case of Egypt" in *International Journal of Middle East Studies*, vol. 12

Ayubi, Nazih (1991): *Political Islam – Religion and Politics in the Arab World* (London: Routledge)

Badil (2002): *Survey of Palestinian Refugees and Internally Displaced Persons 2002* (Bethlehem: Badil)

Baramki, Gabi (1987): "Building Palestinian Universities Under Occupation" in *Journal of Palestine Studies*, Vol. XVII, no. 1

Barghouti, Iyad (1990): *Al-Aslima wal-Siyâsa fî al-Arâdi al-Filastîniyya al-Muhtallah* (Jerusalem: Markaz al-Zahrâ' lil-Dirâsât wal-Abhâth)

Barghouti, Iyad (1991): "Religion and Politics Among the Students of Najah National University" in *Middle Eastern Studies*, vol. 27, no. 2

Barghouti, Iyad (1993): "The Islamist Movements in the Occupied Territories" in *Middle East Report*, July-August

Bauman, Zygmunt (1999): *Globalisering: De menneskelige konsekvenser* (København: Hans Reitzels Forlag)

Bekkar, Rabia (1992): "Taking up Space in Tlemcen – The Islamist Occupation of Urban Algeria" in *Middle East Report*, Nov.–Dec.

Bellin, Eva (1994): *Civil Society and the Prospects for Political Reform in the Middle East*, Conference Report (Sept. 30–Oct. 2, 1994), (New York University)

Bourdieu, Pierre (1986): "Forms of Capital" in Richardson, John (ed.): *Handbook of Theory and Research for the Sociology of Education* (New York: Greenwood Press)

Brynen, Rex (1995): "The Dynamics of Palestinian Elite Formation" in *Journal of Palestine Studies*, vol. 24, no. 3

Brynen, Rex (1995a): "The Neopatrimonial Dimension of Palestinian Politics" in *Journal of Palestine Studies*, vol. XXV, no. 1

Bulliet, Richard W. (1993): "The Future of the Islamic Movement" in *Foreign Affairs*, vol. 72, no. 5

Burgat, Francois (1992): "Les islamistes et la transition democratique: Jalons pour une recherche" in *Democratie et democratisations en la monde Arabe* (Cairo: CEDEJ)

Burgat, Francois (2003): *Face to Face with Political Islam* (London: I.B.Tauris)

Burgat, Francois & Dowell, William (1993): *The Islamic Movement in North Africa* (Austin: University of Texas)

Burke, Edmund, III (1988): "Islam and Social Movements: Methodological Reflections" in Burke, Edmund III & Lapidus, Ira: *Islam, Politics and Social Movements* (Berkeley: University of California Press)

Chaney, David (1987): "Sport as a Form of Mass Entertainment" in Stauth, Georg & Zubaida, Sami (eds.): *Mass Culture, Popular Culture, and Social Life in the Middle East* (Frankfurt: Campus Verlag)

Christiansen, Connie C. & Rasmussen Lene K. (1994): *At vælge sløret: Unge kvinder i politisk islam* (København: Forlaget Sociologi)

Christiansen, Connie C. (1998): "'Vi islamister...'. Distinktion og drama i islamisk aktivisme" in *Tidsskriftet Antropologi*, no. 37

Clark, Janine Astrid (1994): *Islamic Social-Welfare Organizations and the Legitimacy of the State in Egypt: Democratization or Islamization from Below?* Unpublished PhD thesis, Dept. of Political Science, University of Toronto

Clark, Janine Astrid (1995): "Islamic Social Welfare Organizations in Cairo: Islamization from Below?" in *Arab Studies Quarterly*, vol. 17, no. 4

Clark, Janine Astrid (1995): "Democratization and Social Islam: A Case Study of the Islamic Health Clinics in Cairo" in Brynen, Rex; Korany, Baghat & Noble, Paul (eds.): *Political Liberalization and Democratization in the Arab World*, vol. 1 (London: Lynne Rienner Publishers)

Clark, Janine Astrid (2004): *Charity, and Activism: Middle-Class Networks and Social Welfare in Egypt, Jordan and Yemen* (USA: Indiana University Press)

Cobban, Helena (1984): *The Palestinian Liberation Organisation – People, Power and Politics* (Cambridge: Cambridge University Press)

Cobban, Helena (1990): "The PLO and the *Intifada*" in *The Middle East Journal*, vol. 44, no. 2

Cohen, Amnon (1982): *Political Parties in the West Bank under the Jordanian Regime 1948–67* (Ithaca & London : Cornell University Press)

Cohen, Shalom (1980): "Khomeinism in Gaza" in *New Outlook*, March

CPRS (1993): *Public Opinion Poll #1, The Palestinian–Israeli Agreement: "Gaza-Jericho First" September 10–11, 1993*; Survey Research Unit, the Centre for Palestine Research and Studies. http://www.cprs-palestine.org/polls/94/poll1.html#results

Dekmejian, Hrair (1988): "Islamic Revival: Catalysts, Categories and Consequences" in Shireen T. Hunter, *The Politics of Islamic Revivalism* (Bloomington & Indiana: Indiana University Press)

Dekmejian, Hrair (1997): "Multiple Faces of Islam" in Jerichow, A. & Simonsen J. Bæk, *Islam in a Changing World – Europe and the Middle East* (Surrey: Curzon Press)

Denoeux, Guilain (1993): *Urban Unrest in the Middle East – A Comparative Study of Informal Networks in Egypt, Iran and Lebanon* (Albany: SUNY Press)

Detlev, Khalid (1978): "The Phenomenon of re-islamization" in *Aussen politik*, vol. 29, no. 4

DoP (1993): *The Declaration of Principles on Interim Self-Government Arrangements*, 13 September, 1993.

Du'ar, Ghassan (1997): *Al-Muhandis: Al-Shahîd Yahya Ayâsh ramz al-Jihâd wa Qâ'id al-Muqâwama fî Filastîn* (London: Filastin al-Muslima)

Efrat, Roni Ben & Mardi, Diana (1998): "Who killed Muhi ad-din Sharif" in *Challenge*, no. 49

Eickelman, Dale F. & Piscatori, James (1996): *Muslim Politics* (New Jersey: Princeton University Press)

Esposito, John L. (1992): *The Islamic Threat: Myth or Reality* (Oxford: Oxford University Press)

Esposito, John L. & Piscatori James P. (1991): "Democratization and Islam" in *Middle East Journal*, vol. 45, no. 3

Freund, Wolfgang (ed.) (1999): *Palestinian Perspectives* (Frankfurt: Europäischer Verlag der Vissenschaft)

Gharba, Shafeeq (1991): "Voluntary Associations in Kuwait: The Foundation of a New System?" in *Middle East Journal*, vol. 45, no. 2, Spring

Güalp, Haldun, (1999): "Political Islam in Turkey: The Rise and Fall of the Refah Party" in *The Muslim World*, vol. 89, no. 1

Fasheh, Munir (1982): "Political Islam in the West Bank" in *Merip Report*, February

Gershoni, Israel (1989): "The Muslim Brothers and the Arab Revolt in Palestine, 1936–39" in *Middle Eastern Studies*, vol. 22, no. 3

Golan, Galia (1990): *Soviet Policies in the Middle East – From World War II to Gorbachev* (Cambridge: Cambridge University Press)

Guenena, Nemat (1986): "The 'Jihad' – An 'Islamic Alternative' in Egypt" in *Cairo Papers in Social Science*, vol. 9, monograph 2, summer

Hadawi, Sami (1990): *Bitter Harvest* (London: Scorpion Pub. Ltd.)

Haddad, Yvonne (1983): "Sayyid Qutb: Ideologue and Islamic Revival" in John Esposito (ed.), *Voices of Resurgent Islam* (Oxford: Oxford University Press)

Haddad, Yvonne *et al.* (1991): *The Contemporary Islamic Revival – A Critical Survey and Bibliography* (New York: Greenwood Press)

Haddad, Yvonne (1992): "Islamists and "the Problem of Israel": The 1967 Awakening" in *The Middle East Journal*, vol. 46, no 2

Haddad, Yvonne & Esposito, John (1997): *The Islamic Revival since 1988* (Westport: Greenwood Press)

Hamad, Jawad el- & Barghouti, Iyad el- (eds) (1997): *Dirasat fi al-fikr al-siyasi li harakat al-muqawama al-islamiyya (Hamas) 1987–1996*, (Amman, MESC)

Hamas (1988): *Mithâq Harakât al-Muqâwama al-Islâmiya – Filastin*, 14 August

Hamas (1993): "Charter of the Islamic Resistance Movement (HAMAS) of Palestine" in *Journal of Palestine Studies*, vol. 22, no. 4

Hammersley, Martin & Atkinson, Paul (1995): *Ethnography. Principles in Practice*, 2nd edn. (London: Routledge)

Hammoud, Mirna (1998): "Causes for Fundamentalist Popularity in Egypt" in Mousalli, Ahmad (ed.), *Islamic Fundamentalism: Myth and Realities* (Reading: Ithaca Press)

Hanf, Theodor & Sabella, Bernard (1996): *A Date with Democracy – Palestinians on Society and Politics, An Empirical Survey* (Arnold Bergstraesser Institute)

Hawes, Crispen B. (1991): *The Ideology and Development of Hamas – Radical Nationalist Islam*, Unpublished MA thesis, SOAS, University of London

Hebron-Protocol (1997): (Protocol Concerning the Redeployment in Hebron) in *Palestine Report* (Special Edition), vol. 2, no. 32. 17 January 1997

Heiberg, Marianne & Øvensen, Geir (1994): *Palestinian Society in Gaza, West Bank and Arab Jerusalem – A Survey of Living Conditions* (Oslo: FAFO)

Hroub, Khaled (2000): *Hamas: Political Thought and Practice* (Washington: Institute for Palestine Studies)

Hroub, Khaled (2004): "Hamas after Shaykh Yasin and Rantisi" in *Journal of Palestine Studies*, vol. XXXIII, no. 4, Summer

Hroub, Khaled (2006): *Hamas: A Beginner's Guide* (London: Pluto Press)

Hroub, Khaled (2006b): "A 'New Hamas' through its New Documents" in *Journal of Palestine Studies*, vol. XXXV, no. 4, Summer

Hudson, Michael (1996): "Democratization in the Middle East" in *Contention*, vol. 5, no. 2

Huntington, Samuel (1993): "Clash of Civilizations" in *Foreign Affairs*, vol. 72, no. 3

Hylland Eriksen, Thomas (2001): *Bak Fiendebildet. Islam og verden etter 11. september* (Oslo: Cappelen)

Ibrahim, Saad Eddin (1980): "Anatomy of Egypt's Militant Islamic Groups: Methodological Note and Preliminary Findings" in *International Journal of Middle East Studies*, vol. 12

Ibrahim, Saad Eddin (1995): "Civil Society and Prospects for Democratization in the Arab World" in Norton A., Richard (ed.): *Civil Society in the Middle East*, vol. 1 (Leiden: E.J. Brill)

Ibrahim, Saad Eddin, *et al.* (1993): *An Assessment of Grass-Roots Participation in Egypt's Development*, Second draft, August (Cairo: Ibn Khaldoun Center)

Inbari, Pinhas (1996): *The Palestinians between Terrorism and Statehood* (Brighton: Sussex Academic Press)

International Crises Group (2003): *Islamic Social Welfare Activism in the Occupied Palestinian Territories: A Legitimate Target?* Middle East Report no. 13 (Amman/Brussels: ICG)

International Crises Group (2006): *Enter Hamas: The Challenges of Political Integration.* Middle East Report no. 49 (Amman/Brussels: ICG)

International Crises Group (2007): *After Mecca: Engaging Hamas.* Middle East Report no. 62. (Amman/Brussels: ICG)

IPS (1994): *The Palestinian–Israeli Peace Agreement – A Documentary Record* (Washington DC: Institute of Palestine studies)

Israeli–Palestinian Interim Agreement on the West Bank and the Gaza Strip, (1995): Washington DC, 28 September, Ministry of Foreign Affairs, The State of Israel.

Israeli, Raphael (1989): "Islamic fundamentalism among the Palestinian Arabs" in *Survey of Arab Affairs – A Periodic Supplement to Jerusalem Letter/Viewpoints*, 15 August

IUG (1995): *Dalil al-Jami'a al-Islamiyya bi-Ghazza* (IUG: Gaza)

al-Jam'iyya al-Islâmiyya (n.d.): *Qanûn Asâsi* (Gaza)

al-Jam'iyya al-Islâmiyya (1994): *Jam'îyya al-islâmîya* (Gaza) – pamphlet

Jansen, Johannes (1986): *The Neglected Duty – The Creed of Sadat's Assassins* (London: Macmillan)

Jaradat, Muhammad (1992): "Islamic Resistance Movement (Hamas) in the Territories Occupied in 1967" in *News from Within* (5 August)

Jarbawi, Ali & Heacock, Roger (1993): "The Deportations and the Palestinian–Israeli Negotiations" in *Journal of Palestine Studies*, vol. 22, no. 3

Jarrar, Bassam (1994): "The Islamist Movement and the Palestinian Authority" in *Merip Reports*, July–August

Jensen, Michael Irving (1998): "Islamism and Civil Society in the Gaza Strip" in Mousalli, Ahmad, *Islamic Fundamentalism: Myths and Realities* (Reading: Ithaca Press)

Jensen, Michael Irving (ed.) (2001): *På tærsklen til fred? Al-Aqsa Intifadaen og fredsprocessen i Mellemøsten* (København: Gyldendal)

Jensen, Michael Irving (2002): *Hamas i Gazastriben* (København: Akademisk Forlag)

Jensen, Michael Irving (2005): "Youth, Moral and Islamism: Spending Your Leisure Time with Hamas in Palestine, in Simonsen, Jørgen Bæk (ed.): *Youth and Youth Culture in Contemporary Middle East*. Proceedings of the Danish Institute in Damascus III (Aarhus: Aarhus University Press)

Jensen, Michael Irving (2006): "'Re-Islamising' Palestinian Society 'From Below': Hamas and Higher Education in Gaza" in *Holy Land Studies*, vol. 5, no.1

Jensen, Michael Irving & Laursen, Andreas (2000): *Arafats Palæstina: Forventninger og Realiteter* (Odense: Odense Universitetsforlag)

Johnson, Nels (1982): *Islam and the Politics of Meaning in Palestinian Nationalism* (London: KPI)

Karmon, Ely (1999): *Hamas Terrorism Strategy: Operational Limitations and Political Constraints*. www.ict.org.il/articles/hamas-peace_process.htm

Kazami, Farhad & Norton, Augustus R. (1996): "Civil Society, Political Reform and Authoritarianism" in *Contention*, vol. 5, no. 2

Kazziha, Walid (1996): *Civil Society in the Middle East: Some Critical Remarks*, Paper presented during the Conference on Citizenship and the State in the Middle East, 22–24 November 1996, Oslo

Kepel, Giles (1985): *The Prophet and Pharaoh – Muslim Extremism in Egypt* (London: Al-Saqi Books)

Kepel, Giles (1992): *Gud tager revanche* (København: Gyldendal)

Khansan, Hilal (1998): "The Development Programmes of Islamic Fundamentalist Groups in Lebanon as a Source of Popular Legitimation" in Moussalli, Ahmad (ed.), *Islamic Fundamentalism. Myth & Realities* (Reading: Ithaca Press)

Kleiman, Aharon (2000): *Compromising Palestine: A Guide to Final Status Negotiations* (Columbia University Press: New York)

Koran (translation by Yusuf Ali)

Kristianesen, Wendy (1999): "Challenge and Counterchallenge: Hamas's Response to Oslo" in *Journal of Palestine Studies*, vol. XXVII, no. 3

Krämer, Gudrun (1992): "Islam et Pluralisme" in *Democratie et democratisations dans le monde arabe* (Cairo: CEDEJ)

Krämer, Gudrun (1993): "Islamic Notions of Democracy" in *Middle East Report*, no. 183

Krämer, Gudrun (1994): "The Integration of the Integrists: A Comparative Study of Egypt, Jordan and Tunisia" in Saleme Ghassan (ed.): *Democracy without Democrats? – The Renewal of Politics in the Muslim World* (London: I.B.Tauris)

Krämer, Gudrun (1995): "Islam and Pluralism" in Brynen, Rex; Korany, Baghat & Noble, Paul (eds): *Political Liberalization and Democratization in the Arab World*, vol. 1 (London: Lynne Rienner Publishers)

Kurz, Anat & Tal, Nahman (1997): *Hamas: Radical Islam in a National Struggle* (Tel Aviv: Jaffee Center for Strategic Studies)

Lakoff, Georg & Johnson, Mark (1999): *Philosophy in the Flesh: The Embodied Mind and its Challenge to Western Thought* (New York: Basic Books)

Legrain, Jean-Francois (1988a): "Les islamistes palestiniens à l'épreuve du soulèvement" in *Maghreb/Machrek*, no.121, Juillet–Aout–Septembre

Legrain, Jean-Francois (1988b): "Le pouvoir en cisjordanie; un combat à quatre" in *Bulletin du CEDEJ*, vol. 17, no. 23, premier semestre

Legrain, Jean-Francois (1990): "Le leadership palestinien de l'intériur (Document Huseyni, été 1988)" in *Egypte – Monde Arabe (CEDEJ)*, no. 3

Legrain, Jean-Francois (1991a): "A Defining Moment: Palestinian Islamic fundamentalism" in James Piscatori (ed.), *Islamic Fundamentalisms and the Gulf Crisis* (Chicago: American Academy of Arts and Sciences)

Legrain, Jean-Francois (1991b): "The Islamic Movement and the Intifada" in Nasser, J. & Heacock, R., *Intifada – Palestine at the Crossroads*, (Preager)

Legrain, Jean-Francois (1991c): *Les voix du soulèvement Palestinian 1987–88*, (Cairo: CEDEJ)

Legrain, Jean-Francois (1992): "Les élections étudiants en cisjordanie (1978–87)" in *Dossiers du CEDEJ*, Democratie et democratisations dans le monde Arabe

Legrain, Jean Francois (1994a): *Hamas, Legitimate Heir of Palestinian Nationalism?* Conference paper: Political Islam in the Middle East, United States Institute of Peace, Washington, 2–3 March

Legrain, Jean Francois (1994b): "Palestinian Islamism: Patriotism as a condition of their expansion" in Marty, Martin E. & Appleby, R. Scott (eds.), *Accounting for Fundamentalisms: The Dynamic Character of Movements* (Chicago: University of Chicago Press)

Legrain, Jean Francois (1999): "The Successions of Yasir Arafat" in *Journal of Palestine Studies* XXVIII, no.4

Lesch, Ann M. (1985): "Gaza: Forgotten Corner of Palestine" in *Journal of Palestine Studies*, Vol. XV, no. 1

Lesch, Ann M. & Tessler, Mark (1987): "The West Bank and Gaza: Political and Ideological Responses to Occupation" in *The Muslim World*, vol. 77, no. 3–4, July–October

Lesch, Ann M. (1990): "Prelude to the Uprising in the Gaza Strip" in *Journal of Palestine Studies*, Vol. XX, no. 1

Levitt, Matthew A. (2004): "Hamas from Cradle to Grave" in *The Middle East Quarterly*, Winter

Levitt, Matthew A. (2006): *Hamas: Politics, Charity and Terrorism in the Service of Jihad* (Yale University Press)

Lewis, Bernard (1964): *The Middle East and the West* (London: Weidenfeld and Nicolson)

Lia, Brynjar (1998): *The Society of the Moslem Brothers In Egypt: The Rise of an Islamic Mass Movement 1928–1942* (Reading: Ithaca)

Matter, Philip (1988): *The Mufti of Jerusalem* (Columbia: Columbia University Press)

Mayer, Thomas (1982): "The Military Force of Islam: The Society of the Muslim Brethren and the Palestine Question, 1945–48" in Elie Khadourie & Sylvia Haim (eds), *Zionism and Arabism in Palestine and Israel* (London: Frank Cass)

Mcdowall, David (1989): "A Profile of the Population of the West Bank and Gaza Strip" in *Journal of Refugee Studies*, vol. 2, no.1

Milton-Edwards, Beverley (1991): "A Temporary Alliance with the Crown: The Islamic Response in Jordan" in James Piscatori (ed), *Islamic Fundamentalisms and the Gulf War* (Chicago: American Academy of Arts and Sciences)

Milton-Edwards, Beverley (1993): "The Concept of *Jihad* and the Palestinian Islamic movement: A comparison of Ideas and Techniques" in *British Journal of Middle Eastern Studies*, vol. 19, no. 1

Milton-Edwards, Beverley (1996): *Islamic Politics in Palestine* (London: I.B.Tauris)

Milton-Edwards, Beverley & Crooke, Alister (2004): "Elusive Ingredient: Hamas and the Peace Process" in *Journal of Palestine Studies*, vol. XXXIII, no. 4, Summer

Mishal, Shaul & Aharoni, Reuben (1994): *Speaking Stones – Communiqués from the Intifada Underground* (New York: Syracuse University Press)

Mishal, Shaul & Sela, Avraham (2000): *The Palestinian Hamas – Vision, Violence and Coexistence* (New York: Columbia University Press)

Mitchell, Richard P. (1969): *The Society of the Muslim Brothers* (London: Oxford University Press)

Morsy, Soheir A. (1988): "Islamic Clinics in Egypt: The Cultural Elaboration of Biomedical Hegemony" in *Medical Anthropology Quarterly*, December

Moussalli, Ahmad S. (1995): "Modern Islamic Fundamentalists Discourses on Civil Society, Pluralism and Democracy" in Norton, Richard A. (ed.): *Civil Society in the Middle East*, vol. 1, (Leiden: E.J. Brill)

Moussalli, Ahmad (ed.) (1998): *Islamic Fundamentalism – Myth and Realities* (Reading: Ithaca Press)

Mujamma' Islâmî (n.d.): *Qanûn Asasi* (Gaza)

Munson, Henry Jr. (1986): "The Social Base of Islamic Militancy in Morocco" in *Middle East Journal,* vol. 40, no. 2, Spring

Muslih, Muhammad (1993): "Palestinian Civil Society" in *Middle East Journal,* vol. 47, no. 2, spring

Muslih, Muhammad (1995): "Palestinian Civil Society" in Norton, Richard A. (ed.): *Civil Society in The Middle East,* vol. 1, (Leiden: E.J. Brill)

Nasser, Jamal & Heacock, Roger (eds.), (1991): *Intifada – Palestine at the Crossroads* (Praeger)

Nepp, Daniel (2004): "Killing Sheikh Yasin: The End of the Peace Process or the End of Arafat" in *RUSI Newsbrief,* vol. 24, no 4.

Nomani, Farhad & Rahnema, Ali (1994): *Islamic Economic Systems* (London: Zed Press)

Norton, Richard (ed.) (1995 & 1996): *Civil Society in the Middle East,* vol. 1 & 2, (Leiden: E.J. Brill)

Norton, Richard A. (1995a): "Political Reform in the Middle East" in *State, Individual and Civil Society in the Middle East* (Magleås: Middle Eastern Network, CNI, University of Copenhagen)

Norton, Richard A. (1997): "Lebanon: With Friends Like These..." in *Current History,* January.

Nour, Susanne (1998): "På tværs i en polariseret verden" in *Tidsskriftet Antropologi,* nr. 37

Nüsse, Andrea (1998): *Muslim Palestine – The Ideology of Hamas* (Amsterdam: Harwood Academic Publishers)

Pappe, Ilan (2006): *The Ethnic Cleansing of Palestine* (London: One World)

Passia (2002): *Passia Diary* (Jerusalem: PASSIA)

Paz, Reuven (1999): *Sleeping with the Enemy – A Reconciliation Process as Part of Counter-Terrorism: Is Hamas Capable of Hudna?* www.ict.org.il/articles/swte. htm#organisation

PCHR (1995): *Critique of the Second Palestinian Draft Law Concerning Charitable Societies, Social Bodies and Private Institutions of 1995,* Series Study (3) (Gaza: Palestinian Centre for Human Rights).

PCHR (1998): *Critical Comments on the Draft Law of Charitable Associations and Community Organisations,* Series Study (13), (Gaza: Palestinian Centre for Human Rights).

Pelletiere, Stephen C (1994): *Hamas and Hizballah: The Radical Challenge to Israel in the Occupied Territories* (U.S. Army War College)

Perlmutter, Amos (1994): "Arafat's Police State", *Foreign Affairs,* July/August 1994, Vol. 73, no. 4

PFLP (1992): "The Islamic Fundamentalist Movement in Palestine – Focus on Hamas" in *Democratic Palestine,* July–August–September

Piscatori, James (1991): "Religion and Realpolitik: Islamic responses to the Gulf War" in James Piscatori (ed), *Islamic Fundamentalisms and the Gulf War* (Chicago: American Academy of Arts and Sciences)

Qutb, Sayyid (1978): *Milestones* (Beirut: The Holy Koran Publishing House)

Rahnema S. & Behdad S. (1995): *Iran after the Revolution: Crisis of an Islamic State* (London: I.B.Tauris)

Raqab, Salah Hussein (1998): *Hâdir al-'Alam al-Islâmî wa-Ghazw al-Fikrî* (Gaza)

Rashad, Ahmad (n.d.): *The truth about Hamas*, http://www.mafhoum.com/press/52P5.htm

Rashad, Ahmad (1995): *Politics and Justice: The Case of Musa Abu Marzuq*, Occ. paper no. 9, (United Ass. for Studies and Research)

Rasmussen, Lene Kofoed (1998): "Islamiseringen af den nye generation – Rapport fra en islamisk skole" in *Tidsskriftet Antropologi*, nr. 37

Rasmussen, Lene Kofoed (1999): *Den muslimske kvinde genfortalt – Nye narrativer i 1990'ernes kønsdebat i Cairo*, Unpublished Ph.D.-thesis (University of Copenhagen)

Roald, Anne Sofie (1994): *Tarbiya: Education and Politics in Islamic Movements in Jordan and Malaysia* (Lund: Lund Studies in History of Religions)

Robinson, Glenn (1997): *Building a Palestinian State: The Incomplete Revolution* (Indiana University Press)

Roy, Olivier (1993): *Skakmat – Politisk islam: Et alternativ for de muslimske samfund* (København: Eirene)

Roy, Sara (1995): "Beyond Hamas: Islamic Activism in the Gaza Strip" in *Harvard Middle Eastern and Islamic Review*, vol. 2, no. 1

Roy, Sara (1995a): *The Gaza Strip – The Political Economy of De-development* (Washington DC: Institute for Palestine Studies)

Roy, Sara (1995b): "Civil Society in the Gaza Strip" in Norton, R. (ed.), *Civil Society in the Middle East*, vol. I

Rubin, Barry (1994): *Revolution until Victory? – The History and Politics of the PLO* (Massachusetts: Harvard University Press)

Sadowski, Yahya (1993): "The New Orientalism and the Democracy Debate" in *Middle East Report*, July–Aug.

Sahliyeh, Emile (1988): *In Search of Leadership – West Bank Politics after 1967* (Washington DC: Brookings)

Sahliyeh, Emile (1988a): "The West Bank and the Gaza Strip" in Shireen T. Hunter, (ed.), *The Politics of Islamic revivalism*, (Bloomington & Indiana: Indiana University Press)

Said, Edward (1978): *Orientalism* (New York: Vintage)

Samhouri, Mohammed (2007) "The 'West Bank First' Strategy: A Political-Economy Critical Assessment", October 2007, Working Paper 2, Brandeis University, Crown Center for Middle East Studies

Satloff, Robert (1989): "Islam in the Palestinian Uprising" in *Orbis*, Summer

Sayiegh, Yezid (1989): "Struggle Within, Struggle Without: The Transformation of PLO politics since 1982" in *International Affairs*, vol. 65, no. 2

Sayiegh, Yezid (1992): "Turning Defeat into Opportunity: The Palestinian Guerillas after the June 1967 War" in *The Middle East Journal*, vol. 46, no. 2

Sayiegh, Yezid (1997): *Armed Struggle and the Search for State: The Palestinian National Movement 1949–1993* (Oxford: Oxford University Press)

Sayiegh, Yezid, Khalil Shakaki *et al.* (1999): *Strengthening Palestinian Public Institutions,* www.foreignrelations/org/public/pubs/palinstfull.html#list

Schiff, Ze'ev & Ya'ari, Ehud (1989): *Intifada – The Palestinian Uprising – Israel's Third Front* (New York: Touchstone)

Schmidt, Garbi (1998): *American Medina: A Study of the Sunni Muslim Immigrant Communities in Chicago* (Lund: Lund Studies in History of Religion)

Seufert, Günter (1997): *Politicher Islam In Der Türkei* (Istanbul: Franz Steiner Verlag)

Shadid, Mohammed K. (1988): "The Muslim Brotherhood Movement in the West Bank and Gaza" in *Third World Quarterly,* vol. 2

Shadid, Mohammed K. & Seltzer, Rick (1989): "Growth in Islamic Fundamentalism: The Case of Palestine" in *Sociological Analysis,* vol. 50, no. 3

Shadid, Mohammed K. & Seltzer, Rick (1988): "Political attitudes of Palestinians in the West Bank and Gaza Strip" in *The Middle East Journal,* vol. 42, no. 1

Shalev, Areyh (1991): *The Intifada: Causes and Effects* (JCSS: Tel Aviv)

Simonsen, Jørgen Bæk (1994): "The PLO, HAMAS, and the state of Palestine" in Lars Erslev Andersen, ed., *Middle Eastern Studies in Denmark* (Odense: Odense University Press)

Simonsen, Jørgen Bæk (1994a): *Politikens Islam leksikon* (København: Politikens Forlag)

Sivan, Emmanuel (1985): *Radical Islam – Medieval Theology and Modern Politics* (New Haven and London: Yale University Press)

Sivan, Emmanuel (1985a): *Interpretations of Islam: Past and Present* (Princeton, NJ: Darwin Press)

Smilianov, Ivan (2000): *En moderne islamist fra Sudan – Bidrag til forståelsen af nogle aspekter ved Hasan al-Turâbîs tænkning.* Unpublished Ph.D. thesis (University of Copenhagen)

Stenberg, Leif (1996): *The Islamization of Science: Four Muslim Positions Developing an Islamic Modernity* (Lund: Lund Studies in History of Religion)

Strindberg, Andres & Wärn, Mats (2005): "Realities of Resistance: Hizballah, the Palestinian rejectionists, and al-Qa'ida Compared" in *Journal of Palestine Studies,* vol. XXXIV, no. 3, Spring

Sullivan, Antony Thrall (1988): "Palestinian Universities under Occupation" in *Cairo Papers in Social Science,* vol. 11, monograph 2, summer

Sullivan, Denis (1994): *Private Voluntary Organizations in Egypt – Islamic Development, Private Initiative, and State Control* (Tampa: University Press of Florida)

Sullivan, Denis (1995): *Non-Governmental Organisations and Freedom of Association – Palestine and Egypt – A Comparative Analysis,* Palestinian Academic Society for the Study of International Affairs.

Sullivan, Denis (1996): "NGOs in Palestine: Agents of Development and

Foundation of Civil Society"; *Journal of Palestine Studies*, Vol. XXV, no. 3

Taji-Farouki, Suha (1996): *A Fundamental Quest: Hizb al-Tahrir and the Search for the Islamic Caliphate* (London: Grey Seal)

Talhami, Ghada (1988): "Islamic Fundamentalism and the Palestinians" in *Muslim World*, vol. 78, nos. 3–4, July–October

Taraki, Lisa (1989): "The Islamic Resistance Movement in the Palestinian Uprising" in *Merip Reports,* January–February

Turabi, Hassan (1983): "The Islamic State" in Esposito, John L. (ed.): *Voices of Resurgent Islam* (Oxford: Oxford University Press)

United Arab Republic (1962): *The Charter*, 21st May (Cairo: Information Dept.)

UNGA (2007): *Implementation of General Assembly Resolution 60/251 of March 2006 entitled "Human Rights Council"*. Report of the Special Rapporteur on the situation of human rights in the Palestinian territories occupied since 1967, John Dugard.

UNSCO (1997): *Directory of NGOs in the Gaza Strip*, http://www.mcgill.arts.ca./ programs/ polisci/faculty/rexb/directory/index.html-ssi

UNSCO (1999a): *UNSCO Report on Rule of Law Development in the West Bank and Gaza Strip – Survey and State of Development Effort, May 1999*, Jerusalem: United Nations Office of the Special Coordinator in the Occupied Territories

Usher, Graham (1995): *Palestine in Crisis: The Struggle for Peace and Political Independence after Oslo*, (London: Pluto Press)

Usher, Graham (2005): "The Palestinians after Arafat" in *Journal of Palestine Studies*, vol. XXXIV, no. 3, Spring

Usher, Graham (2005a): "The Crises in the Palestinian National Movement and the Struggle for Palestinian Democracy" in Rahbek, Birgitte (ed.): *Democratisation in the Middle East: Dilemmas and Perspectives* (Aarhus: Aarhus University Press)

Usher, Graham (2005b): "The New Hamas: Between Resistance and Participation", *Middle East Report Online*, http://www.merip.org/mero/mero082105.html

Usher, Graham (2006): "The Hamas Triumph", http://www.thenation.com/doc/ 20060220/ usher)

Wendell, Charles (1978): *Five Tracts of Hasan al Bannâ'. A Selection from the Majmû'at Rasâ'il al-Imâm al-Shahîd Hasan al-Bannâ'*: (Berkeley: University of California Press)

Wiktorowicz, Quintan (ed.) (2004): *Islamic Activism. A Social Movement Theory* (Bloomington, Indiana University Press)

Wye River Memorandum (1998): http://www.arabicnews.com/ansub/daily/ ay/981024/ 19981102453.html

Yapp, M.E. (1991): *The Near East Since the First World War* (London: Longman)

Zahhar, Mahmoud (1998): *Ishkâliyât. Al-khitâb al-Siyâsî al-Islâmî al-Mu'âsir* (Khalîl: Dâr al-Mustaqbal)

Zubaida, Sami (1993): *Islam, the People and the State – Political Ideas and Movements in the Middle East* (London: I.B.Tauris)

Newspapers, journals, TV stations and encyclopaedias
Al-Risâla (Weekly Islamist newspaper published by Hamas in Gaza)
Bayânât from Hamas (in Arabic)
CNN
Dagbladet Information (Danish independent daily)
Den Store Danske Encyklopædi (Danish Encyclopaedia)
FBIS (Foreign Broadcast Information Service)
Haaretz
Hayât al-Jadida
Jerusalem Post, International edition (JPI)
Journal of Palestine Studies, Chronology 1987-
Middle East International (MEI), 1991-2004
Middle East Quarterly
New York Times
News from Within
Palestine Report
Press Releases from Palestinian Centre for Human Rights, Gaza
Washington Post

GLOSSARY

al-'Ard: The earth (often used in reference to Palestine)

'Awrah: A term denoting parts of the body not to be exposed in public according to Islamic tradition.

al-Bâtil: Arabic term meaning: futile, vain. The term is often translated and understood as 'falsehood'. Used in the Koran as opposed to *al-Haqq*: the truth.

Bayân: Leaflet.

Dalîl: Directory or guidance.

Dâr al-Islâm: In Islamic jurisprudence used as a term for the areas in which the *sharia* is the basis for law and order. The concept is in opposition to *Dâr al-Harb*, i.e. the areas outside of *Dâr-al-Islâm*.

Da'wa: Arabic term originally meaning a cry for God's help. Often used as a technical term for the educational work various Muslim organisations conduct in order to spread the message of Islam. It is often translated as mission.

Dîn wa dawla: Religion and state. The Islamists argue that Islam is an all-encompassing system in which politics cannot be divided from religion.

Fard: In Islamic jurisprudence a term denoting religious duty.

Fiqh: Islamic jurisprudence.

al-Ghazw al-Fikrî: Arabic term meaning ideological invasion. It builds upon a conspiratorial idea in which the Western civilisation deliberately has infected the way Muslims perceive the world and Islam.

Hadîth: Tradition. Term denoting narratives of the actions and sayings of the Prophet Muhammad and his companions. The Sunna of the Prophet Muhammad is known through a large number of *hadîth* narrating how Muhammad acted in all sorts of contexts.

al-Haqq: The Truth. Throughout the ages God has sent a line of Prophets to ensure the implementation of *al-Haqq* on Earth. Muhammad was the last in line and since *al-Haqq* has not yet been effectuated, Islamists seek to take this task upon their shoulders.

Harâm: A term denoting what is unlawful according to Islamic law.

Hijâb: In the Koran it denotes the meaning curtain or veil. Referring to the garment some Muslim women wear in public space.

Hijra: Refers to the migration of the Prophet Muhammad from Mecca to Medina in AD 622 and is regarded as the stating point of Islam.

Hudna: Islamic concept meaning long–term truce. Hamas is arguing for the need of a *hudna* rather than *de jura* peace. It has a long tradition within the context of Islam since the Prophet Muhammad entered into a truce with a number of his enemies during the seventh century.

Hukm: Denotes a number of meanings as for example legal decision or logical judgement. Here it denotes exercise of authority or to govern.

Ihsân: To do well or to exercise an act in accordance with the Islamic tradition.

Ijtihâd: Interpretation. The concept originally means to exert oneself to the utmost degree. Ijtihâd is based on analogy (*Qiyas*).

Intima': Arabic term describing a close relationship to for example ideology, family or Islam.

Jahiliya: Ignorance. Most often used as describing the period in history prior to Islam. By some Islamist also used as a term characterising the current affairs of the Islamic world, which in their view is out of touch with 'true' Islam.

Jalbâb: Garment often worn by female Islamists.

Jihâd: In Arabic originally meaning exertion, but is often translated as holy war.

Minhâj: Path (God's path). Rule of life or method.

Muhafiz: Governor.

Mujâhidûn: Those who participate in holy war (*Jihâd*).

Mushrikûn: Polytheist or heathen.

al-Nakba: The Catastrophe. Palestinian/Arab reference to the loss of 'Palestine' in the wake of the First Arab–Israeli war in 1948–49.

al-Nashîd al-Islâmî: Islamic hymns. These are popular among Islamists in Palestine and in the region in general.

al-Nasr: The Victory. In this book meaning the victory of God.

Nizâm al-Islâmî: The Islamic order, as it looks within the context of an Islamic state.

Qanûn: Law (most often distinct from religious law, *sharî'a*).

Qudwa: Role model.

Rak'a [pl. Rak'ât]: Term denoting a continous part of the Islamic prayer. According to tradition Muslims must perform at least 17 *Rak'at* daily.

Sadaqât: Voluntary alms.

al-Sahwa al-Islâmiyya: The Islamic revival. Synonymous with Islamism.

Sharî'a: Islamic law. Based on the Koran, Sunna, Analogies (*Qiyas*) and Consensus (*Ijma*).

Shûrâ: Consultation. Some Islamist leaders consider this principle as being equal to democracy.

Sira: Arab term denoting the biographies of the Prophet Muhammad.

Sunna: The norm established by the exemplary conduct of the Prophet Muhammad. The Sunna comprises the deeds and utterances of the Prophet.

Tahrîf: To corrupt or falsify, particularly in reference to Jews and Christians, who according to Islamic tradition have corrupted the words of God. (Cf. Koran 4:47)

Taker: To declare another Muslim to be an infidel.

Taqlîd: Imitation.

Tarbiyya: [Islamic] Education.

Ulamâ [sing. Âlim]: Term denoting the religious scholars within the Islamic tradition.

Umma: The community of the Faithful.

Waqf [pl. Awqâf]: Endowment.

Zâlim: Sinner or someone transgressing the boundaries of God. The term also covers the meaning tyrant or suppresser.

Zakât: Alms tax due to Muslims. One of the Five Pillars of Islam.

INDEX